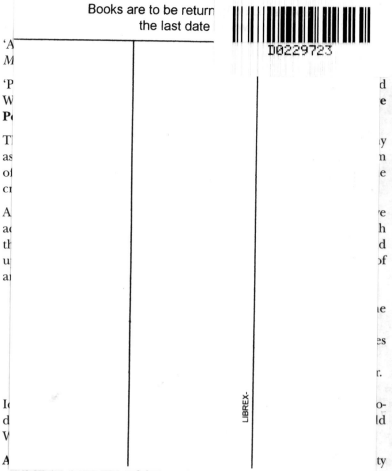
'A
M

'P   d
W   e
P

T   y
as   n
of   e
cr

A   re
a   h
th   d
u   f
a

                                                                     e

                                                                     es

                                                                     r.

I   o-
d   ld
V

A   ty
until his retirement and is now Visiting Professor in History at the
University of Northumbria.

European History in Perspective
General Editor: Jeremy Black

European History in Perspective
Series Standing Order
ISBN 0–333–71694–9 hardcover
ISBN 0–333–69336–1 paperback
(outside North America only)

You can receive future titles in this series as they are published by placing a
standing order. Please contact your bookseller or, in the case of difficulty, write to
us at the address below with your name and address, the title of the series and the
ISBN quoted above.

Customer Services Department, Palgrave Ltd
Houndmills, Basingstoke, Hampshire RG21 6XS, England

The Second World War

Second Edition

A. W. PURDUE

First edition published 1999
Second edition published 2011 by
PALGRAVE MACMILLAN

Palgrave Macmillan in the UK is an imprint of Macmillan Publishers Limited, registered in England, company number 785998, of Houndmills, Basingstoke, Hampshire RG21 6XS.

Palgrave Macmillan in the US is a division of St Martin's Press LLC, 175 Fifth Avenue, New York, NY 10010.

Palgrave Macmillan is the global academic imprint of the above companies and has companies and representatives throughout the world.

Palgrave® and Macmillan® are registered trademarks in the United States, the United Kingdom, Europe and other countries

ISBN 978–0–230–27935–3   hardback
ISBN 978–0–230–27936–0   paperback

This book is printed on paper suitable for recycling and made from fully managed and sustained forest sources. Logging, pulping and manufacturing processes are expected to conform to the environmental regulations of the country of origin.

A catalogue record for this book is available from the British Library.

A catalog record for this book is available from the Library of Congress.

10   9   8   7   6   5   4   3   2   1
20   19   18   17   16   15   14   13   12   11

Printed in China

To Marie

Contents

List of Maps

Chronology

1917	March: Russian Revolution; 15 March: abdication of Tsar
1917	November: Bolshevik Revolution in Russia
1918	3 March: Treaty of Brest-Litovsk
1918	9 November: Abdication of Kaiser and establishment of German Republic. Armistice
1919–20	Versailles (or Paris) Peace Settlement consisting of: Treaty of Versailles 28 June 1918; Treaty of St Germain 10 September 1919; Treaty of Neuilly 27 November 1919; Treaty of Trianon 4 June 1920; and Treaty of Sevres 20 April 1920. The latter was never implemented
1922	30 October: Mussolini becomes Italian premier
1925	16 October: Treaties of Locarno
1929	29 October: Wall Street Crash
1931	September: Japanese occupation of Manchuria
1933	30 January: Hitler becomes Chancellor of Germany
1933	February: Japanese occupy northern China
1934	2 August: Hitler becomes *Führer* and Reich Chancellor
1935	2/3 October: Italian invasion of Abyssinia
1936	13 March: Germany reoccupies the Rhineland
1936	17/18 July: Outbreak of Spanish Civil War
1936	2 November: Rome-Berlin Axis announced
1936	25 November: Anti-Comintern Pact between Germany and Japan (Italy adheres a year later)

1937	9 July: Sino-Japanese War begins. Japan occupies NE and E China
1938	12 March: *Anschluss* of Germany and Austria
1938	30 September: Munich Agreement
1939	15 March: Germany occupies Prague and annexes Bohemia and Moravia
1939	30 March: British guarantee to Poland
1939	13 April: Britain and France give guarantees to Greece and Romania
1939	22 May: Germany and Italy sign Pact of Steel
1939	23 August: German-Soviet Non-Aggression Pact
1939	1 September: German invasion of Poland
1939	3 September: Britain and France declare war on Germany, the Second World War begins
1939	28 September: Warsaw Falls
1939	30 September: Poland defeated and partitioned between Germany and USSR
1939	30 November: 'Winter War' between USSR and Finland begins
1940	12 March: Germany invades Denmark and Norway
1940	10 May: Germany invades Holland and Belgium. Chamberlain resigns and Churchill becomes prime minister
1940	29 May: Dunkirk evacuation begins
1940	10 June: Italy declares war on Britain and France
1940	22 June: Franco-German Armistice
1940	3 July: French Fleets attacked by Royal Navy
1940	10 July: Battle of Britain begins
1940	September: Italians invade Egypt
1940	7 September: The 'Blitz' begins
1940	September 27: Germany, Italy and Japan sign Tripartite Pact
1940	28 October: Italians invade Greece
1941	2 January: British take Tobruk

1941   7 March: British land in Greece

1941   6 April: Germans invade Yugoslavia and Greece

1941   22 April: Greek army surrenders to Germans and British begin to withdraw from Greece

1941   31 May: British defeated in Crete

1941   22 June: Germany invades Russia

1941   12 August: Atlantic Charter signed

1941   5 December: Germans abandon attack on Moscow

1941   7 December: Japan attacks Pearl Harbour

1942   15 February: British surrender at Singapore

1942   4–8 May: Battle of Coral Sea

1942   May 6: American forces in Philippines surrender

1942   4 June: Battle of Midway

1942   21 June: Germans take Tobruk

1942   October: Battle of El Alamein

1942   7 August: Americans land at Guadalcanal

1943   30 January–1 February: Casablanca Conference

1943   31 January: General Paulus surrenders at Stalingrad

1943   9–10 July: Allied landings in Sicily

1943   July: Battle of Kursk

1943   25 July: Mussolini ousted

1943   8 September: Italy surrenders

1943   28 November–6 December: Tehran Conference

1944   6 June: D-day landings in Normandy

1944   June: British defeat Japanese at Kohima

1944   23 June: Soviet offensive (Operation Bagration) begins

1944   1 August: Warsaw Rising

1944   23 August: Romanian government of Antonescu ousted and new government begins peace overtures to Russians

1944   24 August: Allies take Paris

1944   2 September: Provisional Finnish-Soviet Peace Treaty

1944	12 September: Allied troops enter Germany
1944	2 October: Warsaw Rising finally crushed
1944	4 October: British troops land in Greece
1944	17 October: US invasion of Philippines begins with landings at Leyte Gulf
1944	28 October: Russo-Bulgarian Armistice
1944	16–25 December: Battle of the Bulge
1944	27 December: Siege of Budapest begins
1945	17 January: Russians take Warsaw
1945	4–11 February: Yalta Conference
1945	1 April: US forces invade Okinawa
1945	12 April: Death of Roosevelt
1945	28 April: Mussolini hanged by partisans
1945	30 April: Hitler commits suicide
1945	2 May: Fall of Berlin
1945	8 May: Germany surrenders
1945	8 July: USSR declares war on Japan
1945	6 August: Atom bomb dropped on Hiroshima
1945	9 August: Atom bomb dropped on Nagasaki
1945	15 August: Japan surrenders

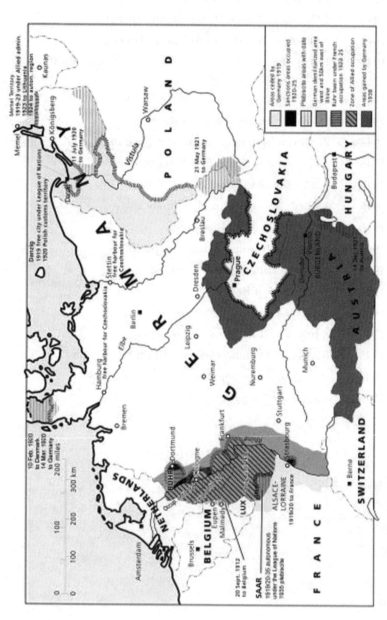

Map 1 Germany 1919–38

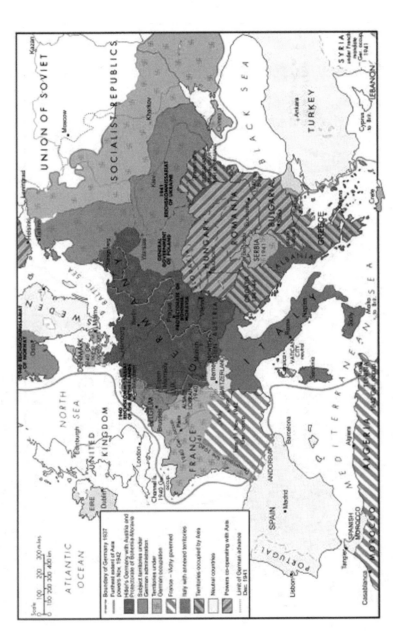

Map 2   Europe at the height of German domination, November 1942

Reproduced by permission of the Open University.

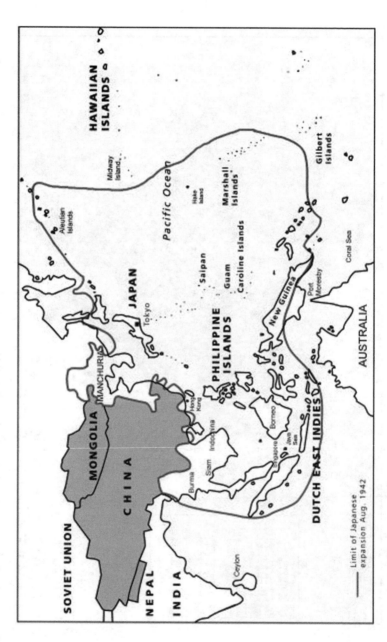

Map 3   The limit of Japanese expansion, August 1942

Map 4   Europe 1945

Reproduced by permission of the Open University.

Preface to the Second Edition

History, some will assert, doesn't change, so why bring out a second and revised edition just over a decade after the first? The answer is, of course, that if the past does not change, our knowledge of it and our view of it do. Salient facts, dates and the course of the Second World War have obviously not changed, but new evidence is continually being discovered as archives are opened, embargoes end, diaries and letters surface, and the old reveal their experiences; the wartime generation was one which knew how to keep secrets as is demonstrated by the decades that passed before the work of Bletchley Park and the deciphering of the Enigma code were revealed. The last decade has also seen new interpretations of the war and its major campaigns by historians, such as Andrew Roberts, Max Hastings and Anthony Beevor. Most importantly, the passage of time continues to alter the perspective on the war and popular perceptions of it. David Cameron's gaffe in referring to Britain as a 'junior ally' of the United States in 1940, a year in which America had yet to enter the war, was, no doubt, a mere slip of the tongue, but not one that Attlee, Macmillan, Callaghan or any prime minister who had lived through the war could have made. Museums, monuments, anniversaries, official remembrances, novels and TV series, keep alive a consciousness of the war but, despite the work of historians, the collective memory is often misty and influenced by the prisms of fiction and faction. Our views of the war continue to change over time. The perspective from early twenty-first century is different to that from the late twentieth century.

My thanks are again due to Jeremy Black for his encouragement and expert advice, to Sonya Barker for being such a helpful editor, and to the two anonymous readers who commented so positively on my draft and whose detailed comments saved me from many errors.

Introduction

Writing 15 years after the end of the Second World War, the historian A. J. P. Taylor wrote that the war, '... like its predecessor, has passed into history' and was as remote to students as the Boer War to their lecturers'. He was, of course, wrong, for in Britain at least, the war cast a long shadow, invading language, and becoming central to that mixture of memory and myth that constitutes the national self-image.

The first edition of this book was published in 1999 and the fiftieth anniversary celebrations of VE and VJ days held in 1995 were in the recent past while I was writing it. They had, I argued, effectively marked the end of one perspective of the Second World War, the lived war in the memories of combatants and those who were young adults between 1939 and 1945. Had the phrase 'the post-war world', familiar throughout most of my life, finally become redundant? Historians had, for decades, treated the war as that paradox, 'contemporary history'; would it now become plain history? A brief survey of the attitudes of the nations most involved in the war suggested that it remained, not just an episode in history but a reference point for national identities.

Britain's affectionate and self-regarding interpretation of the wartime experience, dramatically symbolised by the Queen Mother and her daughters on the balcony of Buckingham Palace in conscious tribute to their appearance with George VI in 1945, was, in 1995, substantially intact and no less revered for being seen across years of national decline. Elsewhere in Europe the great victorious power of 1945, the USSR, no longer existed as such and Russia, although commemorating Soviet victories with a massive military parade, did so across the divide of the disintegration, not only of the union but of the Soviet bloc, while the battles for Stalingrad and Leningrad seemed more distant now that the cities were Volgograd and St Petersburg.

The necessary myths of France's wartime experience had been disintegrating since the seventies as historians questioned the unpopularity of Vichy, the extent of collaboration and the strength of the Resistance. President Mitterand's autumnal testament as to his role during the Vichy regime suggested that the past could be openly confronted.

Germany in the year of the fiftieth anniversary of her defeat was once more the greatest power in Europe, recently reunited and economically dominant. The contrast between present circumstance and the prostrate Germany of 1945 could not have been greater. There was inevitably an ambivalence to German reactions as memories of defeat mixed with national guilt. Could the end of National Socialism be celebrated when the nation had been defeated and could nation and regime be seen as separate? Not quite invited to the succession of anniversaries that marked the allied road to victory, Germany shuffled uncomfortably at their edge.

American veterans and political leaders attended the VE celebrations in large numbers, as they had also attended the anniversaries of the milestones to victory, notably that of the Normandy landings. For the United States the war had meant the end of isolationism and the beginning of a continuous and demanding world role. Yet, for the bulk of US citizens, the Second World War had long ceased to be *the* war, for both the Korean and the Vietnam War had inevitably distanced it.

Throughout what had been the British Empire, commemoration of the war was conducted from a very different position from that of VE and VJ day. Even in the old dominions that retained Queen Elizabeth as their sovereign, it was difficult for younger generations to conceive of a time when the Empire went to war as one under British military command.

For Japan, like Germany resurgent and economically powerful, the VJ anniversary was an uncomfortable time, but not an occasion for great expressions of remorse or guilt. There had never been a great period of national soul searching and *angst*, and Japan had cut off her militarist past and turned resolutely to a future of economic greatness without ever fully confronting the former. School text books had ignored or glossed over the ferocious expansionism of the years 1933–45, while influential political factions stood firmly against any but the most qualified expressions of guilt. Japan also had politically acceptable arguments to hand with which to submerge her particular role in a general condemnation of imperialism and war. That the war in the Far East had been brought to an end by the nuclear destruction of Hiroshima and Nagasaki seemed to some to overshadow Japan's aggression and wartime atrocities.

For one state that had not existed in 1945, memories were not of the war itself, but rather of the attempted genocide of a people, many of whom were contained within it. Israel's Day of Remembrance bore witness not just to mourning but to a determination that the Second World War should not be conceived of as just another war. Was that it? Was 1995 to be the last hurrah, the last time for singing 'We'll meet again', and the last chance for old Red Army soldiers to put on their medals? A similar survey of the way in which combatant states observed the 60th and 65th anniversaries of the end of the war reveals little change in the public ceremonies and commemorations or in popular attitudes. The Second World War has not yet become *history*, at least not in the sense that the Seven Years' War or the Napoleonic Wars are history.

An obsession with anniversaries plays a part here for, although contemporary societies are usually seen as characterised by constant change, obsessed by the new and little interested in the past, special pasts are in practice hugged closely, and their history replayed at every opportunity. June 2004 and June 2009 saw the commemoration of the 60th and 65th anniversaries of D-Day, albeit with ever fewer of those who had landed in Normandy in 1944, while 2005's replication of 1995's celebrations of the end of the war has been repeated in 2010. The anniversary celebrations of 1995 were, indeed the last at which a large proportion of those taking part had their own recollections of the war, but what became evident, both then and at later anniversaries and commemorations, was how enduring were interpretations of the nature of the war first established in the immediate post-war decades.

In Britain, the 2005 commemoration of the war concentrated upon the nation's 'finest hour' and the Blitz with a memorial show in Horse Guards' Parade, rather over-shadowed by a new threat to the nation's security as Islamic terrorists set off bombs in the capital's transport network. May 2010 saw an elaborate homage to the Dunkirk evacuation, while in the late summer the media gave almost blanket coverage to the 70th anniversary of the Battle of Britain. What was apparent at successive British anniversaries was how well those born long after the end of the war knew their parts. They knew their war, not always the real war, though they may have seen documentary compilations of wartime campaigns and battles, but often a war viewed via popular art and culture, a war seen through films, comics and TV programmes. If this war sometimes owed more to *Dad's Army*, or *Allo, Allo!* than to historical fact, the sense of period was impressive. Pubs were able to instantly transform a bar or lounge into a wartime interior with posters warning that Hitler was listening and with Vera Lynn as ubiquitous on CDs as on the 78s of her heyday, while few were at a loss when it came to what to wear to an anniversary or 'Blitz' party or how to dance to Glen Miller.

Each combatant nation has a different collective memory of the war and to a degree of distinct wars as nations have different dates for when the war started. The American War Memorial in Washington has an inscription over its gate reading 'World War II 1941–45', while visitors to Italian war memorials will read of a war beginning in 1940 and for the Chinese 1937 is the significant date. In Russia the celebrations in May 2005 commemorated the 'Great Patriotic War', beginning of course in 1941, and this involved thousands of troops in Red Army uniforms, making it appear, as one historian has remarked, 'as if time had stood still and the Soviet Union was intact.[1] In May 2010 there was the biggest parade in Red Square since the collapse of the Soviet Union in 1991 with Britain providing a contingent of Welsh Guards in dress uniform. This would have been even more of a flashback if Moscow City Council had had its way and the streets been decorated with portraits of Stalin. Celebrations in the US have tended to place a more equal emphasis upon the war in the Pacific and the war in Europe. They have also tended, in the spirit of the 1998 feature film *Saving Private Ryan*, to ignore America's allies and to commemorate a generous and disinterested American crusade to save the world. At the same time an increasing pre-occupation with the Holocaust has tended to distract Americans from other major issues of the war in Europe.

That the war and memories of it have penetrated so deeply into national psyches is not surprising. Both high and popular art had been superimposed on and become part of the Second World War during the actual conflict as artists and film-makers brought ancestral voices, fears and visions to the aid of war efforts (see pp. 126–36), and as they sought to stiffen civilian morale. The Second World War was the first major conflict that could in a sense be replayed because of the vast amount of archive film and the recordings of the speeches of politicians and contemporary commentators; these formed the basis of post-war documentary films and TV and radio programmes. After the war, novels, films and television ensured that the war would be viewed through a succession of prisms to the degree that, even with those who had direct experience of fighting or of living through bombing raids, it was difficult when it came to oral testimony to distinguish between actual memory and received accounts.

Memorialisation and monuments to those who had died for their countries became a psychological necessity after the death toll and horrors of the First World War and, after the Second World War, there was, among the victorious nations, a continuity: town and villages found space on their memorials for new names, the Cenotaph in Whitehall became the focus of British remembrance of both wars, and military cemeteries like Arlington in Washington became national sites of honour and pride. Remembrance and its monuments continue apace and have been affected by contemporary preoccupations and pressure groups. In Britain the natural desire of all the services and wartime units and organisations, whether regiments or civilian 'Home Front' groups like the 'Land Girls' to see their contribution to the war recognised has resulted in new monuments, while feminism has ensured that beside the cenotaph there is now a monument to women's contribution to the war. Military museums abound: in London the Imperial War Museum, first founded to commemorate the First World War, and in New Orleans, the National Museum of World War II, while in Russia most of the Soviet Union's major victories have museums devoted to them. A new development is the museum of experience of war, largely pioneered by the Imperial War Museum and exemplified in its other museum, the Cabinet War Rooms, in which it has recreated the atmosphere as well as the furnishings of Churchill's government's war-time redoubt, and at the Second World War Experience Centre at Leeds. Never has a war been so memorialised, if largely within the boundaries of national perspectives.

One new development, which does cross national boundaries is the way in which, as the Holocaust has come to be seen as a central feature of the war, so Holocaust monuments and museums have been created around the world: in Washington, Berlin, Melbourne, Amsterdam, pertinently at Auschwitz and naturally in Israel. It is noteworthy that the list of Holocaust memorials in the USA is almost as long as the total number elsewhere.

Memorials can be controversial, however, and inconvenient. The British Government for long prevented the erection of a monument to the Polish officers murdered by Soviet forces at Katyn, though one was eventually established at Gunnersbury.

Received memories of the war and the strength of many representations of it are factors in explaining why popular and national attitudes and interpretations have proved so persistent and enduring. What then of the interpretations of historians?

One result of the passage of time has been that the ever more distant perspective means that the special and unique features of the Second World War fade into a wider landscape. The view of the war in Europe increasingly appears as not discrete but is seen, as is discussed in Chapter 1, in the broader context of European history as along with the First World War (once it must be remembered considered the 'Great War) as part of a long 'European Civil War', a 'Thirty Years' War', though many would extend it further to include the Cold War.

Otherwise, what is surprising is the way in which the interpretations of the war that became the consensual view in the 1940s and 1950s continue to be repeated so often in the twenty-first century. In the first edition of this book I argued that a frozen perspective of winners' history' had endured until the collapse of the Soviet Union and the re-unification of Germany and my assumption was that a radical revision would follow. Excellent studies of particular aspects of the war and of great battles and campaigns have indeed in the last decade demolished parts of the of the traditional view of the war but, in 2010, in journalism, the speeches of politicians and some text books there has, at best, been erosion rather than demolition and pillars of its crumbling edifice still stand. Prominent among them are: a caricature of 'Appeasement' and of the foreign policy of Chamberlain's government, which owes more to the authors of *Guilty Men*[2] and Churchill's post-war writing than to an appreciation of the difficulties facing Britain in the 1930s; a collective and selective amnesia as to the actions of the Soviet Union and the fluidity of the war between 1939 and 1941; and a failure to recognise that Germany's east and central European allies in the assault on the Soviet Union had their own individual problems and difficult decisions to make. Revisionism seems partial and hesitant.

Great wars, total wars, have huge death tolls and demand enormous sacrifices on the part of the populations of combatants. It therefore follows, psychologically, if not logically, that they must be fought for great principles, for civilisation and for 'good against evil'. National self-interest, even national survival, is not enough. Thus, the view that the British government declared war on Germany in 1939 because essential British interests and the European balance of power were threatened by Germany's ambitions and actions may well have seemed satisfactory enough to British public opinion at the time, but very different interpretations and explanations of why the war was fought were put forward by the Allied powers in the last years of the conflict and in the immediate post-war period. These were powerful: they drew upon the animosity, the pride and the hatred of years of war, and upon ideologies which reflected the 'common sense' of the time. The idea of 'a war against fascism' became dominant and had the advantage of concentrating upon what the Allies were against as opposed to what they were for.

Such a view never even vaguely fitted the war in the Far East where, although Japan was certainly the aggressor, the label fascist was always a misnomer, and a lopsidedly modernised but residually feudal state, short on natural resources, made a ruthless but misjudged assault upon a weak China, ailing European empires and an economically expansionist but politically quietist USA. The resemblance to National Socialism lies mainly in the extreme cruelty with which Japan waged war and treated the defeated and the conquered.

So far as the war in Europe is concerned, the importance of the Nazi-Soviet Pact and the fluidity of the war between 1939 and 1941 continue to be underestimated as is the degree to which the concept of a war between 'good and evil' was profoundly undermined by the alliance between the Western powers and the Soviet Union. That the Third Reich was a monstrous and evil regime is not in doubt, nor is the fact that Britain was in 1941 in desperate need of a continental ally, so that Churchill's initial view that alliance with the Soviet Union was welcome, even if alliance with the power that had along with Germany invaded Poland in 1939 was a necessary evil, was understandable. It is difficult, however, to remain instrumental about an ally, especially one suffering huge losses, and British and American interpretations of the war remain coloured by attitudes established in 1942 and 1943. The Nazi-Soviet Pact was forgotten as was the fact that, rather than having come to Britain's assistance, the Soviet Union was only in the war because it had been attacked, and the power that had denoted Britain's war with Germany as a conflict between imperialist powers became 'a glorious ally' and its leader 'Uncle Joe'. A similar process took place in the USA, where many began to conceive of the Soviet Union as a progressive force. Such attitudes had become well-established by the end of the war and were not to be totally erased by the Cold War, by Krushchev's denunciation of Stalin in 1956, nor by the increasing evidence that, with its Gulag of concentration camps, its murderous treatment of minority peoples and totalitarian control via its repressive police and security forces, it was every bit as monstrous a regime as Hitler's Germany. With the collapse of the Soviet Union and the opening up of Soviet archives it might have been expected that a parity of evil between the enemy destroyed in 1945 and the ally which sat in judgement alongside Britain and the USA at Nuremberg would have become generally accepted, but the full implications of this for the history of the Second World War are only gradually alter-ing historians' accounts and have yet to modify the popular view of the war. A Manichean division between good and evil is not easily replaced by a more complex picture of two tyrannies wrestling for hegemony, the liberal-capitalist powers seeking a return to order, and the nations of East-Central Europe struggling for survival in a clash between two titans.

It is largely the war in Europe that continues to fascinate. Even in the USA, which was brought into the war by the Japanese attack on Pearl Harbor and whose forces fought Japan back to its home islands, it is the the Holocaust and Hitler, which dominate the view of the Second World War, while in Britain the history of the Pacific War has faded, save for memories of the surrender at Singapore and of the sufferings of prisoners of war, while the Burma Campaign has largely been erased from popular memory. Despite the war's influence upon such developments on Asia and the Pacific as the the decline of Europe's global influence and complementary rise of the USA's power, and the growing importance of Asian economies, the nature and the consequences of the Pacific or Far Eastern dimension of the war have attracted far fewer Western historians than has the war in Europe and, though there have been a number of outstanding stud-ies, in the popular consciousness of Britain and America its history and imagery have faded. The long war between Japan and China was probably as important as that between the Western Allies and Japan and its effects upon relations between modern China and Japan are profound yet, remarkably, few influential accounts have been produced by Japanese or Chinese historians. The paradox may be that, for all the compelling nature of the war in Europe, its place in popular memory, and its role as a reference point for national identi-ties, it can be seen as finished business, while the great issues of the war in the Far East remain raw.

A perspective on the war and its significance in European history must take into account the war outside Europe and its impact upon Europe's place and influence in the world but the very term 'world war' seems increasingly questionable. It is certainly not apposite for the first two years of a war during which fighting was confined to Europe. Did a European war become a world war in December 1941 or were there two largely distinct wars, one in Asia and one in Europe, with the British Empire and the USA the only active participants in both?

Proximity to great events naturally inclines observers to attribute almost every major subsequent development to them. A conflict ranging over most of the world must, it was felt by contemporaries and their children, have made a long-term difference to the course of history. We have only to turn to the counterfactual scenario of an Axis victory that has attracted a number of novelists to see that a different outcome to the war would have had momentous consequences, but many of the analyses of the war's effects, put forward as recently as the eighties, now look dated.

Until the early nineties the most obvious consequence of the war seemed to have been the emergence of two global superpowers, the USA and the USSR, and the associated division of much of the world into two ideologically opposed power blocs. It can now be seen that the superpower status won by the USSR in 1945 was, in the long run, incompatible with the contradictions and weaknesses of its economic system, and led to a crisis in Soviet society which resulted in its collapse in 1991. In that the USSR was not just a great power, but the vanguard power of Marxist socialism, its collapse represented not only a reordering of international power relationships, but the end of an era in which ideology could be seen as the determinant of such relationships. The events of 1989–91 can be seen as the real end, not just of the Cold War, but of the Second World War of which it was the last chapter.

In the wake of the collapse of the Soviet Union and its communist satellites, the American historian Francis Fukuyama wrote of the ending of the Cold War as 'the end of history' (*The End of History and the Last Man, 1992*) but his 'history' was that of war between ideologies. Clearly, the demise of the Soviet regime and of the Eastern bloc weakened explanations of the Second World War that relied too exclusively on ideology. That the war is comprehensible within a history of traditional power politics and international rivalries, or as a consequence of nationalism, could seem a perverse claim in a world divided by political ideology. It seems less so now, especially as greater access to Soviet archives has revealed both the full details of the Hitler-Stalin Pact of 1939 and the peace feelers put out by Stalin to Hitler after 1941, which point to the flexibility of Soviet policy when it came to dealing with its ideological opponent. When the map of Europe resembles more that of the spring of 1918 than that of the late 1940s and where nationalism seems more dynamic than socialism, the continuities of a historical process based on the interests and geography of powers seem more feasible.

At the end of the twentieth century, a number of long-term consequences of the great conflict seemed self-evident. Although Germany and Japan had failed in their bid to dominate the world militarily, they were, next to the USA, the world's leading economies. Britain and France had emerged among the victors, but had within decades lost their empires and their positions among the great powers. The Soviet Union, having seemed for over 40 years to be the power that had benefited most from the war, was no more and an attenuated Russia did not promise to be militarily or economically a first rank power. The USA had become the only super-power and the world was heading ineluctably towards forms of liberal-capitalism and democracy. The European states had, largely as a result of the trauma of great divisive wars, bound themselves together in an ever-tightening union in which social democracy and state welfarism was the norm. Almost all of these conclusions seem, in the light of the events of the first decade of the twenty-first century, to be questionable or in need of modification.

Central to most analyses of the collapse of the Soviet empire was the conclusion that the world was now to be dominated by a single super power, the USA and its political ideals, ideals which had directed American participation in the Second World War. Arguably, the end of the Cold War gave a third wind to the Wilsonian and Roosevelt belief that the world could be re-made on an American liberal model. The events of the first decade of the twenty-first century have put in doubt the durability of an American hegemony, while the new economic and political strength of Asian powers, amongst which China, rather than Japan, now seems the most formidable, give the history of the war in the Pacific and the Far East a new pertinence. At the same time, Islamism and international terrorism direct attention to the dog which hardly barked in the Second World War, religion, and, to what most historians have seen as a minor factor in a war fought between the armed forces of states, the actions of resistance movements and sabotage, now seen when used against conventional forces as part of asymmetrical warfare.

The creation of the European Union has been widely ascribed to the experience of the war, which, it is held, impelled the western European states in the direction of greater unity. The movement, so the almost sacrosanct version of its origins goes, gained strength in the post-war period with the vision and fears of Christian and Social Democratic politicians. The war had both demonstrated the horrors that resulted from the rivalries of a Europe of nation states and shown that older notions of a concert of Europe or of a balance of power, were inadequate safeguards of stability, so that a European Union seemed to be the answer.

There are, of course, other versions of the formation of what eventually became the European Union. Some would argue that it was the common membership of NATO of the principal European states and the experience of the Cold War that brought about the move towards union. A less elevated scenario places it in the context of Franco-German rivalry over more than a century and sees French politicians and industrialists as realising after the Second World War that intimate economic bonds were a better way of coming to terms with Germany's latent power than political and military opposition, while the common economic institutions set up in Hitler's Europe after 1940, provided a rarely acknowledged precedent. An emphasis upon the liberation of Hitler's Europe, with an important role given to the Resistance provides a very different picture to accounts which point to the relative stability of France, the Netherlands and Belgium between 1940 and 1943. Interpretations of the Second World War are therefore crucial in an evaluation of the EU's development and antecedents. The social democracy and generous state welfare systems which have character-ised the states of the Union have also been seen as emanating from the war, the consequence, it has been argued, of the need for wartime governments to maintain the support of all sections of society and of the search for a European way between capitalism and socialism. The crisis of the Euro in 2009–11, the reactions to immigration, particularly Muslim immigration, and the associated worries over the viability of economies with generous welfare systems cast some doubt on the more eirenic accounts of post-war Europe and the impact of the Second World War on society.

If the old certainties about the causes, nature and consequences of the war are no longer compelling, this should not lead to a dismissal of the war's importance in the creation of the modern world. It does mean, however, that its significance needs to be constantly evaluated afresh, placed in a long-term context, and approached as history.

Chapter 1: The Origins of the Second World War

A Thirty Years' War?

Two statements which generations of students have been invited to discuss as essay questions encapsulate the most popular and contradictory explanations of the causes of the Second World War: 'The origins of World War II lie in the Versailles Settlement' and 'The causes of the Second World War can be summed up in one word, Hitler'. A third thesis, which has recently gained ground, is that the First and Second World Wars were inextricably linked with a common cause, the upsetting of the balance of power of Europe by the emergence of a united Germany with expansionist ambitions.

Insofar as the Versailles Settlement provided the geopolitical context for the international relations of the inter-war period, even down to providing some of the cast of nation states, the centrality of the Settlement to discussions of the origins of the Second World War has never been in doubt. Whether the Settlement was to be blamed for causing instability and leaving Germans angry and vengeful, or whether British and French politicians were at fault in not upholding its provisions firmly enough, Versailles's importance has always been recognised. To that extent it is inaccurate to state, as it so often is, that until the 1960s historians saw the origins of the war as simply synonymous with Adolf Hitler. Hitler had had to gain power and had been able to use supposed grievances that were to hand, while even the most single-minded and ruthless of expansionist policies confronts other powers with the decision as to whether to accede or not.

The interpretation that achieved the status of consensus was more complex than 'the one-man Hitler' caricature. It was essentially that put forward by Winston Churchill in his massively influential book, *The Gathering Storm* (1948). History and the writing of history came together as one of the war's major figures justified his record and shaped perceptions of the conflict. As a recent study has demonstrated, Churchill was ever 'in command of history'.[1] His argument was, in essence, that the war arose out of a combination of Hitler's ambitions and a failure to prevent the German revision of Versailles. Churchill was selective in his attitude to Versailles, condemning the reparation clauses, but defending the modified Settlement as it existed after the Locarno Treaty of 1925. He argued that war could have been avoided if German rearmament, contrary to the disarmament clauses of the Versailles treaty, had not been allowed in 1934. After that date, he considered, war was inevitable. Others saw the stage at which war became inevitable as the failure to oppose the remilitarisation of the Rhineland in 1936, but the essential thesis was the same: the war arose because of Hitler's ambitions and the failure of Britain and France to stand up to him in the early stages. The development of the Cold War introduced subsidiary debates: arguments from Soviet historians that the machinations of finance capital had produced both Hitler and Anglo-French appeasement of him; and from Americans that Stalin and pre-war Soviet-German co-operation had some responsibility for the outbreak of war. Such arguments did not displace Hitler from the central role.

There can be no doubt, however, that the publication of A. J. P. Taylor's *Origins of the Second World War* (1961) marked a massive widening of the debate, not just in its denial that Hitler proceeded to war deliberately and according to a plan but also in its view that Hitler's ambitions were a continuation of traditional German policies. It is a testimony to the power and originality of the work that Taylor's bibliography included no book titled *The Origins of the Second World War*, while any reading list today would inevitably include at least half a dozen. *The Origins* remains controversial even 35 years after its publication. If Taylor's coat-trailing remark that Hitler was 'just an ordinary German politician' detracted from his less extravagant argument that his ambitions were essentially a continuation of traditional German foreign policy, it did encapsulate it.

Not only did Taylor's book turn the spotlight back upon the Versailles Settlement, the revision of which was the aim of most inter-war German politicians, but in doing so it connected the First and Second World Wars. To see the Second World War as, in large part, a repeat performance of the First World War was scarcely original and had been the common sense of popular opinion in 1939. That it was unpalatable to the consensus of the post-war world can be explained by several factors: the course of the war, rather than its origins, had revealed the extent of Hitler's ambitions, which went far beyond those of the Kaiser or his generals; it demoted ideology, which in the context of the Cold War, seemed self-evidently the dominant force in twentieth-century world politics; and, within a polarised Europe where a West and East Germany were recruited to the Western and Soviet blocs, it was far more convenient to conceive of the Second World War as having been fought against Hitler or against fascism than against Germany.

The number of books and articles that have been written on the subject of the causes of the Second World War is enormous and a brief guide to influential works is given in the bibliography, but the principal interpretative divide remains between those who see the war as separate from the First World War and unique in its causation and those who stress a continuum not only between the two wars but also in the interaction of great power rivalry since the emergence of a united Germany in 1870. The sides of this debate are by no means fixed by national sympathies and the idea of continuity in German ambitions has found support among German historians, some of whom have emphasised Teutonic expansionism further back in German history.[2] Ideological and professional sympathies have probably been as influential as national ones in forming opinions. Those committed to a view of twentieth-century history as a battleground of political philosophies have been reluctant to see its great events reduced to an extension of great power rivalry and the imperatives of geography. Economic, diplomatic, military and social historians have brought their own methods, preoccupations and expectations to the debate. There are some strange bedfellows, those normally concerned in pointing to deep socio-economic currents dictating historic change have found themselves implicitly emphasising the difference made by the charismatic leader, Adolf Hitler, while those given to accepting the role of the individual in history have been forward in pointing to the inter-generational continuities of foreign policies.

Changes in the present from which we view the past have probably been more important. To those who went to war in 1939 a continuation of the 1914–18 conflict seemed the explanation. To those who had fought between 1939 and 1945, the special nature of their war and its personification as 'Hitler's war' seemed the obvious truth. Until the late eighties the results of the war in terms of creating a different and politically divided Europe seemed so complete and permanent that continuity with 1918 or 1870 seemed unthinkable. The collapse of the Soviet bloc and of east-European socialism has shifted perceptions. The enduring interests of nation states now appear more important than political ideologies, while nationalism seems to remain a dynamic force. The concept of an 'end to history' implies in reality a return to history with competing ideologies as a component, rather than the framework, of historical change.

A combination of distance from the events and *déjà vu* at the sight of the emerging landscape of the late twentieth century made for the increased plausibility of the concept, not of two linked wars fought for similar reasons but of one war,[3] a 30-years war, a concept that remains compelling in the early twenty-first century. The Second World War was, it can be argued, simply stage two of a Thirty Years' War, the second military phase of a European civil war to determine the mastery of Europe.[4] A wider context, and an even longer scenario, is possible if one considers the emergence of the German Empire in 1871 to have destroyed the balance of power in Europe at a time when the global influence of Europe, most concretely manifest in overseas empires, was increasing. From 1871 the basic European problem was to be how to accommodate or contain Germany, while European influence in Asia, Africa and the Middle East, enhanced during the high 'age of imperialism' of the late nineteenth century, ensured that the success or failure of such accommodation or containment would have a global impact.

From such a point of view, 1871 affected all participants in the Second World War. It saw the birth of a German Empire, populous and with a developing economy and a strong army, which inherited from Prussia a tradition of respect for the power of government and an inclination towards protectionism rather than free trade in economic policy. It diminished Russia's preponderant power in Eastern Europe. It propelled France into both a feverish search for colonial aggrandisement as a compensation for diminution of status and power in Europe, most piquantly illustrated by the loss of Alsace and Lorraine, and a search for European allies against Germany. This in turn changed Britain's reluctant imperialism into an expansionism which overstretched her resources and led to the Anglo-Japanese Alliance of 1902, bringing an Asian power for the first time into an equal relationship with a Western power, and able to benefit or lose from changes to the European balance. The penetration of European power, together with European conflicts into the wider world, disturbed the USA and its South American and Pacific interests leading to her determination to build a large navy. Thus the coming of the German Empire posed the problem and determined many of the parameters of international relations for the next century or more.

The First World War was fought by Britain, France and Russia in order to contain the powerful German state, much as the same essential reason was to dictate Britain's and France's declaration of war in 1939. Germany conversely went to war to destroy a containment she felt threatened the rightful place her strength entitled her to as the dominant European power, making her bid for pre-eminence in the calculation that time was against her and delay would see a stronger Russia. Germany had extensive annexationist aims before and during the war, and deliberately went to war to achieve them. Bethmann-Hollweg's memorandum of war aims of September 1914 has been much cited as sketching out a map of political and economic control foreshadowing that established by the Third Reich in 1940.

If the First World War was essentially a European conflict, its reverberations were on a world scale, not just because fighting took place in Africa, the Middle East and Asia, as well as on all the oceans, but in that the USA was eventually drawn in and Britain had to rely on her Japanese ally to bolster her naval position in the Pacific.

The 'German Question' was not solved by the First World War. Versailles was either too lenient or too severe for that, and from the 'Thirty Years' War' perspective, the so-called inter-war years marked merely the recovery of German strength and the revision of much of the peace settlement. The second military phase was embarked on by Germany in much more propitious circumstances, as the effect of the Bolshevik Revolution resulted in the Western allies having no eastern partner of the weight of imperial Russia.

Compelling as the Thirty Years' War thesis is, it can be challenged on a number of grounds. It neglects the real possibility that by the late twenties Europe had achieved a degree of stability; some of the most pressing problems that had arisen from Versailles had been solved, and, while France had desisted from her forward policy of upholding every letter of the Settlement by force of arms, German generals were reconciled to the impossibility of revisionism by military means. It ignores the economic dimension and the argument that economic recovery in the twenties had produced a less-turbulent Europe and that it was economic depression from 1929 which destroyed this. It takes no account of the role of ideology and of the view that communism and fascism radically changed the nature of international relations. Above all, of course, it takes little account of Adolf Hitler.

Versailles

The strongest and most obvious argument for seeking the origins of the war in Versailles is that the years between 1919 and 1939 were punctuated by a series of crises which concerned the provisions of the peace settlement, and they can retrospectively be seen as steps towards a war which, after all, started over one of those provisions, the free city of Danzig. The Versailles Settlement was central to the territorial changes to the map of Europe that took place at the end of the First World War and did much to determine the context of the international relations of the European powers in the twenties and thirties. It was not, however, Versailles alone that shaped post-war Europe. Two factors of crucial importance pre-dated the peace conference. The decision to keep Germany in being and largely intact had already been taken and Germany had won the war in the East.

By concluding an armistice while a German state and army were still intact, the Western powers provided for the continued existence of Germany. Given that Britain, France and Russia had gone to war to contain the ambitions of the German Empire and that the strength of a unified Germany could be seen as a threat to the European balance of power, the most drastic solution to the German, or rather the Germany, problem would have been to dismember the German state. A secret treaty between France and Russia of March 1917 had in fact provided for a Rhineland under French control, but by November 1918 not only was Russia out of the war but the USA was in it, and any chance of breaking Germany up had passed.

It must also be realised that neither the Versailles Treaty nor the wider Versailles Settlement, encompassing the Treaties of St Germain with Austria, Trianon with Hungary, Neuilly with Bulgaria and Sèvres with the Ottoman Empire, was synonymous with the great reconstruction of Europe that took place at the end of the war and in the immediate post-war years. Sèvres was never ratified nor fully implemented, and after the emergence of a secular national Turkish state under Kemal Ataturk, whose armies decisively defeated those of Greece, it was made redundant by the 1923 Treaty of Lausanne.

Germany had won the war in the east by the end of 1917 and this victory was reflected in the Treaties of Brest-Litovsk and Bucharest early in 1918. Although Germany went on to lose the war in the west, what may be termed the afterglow of Brest-Litovsk was to influence Versailles itself, the shape of inter-war Eastern Europe and the course of the Second World War. The combined effects of the Bolshevik revolution and Brest-Litovsk made a great difference both to the dispositions and scope of the post-war peace settlement. A peace settlement in which Russia ranked among the victorious powers would undoubtedly have provided for areas in eastern Europe not covered by Versailles, and might have made very different provisions for the areas that were covered by it. The consecutive defeats of Russia and Germany, together with Russia's continued weakness, meant that not only did Finland and the Baltic States continue to be independent of Russia but they were also able to be independent of Germany. The simultaneous weakness of the two great powers meant that, like two great boulders, they were temporarily rolled back, allowing small eastern European states a brief independence between them. The same developments allowed the Poland established by Versailles to establish frontiers beyond those of the Treaty by its successful war with Russia in 1920. Brest-Litovsk had, however, demonstrated German power in Eastern Europe and her politicians and public remembered the lost victory, while for Russia, after 1922 the Soviet Union, the permanent loss of territory had never been accepted. Any debate over Versailles's role in causing the Second World War has to take account of the fact that Versailles by itself did not draw the geopolitical map of inter-war Europe.

The argument that the Versailles Settlement led to the Second World War relies both on the view that the treaty with Germany was harsh and vindictive, and that the demise of the Austro-Hungarian Empire, made manifest in St Germain and Trianon, led to an unstable east-central Europe composed of mutually hostile small states. The Treaty of Versailles thus led to a vengeful Germany and the instability to the east provided the path to revenge.

The critique of Versailles which became the received wisdom of the twenties was that Germany, contrary to the promises of Woodrow Wilson's Fourteen Points, was treated as defeated and uniquely culpable, saddled with 'war guilt', made to pay exacting reparations, stripped of territory in defiance of the concept of the principle of national self-determination and subjected to compulsory disarmament and partial military occupation. Yet, if Germany had to submit in 1919, Versailles did little to weaken her position in the long term. Germany had not been invaded and remained Europe's foremost industrial power. The breaking up of the Austro-Hungarian and Russian Empires, together with the Soviet Union's internal problems, presented her with a much weaker east-central Europe than had existed before the war. This, together with the USA's withdrawal into isolationism, meant that in essentials the balance of power had shifted in her favour. As A. Lentin has commented:

> It was a wise precept of Machiavelli that the victor should either
> conciliate his enemy or destroy him. The Treaty of Versailles did

neither. It did not destroy Germany, still less permanently weaken her, appearances notwithstanding, but left her scourged, humiliated and resentful.[5]

The humiliation of the potentially strong is rarely wise. There can be no doubt that most Germans regarded Versailles as a *diktat* and that almost all German politicians were committed to overturning the majority of its provisions. At the same time, France was the only great power dedicated to upholding every aspect of the Treaty. When no American guarantee for Versailles was forthcoming, Britain too refused to underwrite it and 'progressive' British public opinion soon began to feel that it had been unfair to Germany.

The attempt to enforce the letter of Versailles strictly did not last long. The French occupation of the Ruhr in 1922 in order to extract reparations payments was its high point. Reparations were reduced in 1924 (the Dawes Plan) and again in 1929 (the Young Plan), before being discontinued altogether in 1932, though, bizarrely, the last payment on the interest was made in 2010. Some aspects of the Treaty had always been intended to be temporary with provision for the withdrawal of occupying armies and a plebiscite in the French occupied Saar within 15 years. By 1925 France had accepted that it could not by itself enforce Versailles and the Treaty of Locarno seemed to mark a return to stability. France would not seek to maintain every detail of the peace settlement, while Germany sought its revision by diplomatic means. Britain took up an honest broker position, concerned to appease French fears and German grievances. Germany freely recognised the 1919 borders with France and Belgium and the permanent demilitarisation of the Rhineland. Taken together with the scaling down of reparations, Germany's joining of the League of Nations in 1926, and the withdrawal of the allied inspectorate from Germany in 1927, Locarno marked a considerable conciliation of Germany.

Was Locarno the success it appeared at the time? Some have argued that it was irredeemably flawed by its lack of provision for Eastern Europe. The eastern frontiers of Germany and her neighbours were not guaranteed by Locarno, and it was to the east that the territorial provisions of Versailles had left the most dangerous problems. Here the 1919 Settlement had vacillated between the principle of national self-determination and the need to reward allies, leaving not only a division between revisionist states (Germany, Hungary and Bulgaria) and those who had gained from or emerged from the Settlement (Romania, Czechoslovakia, Poland and Yugoslavia), but a simmering dispute over Teschen between two successor states, Poland and Czechoslovakia. It was not the eastern dimensions of Versailles which had caused most

trouble up to 1925 but it was those dimensions which were to dominate the years after 1935. In the intervening decade came depression
in 1929 and Hitler's rise to power in 1933. Locarno left unfinished
business, but the arbitration treaties Germany signed with Poland and
Czechoslovakia could be interpreted as leaving open paths to an eastern Locarno. Gustave Stresemann, the German foreign minister, was,
of course, dedicated to further revisions of Versailles. His signature on
the pacts was analogous to one on a post-dated cheque; payment would
only become due when Germany was strong enough to break the
agreements. Yet, with continued moderate German governments, such
revisions might have been accomplished by diplomacy and agreement.
The coming to power of Hitler in the wake of the Depression altered
the position considerably.

Locarno, from one point of view, marked merely an interval, lasting from 1925 to 1936, in which the interests of France, on the way
down, and Germany, on the way up, happened to coincide with those
of Britain, which just wanted a quiet Europe. From another viewpoint, it inaugurated a genuine period of stability and of co-operation
between Germany and France.

Locarno was essentially an achievement of traditional diplomacy,
but, insofar as one of its provisions was the admission of Germany to
the League of Nations, it appeared to strengthen the greatest ideal-
istic innovation of Versailles, an international structure for the resolution of disputes between powers. Although the League had been
dealt a severe blow by the US Senate's rejection in 1920 of the vision
shown in a US president's proposal, every European state except the
USSR was a member by 1928, while Japan's membership of its Council
underlined its claim to be truly international. In the late twenties the
prestige of the League was high.

The demise of the authority of the League of Nations began in
September 1931 in Manchuria, when the Japanese Kwantung army
put into action its plot to seize Manchuria and quickly occupied the
whole country. The situation in Manchuria had long been confused,
with the Japanese enjoying special rights and control by Chiang Kai
Chek's Republic of China amounting to little more than a vague
admission of suzerainty by the local warlord. Nevertheless the
Chinese government appealed to the League of Nations. Any effective action by the League would have depended upon the support of
a non-member, the USA, which was not forthcoming, but the failure
of the League to take action was both a blow to its reputation and an
indication that military force could bring rewards.

The next blow, both to the principle of collective security represented by the League of Nations and to international stability, came in 1935 with Italy's invasion of Abyssinia (known today as Ethiopia). Although on this occasion economic sanctions were applied, Italy's eventual success again seemed to show the ineffectiveness of collective security. It is often said that the failure of the League marked a return to power politics. This is largely nonsense for an effective League would have depended upon the armed forces and political will of great powers. Its failure simply demonstrated the refusal of Britain and France to go to war over issues that did not threaten their essential interests and took away from power politics the fig leaf of collective security.

Both Japan's takeover of Manchuria and Italy's conquest of Abyssinia were, essentially, outmoded imperialist acts. The two powers could respond, with some justice, that the rules had been changed by states that had secured their own imperial interests. Both cases of expansionism can only be seen as harbingers of the Second World War with hindsight. Neither threatened the essential interests of Britain and France, the states which declared war on Germany in September 1939. What they did do was diminish faith in the League and in the capacity of the great powers to support collective security. Two members of the League's Council had been aggressors and the other two had done little to resist that aggression.

The next crisis was, however, one which directly concerned the European order established by the Versailles Treaty and reaffirmed by Locarno. On 7 March 1936 Germany announced the remilitarisation of the Rhineland, and German troops marched into the demilitarised zone. This action was a flagrant breach of Locarno and destroyed the main buffer against a German westward offensive, but neither Britain nor France was prepared to take military action. Germany had rearmed beyond treaty provisions, but its rearmament was superficial and it was far from ready for war. Its air force, for instance, was in no position to contest the French in the air and it seems certain that a determined France could have acted alone with success. In the end, however, France was faced down in the absence of support from Britain, blaming Britain's refusal to enforce its treaty obligations and act in concert. Germany had already discontinued reparation payments but the remilitarisation of the Rhineland can be seen as the real beginning of the retreat from the Versailles Settlement, which was to end in September 1939 with war over Poland.

What is most beguiling about the view of Versailles as a cause of war in 1939 is that Germany's steps towards war can be seen as a progressive demolition of what, by 1933, remained of the treaty. This was a process facilitated by the lack of appetite displayed by Britain and France for preventing the demolition, if this meant the risk of war, and divisions between those two powers; the Anglo-German Naval Treaty of 1935, which permitted a parity between the German and the Royal Navy in submarines, was concluded, despite Britain's promise to France that she would not conclude a separate treaty with Germany. The seemingly inexorable steps were German rearmament; the remilitarisation of the Rhineland in March 1936; the *Anschluss* (the incorporation of Austria within the German state), March 1938; Munich, September 1938 and the incorporation of the Sudetenland into the Reich, October 1938; the breaking up of Czechoslovakia, March 1939; the retaking of Memel from Lithuania, March 1939; and, finally, the very immediate cause of war, the invasion of Poland over the issue of Danzig, September 1939. Yet, although Hitler's methods were bombastic and threatening, all save the last were accomplished without war. Germany went to war with Poland over what was the last major German grievance of Versailles, a grievance which it seems probable could have been resolved by diplomatic means had Hitler been prepared to exercise patience, and the one which Britain had at the time of Locarno been least prepared to commit herself to upholding. It seems odd to see Versailles as causing the Second World War when so much of the Settlement had been overturned without war.

The Economic Causes of the War

Between the optimism of the late twenties and the remilitarisation of the Rhineland came the depression. The case that the economic depression of 1929–35 did much to cause the war is a strong one. It is seen as destroying economic co-operation and trading relations between the powers, an early casualty being co-operation between French and German business interests. Unemployment threatened political stability, while the decrease in trade led to competitive devaluations of currencies, a search for economic self-sufficiency and protectionism, a kind of economic nationalism. Above all the growth of German unemployment from two million in 1929 to over eight million in 1932 can be seen to have paralleled the rise of the National Socialist Party and Hitler to power, the Nazi vote going up from 800,000 in 1928 to 13 million in July 1932. This latter vote made the National Socialist Party, the Nazi Party, the largest in the German Parliament. Improvements in the economy may well have been responsible for a decline in the Nazi vote at elections in November, but the Nazis remained the biggest party. A combination of Hitler's skilful exploitation of his position and the miscalculation of other right-wing politicians that they could use the Nazis resulted in Hitler becoming chancellor in January 1933.

The hyperinflation of 1923 had already dented the capacity of many of the middle classes, whose savings had been lost, to act as a force for stability and the effect of the depression years was to induce a great swathe of the German population to look for radical or revolutionary solutions to their plight. Voters turned to the extremist parties and it was the extremists of the right who won. It is difficult to argue that the depression caused the Second World War in any straightforward sense as Europe had largely emerged from depression by 1939, but it did much to create a climate of desperation, hostility and political extremism in Germany and elsewhere. It was in this climate that Hitler, leader of what had been a minor party in the relatively prosperous economic climate of the late twenties, came to power.

Marxist analysts of the causes of the war have for long argued that it was the inevitable outcome of the contradictions of the capitalist system and of the international competition for markets and resources of the capitalist powers. Ironically, it can be argued that it was this very analysis of the inevitability of a capitalist war by Marxists of the thirties and its influence on the policies of the USSR that did much to bring about war. Although Hitler and Mussolini were portrayed at times as representing a particular stage of advanced capitalist decay, no basic distinction between their regimes and those of Britain and France was allowed for in the Soviet view of the world; all capitalist powers were enemies of the Soviet Union which had no long-term interest in which of them survived an inter-capitalist war. One result of this was the refusal of the German Communist Party, the KPD, to co-operate in any way with the Social Democrats, the SPD, who were portrayed by the communists as 'social fascists'. This greatly facilitated the Nazi rise to power.

It can, indeed, be argued that it was the departure from orthodox capitalist economics by most powers in the thirties and the subordination of economics to politics that exacerbated international relations. The decade saw a marked decline in world trade as states turned away from free-trading policies towards protectionism, and even attempted self-sufficiency. Such policies worsened relations between states and led to armaments programmes, which in turn produced further economic problems. The need to attempt to balance budgets, and to worry about trade deficits, is at least as impelling a reason for eschewing expensive armament programmes as a desire for world peace, while, with accountable governments, a popular appetite for a decent standard of living is a further curb and the armaments programmes of France and Britain were limited by the need to protect their currencies, to keep down taxation and maintain welfare expenditure. Only in the Soviet Union was the state able to subordinate the economy entirely to the goals of leader and party with Stalin sacrificing living standards to the programme of industrialisation and armaments. It has been argued that 'the Third Reich shifted more resources in peacetime into military uses than any other capitalist regime in history',[6] but 'capitalist' is the operative word here and is one that needs to be carefully qualified in relation to Nazi Germany; it was the extent to which Germany was capitalist that explains the Nazi failure to establish a command economy on Soviet lines, while Hitler unlike Stalin felt a need to retain popular support and demanded that, in the short term, the economy provide both guns and butter. In the long run, Germany's economic potential was not up to the task and Hitler's demands could only be met by conquering neighbouring states and integrating their economies with Germany's. The state that having demonstrated its capacity to provide consumer goods for its citizens was to go on to demonstrate the greatest ability to provide the resources for modern warfare was the archetype of capitalism, the United States.

A War of Ideologies?

A somewhat tattered, but still influential view of the Second World War is that it was 'a war against fascism'. A more complex interpretation is that it was forged in a triangular crucible in which liberal-democracies, fascist states and the Soviet Union formed the three sides and, after preliminary hesitations and side changing, the liberal-democracies and the communist Soviet Union joined forces to defeat the fascist powers. Afterwards the two victors fell out and proceeded to establish their own ideologies in the areas they had conquered.

An alternative view is to see the great divide as between the liberal-democracies together with the semi-authoritarian states, such as the kingdoms and republics of east and central Europe, on the one hand, and *totalitarian* states on the other. Stalin's Russia, Hitler's Germany and even Mussolini's Italy had many striking similarities. The greatest of these was that the state, itself synonymous with party and leader, aspired to total control of every aspect of an individual's life and the elimination or incorporation of any institution that was not a state or party organisation. Stalin was far more successful than Hitler in establishing a state where civil society virtually disappeared, for in Germany private industry, the churches and even the armed forces continued to have some independence; it was, for instance, only in the last months of the Reich that the *Wehrmacht* had the equivalent of commissars imposed on it. In Italy, where the monarchy coexisted with the regime and the Catholic Church had considerable autonomy and influence, a totalitarian state remained an aspiration. The aim, however, was the same in all three states, and it distinguished them from the liberal-democracies and old-fashioned authoritarian states alike. On this basis there was no moral distinction between communism and Nazism/fascism and, if Britain and France had to choose between them or ally with one against the other, the sensible reason for the choice was which was least dangerous.

A further and parallel distinction is between states which were interested in preserving the existing order and those concerned to overturn it. Britain and France were in the former category; their enemies might well say they had good reason to be satisfied with the existing order, rather as the rich man sees little reason to interfere with the prevailing distribution of property and wealth. They were the 'haves'. The 'have not' powers took a different view. Foremost among the 'have nots' were Germany and Italy and, in the Far East, Japan. They also saw themselves as the dynamic powers as opposed to the static powers, Britain and France. The smaller states of east and central Europe could be categorised in a similar way, those who had done well out of Versailles or the contraction of Russia being essentially defensive, while those who had lost territory were hungry for its recovery.

The USA was, like Britain and France, essentially a power content with the existing world order; indeed, because its size and enormous internal market enabled 'isolationism' to seem a feasible policy, it seemed not to have to intervene to protect its interests, though its demands for an 'open door' policy for all states to world markets appeared to many to disguise a consistent support for American business interests.

The USSR was in essence, indeed by definition, a power dedicated – like Germany and Italy – to the upset of the existing order of things. One view of the USSR in the circumstances of the thirties is that it was not in practice an aggressive power, but one content to wait on events in the confident expectation that history was on its side; the capitalist powers, and this included Germany and Italy, were bound to fight each other and war was 'the locomotive of history' which would give the USSR and world communism opportunity. Another view is that Stalin's stance was rather that of thwarted aggression in that he realised he did not yet have the strength to embark upon war against the established European order and calls for proletarian uprisings in western Europe had proved disappointing. In these circumstances the coming to power of Hitler was to be actively, if secretly, welcomed for, in disturbing the European order, he would give Stalin his opportunity.[7]

The view of the major cause of the war as the clash between the upholders of the existing order and those determined to overthrow it embraces ideology, in that Nazism, fascism and Marxism were all opposed for ideological reasons to the existing order, but it also takes us back to geography, history and to *national* interests: a powerful German state determined to expand to greater boundaries and influence and conscious of the dangers of war on two frontiers; a greater Russia, also conscious of two frontiers with a Japanese army on one and a number of small, but hostile states on the other; a France in demographic and military decline, torn between defiance and defence; a fascist Italy with the traditional Italian ambitions in the Mediterranean, Africa and the Balkans; and a Britain, overstretched by imperial commitments, but determined, as in so much of her history, to prevent Europe being dominated by a single great power.

The view of the twenties and thirties as a period dominated by competing political ideologies has some substance but cannot by itself explain the origins of the Second World War. The path to war was tortuous and involved shifting associations between disparate ideological partners, while the foreign policies of the powers were determined by national interests and ambitions as well as by ideology. The question as to which predominated, national interests or ideologies, is not susceptible to an easy answer. Hitler and Mussolini substantially devised their political philosophies which, in any case, gave pride of place to national interests. Stalin's twisting path can be interpreted quite easily in terms of a pragmatic pursuit of Soviet interests, yet he always came up with a suitable Marxist–Leninist explanation for every change of policy, and could justify apparent inconsistencies by the claim that the interests of the Soviet state were identical with those of world socialism.

A consequence of the First World War had been to make incarnate political ideas which were profoundly destabilising and which weakened established authority almost everywhere, and most obviously within the defeated states. The years 1917–22 saw successful and unsuccessful revolutions, economic hardship and the rise of movements hitherto confined to the fringes and backstreets of political life. The liberal-democracies had won the war, but had not made a world safe for their political and social systems.

All over early-twentieth-century Europe, there were socialist parties and socialism was widely perceived as a threat and an alternative to authoritarian and liberal governments alike. As a revolutionary force before 1914, socialism was blunted in a number of ways: by its association, particularly in Britain and France, with a liberal-radical parliamentary tradition; by the growth of revisionism, even within formally Marxist-Socialist parties such as the German Social-Democratic Party, which accepted the possibilities of reform and progress under capitalist systems; and, conversely, by the faith of even outlawed parties, such as the faction of the Russian social-democrats, the Mensheviks, in the inevitable triumph of socialism when the unfolding course of history had created the right socio-economic circumstances. However, the Bolshevik Revolution in Russia saw the success of a disciplined revolutionary party which had seized power and claimed to be taking charge of the course of history, rather than waiting for the 'inevitable' succession of socialism.

There can be little doubt that the Bolshevik Revolution and the setting up of an avowedly revolutionary state, the Soviet Union, were profoundly threatening to other European states. It is true that by 1922, the year the USSR was formally established, expectations that the rest of Europe would quickly follow the path to socialist revolution had been confounded and policy was increasingly based on the defence and protection of socialism in one country, but the Soviet Union remained an open enemy of all other states. Although its existence became warily accepted by other states, here was a state that adopted the normal institutions and apparatus of diplomatic relations, but was formally dedicated to the export of revolution and, in the name of class solidarity, made claims on the allegiance of the citizens of other states. If the one face was represented by foreign ministers and ambassadors, the other showed itself both in the shape of the Comintern, or Communist International, and in support for and control of communist parties. Contemporaries and historians who argued, and argue, that the obvious course for Britain and France was to ally with the USSR against Germany underestimate this factor.

The other developments disruptive to both the internal stability of states and to relations between them are usually grouped together as 'fascism', but here we run into a quagmire of conflicting definitions and analyses. What was fascism, and which parties, movements or regimes can accurately be classified as such? Fascism has been variously described as simply a virulent species of nationalism, a reaction against the modern world, a radical variant of modernism, a deviant form of socialism, or, by Marxists as a late, desperate inspiration of monopoly capitalism.

Certainly nationalism, though national self-determination was embodied in principle by many of the provisions of Versailles, can be seen as a destabilising force. For much of the nineteenth century it had been seen as compatible with liberalism, but had, in the later decades of that century, in some countries acquired a pronounced racialist tone. In the circumstances of the immediate post-war world, nationalism became a more radical and less-conservative force, no longer subservient to elite leadership and finding its support among ex-servicemen, the unemployed and discontented members of the lower middle classes. Extreme nationalist movements are sometimes lumped together by historians with Italian fascism, which gained power in Italy in 1922, and with political groups in other countries which emulated Italian fascism. A further extrapolation sees Germany's National Socialists, Japan's militarists and right-wing factions and Spanish Nationalists as one and all fascists. A tighter definition of fascism confines the term to a small number of movements of which only the Italian variety exercised unchallenged political power for any length of time.

The Italian Fascist Party came to power in 1922 and soon inspired imitators in most European states, but did not initially appear a threat to diplomatic stability. The problem for Benito Mussolini was that, although he glorified dynamism and force in foreign policy, Italy was not a first-class military power. The bombardment and occupation of Corfu in 1923 epitomised what the British diplomat Harold Nicolson called Mussolini's 'exuberant petulance' but the main foreign policy success of his early years in power, the acquisition of Fiume in 1924, was the result of diplomatic negotiations and for the next decade his foreign policy was relatively cautious and conventional.

Where international communism was monolithic, an international fascism was intrinsically something of a contradiction in terms. An International Fascist Conference was held in 1934 and there were links between the Italian fascists and fascist parties in other countries, but – in that fascism, in many ways a socialist heresy, put its faith in the nation, rather than a notional international identity like a class, and espoused the concept of struggle and force – the problems for co-operation between fascist parties are obvious. Yet there was a supranational European dimension to Italian fascism and the aspirations of other European fascist parties. Mussolini in the early and, indeed, in the late days of the movement talked of uniting the nations of Europe and found a response in those throughout Europe who feared that European power was in decline and that unity alone could enable the continent to compete with the USA. Fascism, indeed, hovered between the ethos of the nation and that of Europe.

If fascism was primarily national, there could only be pragmatic alliances and empathy but no long-term unity of interests between fascist movements. Italy, for instance, gave some financial assistance to Oswald Mosley's British Union of Fascists, just as the British Communist Party was financed and its newspaper, the *Daily Worker*, subsidised by the Soviet Union. But, whereas British communists could openly declare subordination to the Comintern and the socialist motherland, the BUF might emulate Italian fascism, but its nationalist ethos denied, at least in theory, subordination to foreign direction. Yet, just as fascists in Vichy France hoped for a new order that would be genuinely European rather than a mere German hegemony, so Oswald Mosley after 1945 attempted to build a European Movement on the ruins of the old BUF.

As well as style, a liking for uniforms, salutes, youth sections, angry rhetoric and street fighting, fascist movements had a rather loose philosophy in common: belief in dynamism, action, strong leaders, nationalism, an interventionist and directive state, together with a distaste for both capitalism, liberal-democracy and communism. 'Fascism', as we have seen, is a term often used very loosely, but an authoritarian regime, even with a dictator in a uniform, does not constitute a fascist regime. There were plenty of dictators around in inter-war Europe and, indeed, in Latin America and elsewhere, but most of them were clerical conservatives or straightforward nationalists, even if some, like Salazaar in Portugal and Franco in Spain, had fascist trimmings or fascist supporters.

Mussolini attempted to forge his country into a strong state with most aspects of life controlled by the Fascist Party and opposition crushed. The positive method of eliminating conflict and dissension within the state was the corporatist state: all interests within the state, workers, employers, even the professions, were to be organised in corporations, their interests harmonised and synthesised under a Ministry of Corporations. Much of Mussolini's and his party's dream of a united, unitary, dynamic and efficient Italian state was not translated into reality. Pragmatism demanded the retention of the monarchy, and the Lateran Treaty of February 1929 gave a separate and privileged position to the Catholic Church, while the recognition of the Confederation of Industry ensured that employers retained

considerable freedom of action. It may well have been that disillusionment with the attempt to transform Italy and lack of economic
success impelled Mussolini towards a more aggressive foreign policy
in the mid thirties.

Until 1935 Mussolini's foreign policy was generally unadventurous
and, even though Italians had been greatly disappointed by their gains
from Versailles, Italy was a guarantor of Locarno. Mussolini pursued
the aim of greater influence in the Mediterranean and had ambitions
in the Adriatic and North Africa, but so had previous Italian governments. Nor were relations with Germany particularly close, with Italy
supporting Austrian independence and enjoying reasonable relations
with France and Britain.

The meeting at Stresa in April 1935, at which Britain, France and Italy
upheld the sanctity of treaties and condemned Germany's breaches of
them was the high point of Mussolini's co-operation with Britain and
France and seemed to suggest that Italy's opposition to Hitler's aim of
incorporating Austria into the Reich was stronger than any ideological sympathy with him. Even before the Stresa talks began, however,
Mussolini had begun his moves towards an African conquest and had
insisted on the insertion of the words 'in Europe' in all mentions of
support for the sanctity of treaties and for the peaceful resolution of
conflicts.

On 3 October 1935 Mussolini plunged Europe and the League of
Nations into crisis with his invasion of Abyssinia, an old-fashioned
imperialist act. This and the reactions of Britain and France to the
invasion led to a sea change in his foreign policy. From 1936 Italy
intervened on the side of the Nationalists in the Spanish Civil War
and was soon joined by Germany. In the same year, Mussolini moved
closer to Hitler and announced a Rome–Berlin Axis. The price of
German friendship was to cease giving support to an independent
Austria. When, in 1934, Hitler had threatened to invade Austria,
Mussolini had sent troops to the Brenner Pass, but in 1938 he made
no attempt to prevent the incorporation of Austria into the Reich.
In April 1939 Italy occupied Albania, and in May a formal German–
Italian alliance, the Pact of Steel, was signed. By this time Mussolini's
goals were clear and, just as importantly, so were his methods. He had
built on the traditional aspirations of Italian policy. Previous Italian
governments, and indeed the earlier Mussolini, had sought a greater
share of power in the Mediterranean and Adriatic, now Italy wished
to dominate. He argued in 1939 that Italy was imprisoned by the
Mediterranean, the bars of the prison being provided by British and
French possessions such as Corsica, Tunis, Cyprus and Malta, while

the sentinels were Gibraltar and Suez. Once the bars were broken, Italy could march to the Indian Ocean or the Atlantic. Such ambitions could only be achieved by conflict with Britain and France and in alliance with Germany. Too little attention has been paid to Mussolini's foreign policy and expansionist ambitions. Because the Italian army was not up to the tasks he gave it, and had to be rescued by Germany in both Greece and North Africa, the role of Mussolini in ensuring that the war had a southern European and North African sphere has tended to be underestimated. Without Mussolini's initiatives, Britain in 1941 would have had nowhere to fight a land war. To what extent his foreign policy was fascist or just an extension of traditional Italian policies is, however, debatable. Perhaps it is best characterised as a union of established Italian aims and the fascist ethos made wilder by failures in domestic policy and emulation of Hitler.

Hitler had earlier emulated Mussolini, taking many of the trappings of Italian fascism for his own party and launching the unsuccessful Bavarian *Putsch* of 1923 in imitation of Mussolini's march on Rome. Increasingly from 1936 it was Mussolini who followed Hitler. How much did Italian fascism and German Nazism have in common? Obviously quite a lot: the cult of a charismatic leader; an emphasis on action, dynamism and youth; extreme nationalism; the same sort of paramilitary trappings and so on. There were also major differences: whereas fascism saw itself as a thoroughly modern movement born of a new industrialising Italy and as welcoming urbanisation and technology with little time for the cultural and social traditions of the past, the Nazi attitude to the modern world was ambiguous and involved a yearning for a rural past, a Teutonic bond with nature and a *folk* rooted in the land; bound up with this was the Nazi obsession with race, whereas fascism was nationalist but not racialist; and when it came to economic and social questions, fascism had a greater claim to a coherent philosophy with its corporatism in comparison with Hitler's somewhat *ad hoc* policies.

The Nazi Party's 25-point programme, drawn up in 1920, had three main features: it was nationalistic, seeking the dismantling of much of Versailles and aiming for a greater Germany; it was anti-capitalist, but it called for class unity instead of class war; and it was anti-Semitic. The combination of nationalism and socialism were enduring themes during Hitler's rise to power, though once power came close, he was prepared to make accommodations with big business. The social radicalism of Nazism should not, however, be underestimated; social unity was an essential aim of Hitler's and, though he made tactical accommodations with manufacturers and the aristocratic army command alike, Nazi government was to see a more fluid and less class-based society develop. Anti-Semitism was undoubtedly central to Hitler and the Nazi Party's world view, bizarrely so, as to see the Jews behind Bolshevism *and* the capitalism of Wall Street and the City of London was a feverish conspiracy theory, but, if there was a consistent purpose leading from *Mein Kampf* and the early twenties to the programme of genocide begun in 1941, it was not one that was perennially prominent in Hitler's speeches. Nor was anti-Semitism a major factor in Hitler's rise to power. Many Germans were anti-Semitic but, although hatred of the Jews figured prominently in the mind sets of individual Nazis and engaged much of the party's rank and file, Hitler seems to have realised that to make anti-Semitism a main plank of the Nazi programme was not, before 1933, a way to gain mass support nor, after that date, a way to consolidate support for his regime.

Perhaps the Nazi Party's anti-Semitism should be seen as part of its ambiguous relationship with modernity. It has been suggested that secularised Judaism was a major modernising force in the early twentieth century, propelling capitalism and the arts alike.[8] National Socialism, like socialism itself, was basically a collectivist reaction to the individualism of capitalism and liberalism, and the Nazi emphasis on national unity and opposition to capitalism included anti-Semitism in its psychological baggage. As we have seen anti-Semitism was not a feature of Italian fascism before Mussolini began to imitate and be led by Hitler. In fact, the proportion of the small Jewish population of Italy who were members of the Fascist Party in the twenties and early thirties was high and Mussolini, who himself had a Jewish mistress, Margherita Sarfatti, until the early thirties, experienced considerable difficulty in persuading his followers to adopt anti-Semitism.[9] There was little that was universal or internationalist about Nazism, unless anti-Semitism is taken as such. Hitler was a radical German nationalist and Nazism was not for export except as German hegemony. In this it parted company with fascism which mixed nationalism with Europeanism. Those European fascists who mistook Hitler for a leader of a new Europe, instead of a German empire, were to be disappointed in the new European order that Hitler briefly imposed from 1940.

If the differences between Mussolini's Italy and Hitler's Germany were distinct, what of that other partner in the supposed fascist alliance? The notion that the Japanese Empire was fascist or became so in the thirties, as extreme nationalist political and military factions jostled for power and impelled Japan into expansionist policies, has little substance. There were some similarities: a rejection of parliamentary democracy, a central direction of the economy in the interests of military production, extreme nationalism and an adulation of the armed forces. Japan had, however, no charismatic leader, nor a one-party state. The Meiji period had seen an attempt to add a political and military dimension to the traditional theocratic role of the Emperor but Hirohito exerted little positive authority. The Japanese were nationalistic, authoritarian and imperialistic, and they threatened the established order in the Far East. Fascism was a word that happened to be at hand. It is probably better to confine use of the term 'fascism' to Mussolini's movement and to those other movements which accepted the label and think instead of an empathy between states which were authoritarian, militaristic and nationalistic.

That the Italian–German alliance grew ever closer from 1935 and that Japan joined Germany and Italy in the vague Anti-Comintern Pact of November 1936 are not the only reasons for the influential perception of the need for an anti-fascist alliance that was current in the late thirties. A parallel development was a change in the Soviet attitude towards Italy and Germany. The Soviet Union in its twin roles of power and revolutionary agent persisted until 1935 in seeing fascism and National Socialism as merely another face of finance capitalism and viewed even non-Marxist socialists as 'social fascists'. Soviet–Italian relations were good in the late twenties and there were mutually beneficial trading links. Communist ideology initially saw Hitler's rise to power as a hopeful sign of the impending collapse of capitalism. In August 1935, however, the ideological line was redefined with the Comintern deciding that if Nazism was still an example of finance capitalism, it was a particularly dangerous specimen, so a popular front embracing all anti-fascist forces was necessary. From 1935 to 1939 the popular-front philosophy was promoted by Moscow, finding its greatest success and symbol in its support for the Republican side in the Spanish Civil War.

The popular front propaganda campaign was remarkably successful in attracting the support of socialist and even of much liberal opinion. Non-Marxist socialists had had an ambivalent attitude towards communism and the Soviet Union, intensely suspicious of the communist parties in their own countries, but attracted by the image of the Soviet Union as an avowedly socialist state. Hurt and angry at being described as social fascists, they welcomed the concept of a front against fascism even to the extent of turning a blind eye to the export of Stalinist purges into the Spanish arena where the NKVD, the Soviet secret police, took every opportunity to eliminate Trotskyists, anarchists and other deviationists from the Soviet line.

The success of the popular front propaganda was responsible for one of the most enduring myths of the thirties, that of a united alliance of all right-thinking, or rather left-thinking, men and women against fascism. Fractured and shaken by the Hitler–Stalin Pact of 1939, it was dusted down in 1941 and formed the basis of that other myth – that the Second World War was a war against fascism.

Hitler's War?

Adolf Hitler dominates any discussion of the Second World War. Without him it seems possible that the rivalries between the powers over ideology, land or resources could have led to a war or wars, but not to a world war involving all the great powers. How responsible was Hitler for the war that began in 1939?

By the summer of 1939 Germany, as we have seen, had been successful in reversing most of the provisions for central Europe made by the Versailles Treaty. No doubt any German politician would have been glad to accomplish such a demolition of the hated Treaty, if few would have used Hitler's methods or taken the risks he did. Gustave Stresemann's foreign-policy aims certainly seem to have been far-reaching. He informed the German cabinet in 1925 that he wished to create a greater Germany in central Europe[10] and declared in 1926 that 'Naturally we refuse to see any justification for the continued existence of the present Polish state.'[11] It seems fair to conclude that what Stresemann envisaged went beyond a comprehensive revision of Versailles. Such ambitions might well have been accomplished without a war, or even by a limited war with Poland, and it is possible to see war in 1939 as caused by Hitler's methods rather than his aims.

But was Hitler's aim the extended German hegemony in Europe that Stresemann, like many imperial German statesmen before him, aspired to? Were his aims, rather than being in the tradition of German foreign policy and those of an 'ordinary German politician', those of an extraordinary Austrian political extremist who was given – by virtue of will, ability and chance – the opportunity to turn into reality the wilder pan-German and racialist ideas that had been current in the bars and coffee houses of turn of the century Vienna? Was the revision of Versailles no more than a first step towards world conquest or even a mere tool to inveigle a reluctant German population into a major conflict? We come back to the big question: just how much difference did Hitler make?

Rarely has so much been written on a man and less of a consensus emerged as to his aims, motives and dynamics than in the case of Adolf Hitler. There is no disputing that Hitler always wanted to undo Versailles and unite adjacent German peoples into the Reich, but as to how far his ambitions extended beyond this and how consistently throughout his career he pursued a definite plan, there is no agreement. The main division is between those who believe that from early in his career, Hitler was determined on conquests which went far beyond any traditional German foreign-policy aims and those who consider him an opportunist, albeit a ruthless one, who reacted to events and took advantage of the chances they offered to extend his and Germany's power.

In the former camp are those who see his ambitions as essentially Eurocentric and those who perceive a plan for world domination. Much stress has been laid on Hitler's book *Mein Kampf* as revealing his aims and intentions; he may have weaved and tacked along the way, but what he wanted, it has been claimed, was a great German empire in eastern Europe which would provide *Lebensraum* (living space) for the German people. A reliance on *Mein Kampf* goes hand in hand with the view that Hitler's early hatred of Bolshevism and of the Soviet Union was maintained throughout his career and that his invasion of the Soviet Union in 1941 was intended to bring about the culmination of his ambitions. But was a greater Germany bestriding Eastern Europe the limit of his aims? Some have seen Hitler's aim as global rather than European mastery: the defeat of France and the attack on Russia were merely the continental phase in an attempt at world conquest, and were meant to be followed by the defeat of the British Empire and a final showdown with the USA.[12] This view has gained support from Gerhard L. Weinberg's *A World at Arms: A Global History of World War II* (1994), which argues that Hitler always aimed at a total reordering of the globe. A variant is Adam Tooze's argument that the United States always loomed large in Hitler's thinking, in that he realised and hated the increasing economic power and cultural influence of America; he knew that without extreme action Germany and Europe were going to be overshadowed by American capitalism and his attack on the Soviet Union and its corollary, the establishment of *Lebensraum*, were a desperate attempt to prevent this.[13]

Taylor's view that Hitler had no great programme and that the main sources for Hitler's intentions, *Mein Kampf*, *Hitler's Secret Book* and *The Table Talk*, need not be taken too seriously has received some support from German historians, who have argued that Hitler's foreign policy was often a reaction to domestic pressures. It is too easily assumed, they argue, that Hitler was effortlessly in charge and that the Nazi Party and, indeed, Nazi Germany were his mere tools. He needed to satisfy demands from within the Nazi Party for action, and his and German policies need to be seen in the context of the structure of German society in the Third Reich. Such 'structuralists' argue that the Nazi regime was more than just Hitler and that the *Führer* had to react to internal pressures, while the unstable competing agencies, over which he presided rather than directed, produced results that he went along with rather than willed.[14] The attention given to the overlapping and rival bureaucracies of the Third Reich has, in many accounts, replaced the image of an efficient dictatorship with one of considerable administrative chaos under the aegis of a remote, if charismatic, *Führer*. Hitler becomes a 'weak dictator' and an opportunist responding to external pressures.

Even if there was a fair amount of administrative chaos in the Third Reich, with Nazi leaders controlling their spheres of power like so many feudal barons and the state kept going by the old regime of civil service, army and private industry, it is difficult to see Hitler as a weak leader, though he may have been a leader with weaknesses. His personal power and the administrative failings of the regime went hand in hand, founded as both were on institutions and individuals competing for his favour and power. There is, however, little reason to believe that he was not in control of foreign policy. The German people had no great enthusiasm for a prolonged war, but he led them into one; the satraps of the party would have been content to strut on the middle European stage, but followed him to a wider theatre.

Whatever Hitler's long-term aims, did he intend to fight a war in 1939? Much depends on what sort of war one means. He would probably have welcomed a war with a minor power at any time from early in 1938 – the ethos of National Socialism dictating a preference for violent rather than peaceful acquisitions of territory – but had hoped to postpone a war with France and avoid a war with Britain.

The state of the German economy and the level of German rearmament have been seen as crucial to the question of Hitler's plans for war. On the one hand there is the view that the very weakness of the economy and its need for expensive imports impelled Germany towards war.[15] Against this is the argument that if Hitler had expected to fight a great war in 1939, he would have attuned his armament and economic strategy to that end.

Germany, it seems clear, did not have an economy mobilised for total war in 1939. Contemporaries were often convinced by Germany's great military parades that Hitler had created a war economy, but this was far from the case. One explanation of this is that he did not expect a war with a major power or powers, and was content with an army and air force that could fight short lightning wars, or *blitzkreigs*, in central Europe.[16] Such 'superficial' rearmament fitted in with an economic strategy designed to keep the German population prosperous and contented. To spend too much of the German national income on armaments risked weakening the support of the German people for the Nazi regime. Hitler, it has been argued, had never forgotten the collapse of the home front in 1918 and distrusted the capacity of Germans to suffer hardship in the national cause. He thus sought an armaments programme that was not extensive enough to interfere with consumer spending so that even after the outbreak of war the economy was not fully mobilised until 1942.

Germany had tackled the massive unemployment of the early thirties by stimulating the economy with public spending on the chemical and steel industries, on roads and on rearmament. Paradoxically, however, even the armaments industry posed problems for rearmament. If workers made good money working in the armaments industry, were they to be allowed to spend their money on consumer goods and better food? If so, how was the state to pay for the raw material imports necessary for the armaments programme? This dilemma resulted in an overheating of the economy which could only be resolved by cuts in the standard of living or by expansionist wars.

An alternative explanation is that Hitler was indeed bent on a total mobilisation of the economy for war and that this process was inaugurated with the Four Year Plan of 1936.[17] This plan, behind schedule because of the inefficiencies and rivalries within the Reich and the reluctance of private industry to co-operate, was only the first stage in preparation for a major war Hitler expected to fight sometime in the mid-1940s. Germany found itself at war in 1939 at a half-way stage in a rearmament programme which involved the restructuring of the entire economy. There had been no deliberate plan to rest content with a capacity for *blitzkreig* operations.

The weight of the diplomatic, military and economic evidence is against Hitler desiring or planning a war with Britain and France in 1939. The much-argued-over Hossbach Memorandum, the minutes of a secret meeting at the Reich Chancellory on 5 November 1937, demonstrates that Hitler was determined to overthrow Austria and Czechoslovakia and incorporate them within the Reich. It also reveals that he did not expect to achieve this until 1943–5 and, though he saw Britain and France as 'hate-inspired antagonists', did not necessarily expect them to intervene. He was, however, prepared to act earlier if opportunity, in the shape of French weakness, beckoned. By early 1939 he had achieved his aim as regards Austria and Czechoslovakia. Overconfident now that an understanding with the Soviet Union was achieved, he blundered into a war with Britain and France over Poland that he did not really want.

The overturning of the Versailles Settlement in central Europe was there for Germany's asking. Another German government would have probably achieved it more slowly. Hitler's contribution was to speed up the process, rob it of any shreds of diplomatic decency, and stumble into war with Britain and France in the final stage. His expansionist aims went far beyond a greater Germany in central Europe, but if they explain his actions in 1941, they had little to do with the outbreak of war in 1939.

A War Caused by Appeasement?

That it takes two to make a war is only true in the sense that surrender to aggression avoids war, as in the case of Czechoslovakia, and resistance ensures one, as in the case of Poland. It can, however, be argued that the policies of the other European powers and their reactions to Germany's unilateral and incremental demolition of the Versailles Settlement did much to contribute to the outbreak of war. To what extent were the policies of the other European powers responsible for the Second World War?

The most well-established view is that Britain and France should have intervened militarily long before September 1939. The time favoured retrospectively is the point where Hitler abandoned Stresemann's policy of negotiating a revision of Versailles and moved to one of forceful dismemberment of it, either when he openly disavowed the rearmament clauses of Versailles or when he moved troops into the demilitarised zone of the Rhineland. In 1935 and 1936, it is argued, the German armed forces were in no position to take on those of Britain and France, and Hitler would have had to climb down or would have been overthrown by the army. Even in 1938 military opposition at the time of the *Anschluss* or, later in the year, in support of Czechoslovakia could have succeeded in arresting Hitler's progress and perhaps led to his fall from power.

This view of the failure of Britain and France to take effective action as a major cause of the war was the 'common sense' of 1945 and of the immediate post-war world. It still commands much support. The villain of the peace is an Anglo-French policy of 'Appeasement': not only did the two powers give way tamely to Hitler's demands, but they failed to do so early or thoroughly enough. An ancillary charge is that they refused effectively to pursue alliance with the one power that could have counter-balanced Germany, the Soviet Union.

It is important to see the policies and reactions of Britain and France in the context not of a war that was in the future, but within the circumstances and restrictions that surrounded events which can only retrospectively be seen as steps towards that war. Only a handful of contemporaries considered in 1933, or even in 1936, that the fundamental nature of Europe's problems had been changed rather than merely exacerbated by Hitler's accession to power. There was thus, unsurprisingly, considerable continuity in the foreign policies pursued by Britain and France both before and after 1933.

Locarno had marked a French acquiescence in a partial erosion of the Versailles Settlement and a move towards a defensive approach to Germany, which was to be concretely expressed in the Maginot Line. What would later be called appeasement, a readiness to give way to German demands for further revisions to Versailles, was already established British policy by the mid-twenties. There was no consensus between the two powers when it came to the German problem, but two distinct analyses and policies.

French appeasement is perhaps better described as pessimistic realism. There were few in France who believed that Germany had been badly treated in 1919, but many who doubted France's chances of success in a future war with her powerful neighbour. The French population had for long been in relative decline compared to Germany's, but the low birth rate now brought it close to absolute decline. The economy had been gravely weakened by the war and France had lost most of her overseas investments; rescued by the devaluation of the franc and a brief export boom in the late twenties, France went into depression later than the other powers, but by the mid-thirties her industrial production had declined by a third and the countryside was plunged into poverty as agricultural prices fell. A polarisation between left and right marked politics, with right-wing riots in 1934 and the election of a popular front government in 1935. Worried by the revival of German power, traumatised by the great loss of life in the late war, her economy in recession after 1932, and socially and politically divided, France perceived dangers she had not the will to confront.

Prior to 1914 France had found the answer to her relative weakness compared to Germany in an alliance with Russia. A standard criticism of French and, to a degree, British foreign policy in the thirties has, as we have seen, been the failure to come to a firm understanding with the USSR. Such a view neglects the fact that the USSR, if further away than Germany, was as hostile in long-term intent towards the Western democracies, and that many of the eastern and central European states France was allied with were as opposed to the USSR as they were to their other big neighbour. France did, in 1934, sign a pact of mutual assistance with the USSR, but it was only ratified after stiff resistance from the French right. Britain was hostile to a consolidation of Franco-Soviet ties, considering that Germany would see this as a policy of encirclement and it would impede the settlement of German grievances which was Britain's aim.

British policy, too, was constrained by her diminished economic and military strength and by strong strands of neo-pacifist feeling among the electorate. Rearmament was made difficult by a combination of democracy and economics: it was not just that much of the electorate opposed rearmament on the grounds that it led to war, but that the electorate demanded spending on social policies which reduced the money available for defence spending, while any rapid expansion in armaments was likely to lead to balance of trade deficits. The major constraint upon Britain, however, was that she had military commitments around the world which were ill-matched by her capacity to fulfil them. Both Britain and France had great empires, but imperial considerations counted for much more in the minds of British policymakers. France was a continental power with long borders and potential enemies. German forces had invaded French territory twice in 50 years. She had a network of alliances with the Versailles states of central and eastern Europe. Important as her empire was to France, there could never be any question of choosing between it and her European interests. This was not the case with Britain.

Britain was a European power with a strong interest in the stability of the continent, but to both government and people her political and economic interests seemed more dependent upon her empire and her worldwide role. This was no fading vision, for the experience of the First World War had increased enthusiasm for an empire which had loyally supported Britain, while, as Britain pulled out of depression in the early thirties, her economic interests were more bound up with the imperial trading area than ever before. The Empire was led by Britain, but much of it was not ruled by the British government and in a very real sense, British foreign policy cannot be seen as entirely autonomous, but had to take account of the views of the governments of the dominions.

Britain's position in the inter-war period has been seen as a classic example of the way in which great powers tend to increase their military commitments in the defence of their manifold possessions and interests beyond their economic strength. An early manifestation of British weakness had been the signing of the Anglo-Japanese Alliance in 1902, a tacit acknowledgement that Britain by herself could not fulfil all her Far East commitments against all corners. Twenty years later, when defence spending was being sharply cut back and the Empire was wider than ever, Britain under pressure from the USA gave up this, her only alliance. From 1921 to 1941 Britain had no ally in the Pacific, making her extended commitments more worrying and diminishing any chance that she could overawe any threats to the European balance of power. Unable to maintain an adequate Pacific fleet or to prepare proper defences for the most important base, Singapore, British governments were acutely aware that a war in Europe would expose their vulnerability in the Far East.

A further distinction between British and French appeasement of Germany was that, while for France appeasement was essentially negative, a policy forced upon her by her weakness, there was a positive side to British appeasement. The view that Germany had real grievances, particularly over the position of Germans outside the German state, as in the Sudetenland and Danzig, commanded considerable support among government circles and the general public alike.

The reasons why Britain and France did not oppose Germany's remilitarisation of the Rhineland must be seen in the context of the above and of the immediate circumstances. Italy, one of the guarantors of Locarno, was estranged from Britain and France because of their opposition to her invasion of Abyssinia and was rapidly growing closer to Germany when, in March 1936, Hitler ordered troops into the Rhineland; this was no large army and it consisted of no more than 30,000 regular troops, a mere 3000 of whom were to penetrate deep into the zone with orders to retreat immediately in the event of contact with French forces. They were enough for there was little likelihood of their being opposed.

Baldwin's government was committed to rearmament on a limited scale, and to collective security via the League of Nations, while it was preoccupied by the Abyssinian question. Public opinion was strongly against intervention and among politicians of influence only Austin Chamberlain, an architect of Locarno, spoke out for it; Churchill gave no indication at the time of the importance he later attached to Britain's and France's failure to intervene. In France a left-centre government had only been in office for a few weeks and was struggling with social and financial problems; an international crisis seemed likely to result in a devaluation of the franc. The advice from both British and French generals was that the forces required for intervention were not available. Whether military intervention would have led to a war with Germany was never put to the test, but it is important to realise that in the circumstances of the time such intervention was never likely. Germany was allowed, in Lord Lothian's phrase, to walk into her 'own back garden'.

France's defences were drastically weakened by the remilitarisation of the Rhineland. The Maginot line had not run along the Belgian frontier because Belgium was allied to France by a treaty of 1920 and France had relied upon Belgium's own defence line on the Belgian-German border. Belgium, now exposed on her frontier with Germany, declared herself a neutral power and France was open to invasion if, as in 1914, Germany invaded via Belgium.

If France was not prepared to take military action over such a threat to her own immediate border with Germany, it was hardly conceivable that she would have intervened when, in March 1938, Austria was absorbed into the German Reich. Hitler's support for the German separatist movement in Czechoslovakia's Sudetenland seemed much more likely to provoke French intervention when he encouraged the indigenous Nazis there to demand full autonomy and threatened force if the Czech government did not comply. Edouard Daladier, at the head of a centre-right coalition, had become premier a few weeks after the *Anschluss*. He was the man who in the end steeled the French nation for war, but in 1938 his government was divided over support for the Czechs, his foreign office advisers were against it, the generals were pessimistic and public opinion demanded peace at almost any price.

Throughout the long drawn-out crisis, which lasted from March till September, Europe was near to war on two occasions when, in May and September, German invasions looked close. Hitler would probably have preferred to resolve the matter by war, but not by a war against Britain and France. Each time this threatened he drew back. France, bound by a treaty commitment going back to 1924 to go to Czechoslovakia's aid if she was attacked, was largely concerned to escape her obligations with the minimum of dishonour, but would probably have honoured them in the event of a German invasion of the Sudetenland. The USSR was treaty bound to aid the Czechs if the French honoured their commitment. Whether she would have done so is debateable: Soviet ground forces could only have reached Czechoslovakia via Poland or Romania and both states would have opposed their passage, In addition, the USSR was fighting Japanese forces on the Manchurian border at the time, while the Red Army was demoralised and disorganised by a purge of the senior-officer corps. Britain's role was crucial. Neville Chamberlain had succeeded Baldwin as prime minister the previous year. Chamberlain had a shrewd appreciation of Britain's strength and realised that a major war was likely to lead to economic decline and the loss of the empire. His main aim, however, was to safeguard the power and influence of Britain, and he was no defeatist. If he was prepared to make concessions in the face of German demands, he made them in order to achieve a settlement which he thought could be the basis for a wider European stability. Such a settlement would provide for an enlarged German state, but not for a German super-power.[18]

To this end, throughout the summer and autumn of 1938 he pursued a double strategy, putting pressure on the Czechs to come to an accommodation with Hitler while at the same time demonstrating to him that an invasion could result in Britain and France coming to Czechoslovakia's aid. The former was pushed more firmly than the latter and the Czechs were more malleable than the Germans. A crucial factor was the way the Czechoslovakian government was pushed aside. Czechoslovakia's best chance was, paradoxically, a German invasion, which might have impelled France and Britain to come to her aid, but a merely threatened invasion simply put the pressure on the Czechs to make concessions and eventually marginalised them. Every time they made concessions at British and French insistence, they made British and French support less likely.

At the time, Chamberlain's three journeys to Germany in September 1938 seemed heroic attempts to save the peace of Europe, but to posterity his efforts have often seemed futile and naive. He did believe both that Germany had a genuine claim to the Sudetenland and that a settlement with Hitler was possible. The likelihood that Britain would have gone to war if no agreement had been possible should not be underestimated. Britain and France were preparing for war when Hitler, having already gained British and French agreement to an annexation of the Sudetenland by Germany, in late September upped his demands to the immediate occupation of the area, plus consideration of Slovak autonomy, and Polish and Hungarian claims to Czechoslovak territory. In the end war did not break out because the Czechs were not prepared to fight without allies and the Germans were not prepared to invade, and risk a war with Britain and France. Of course, Hitler got what he ostensibly wanted, the Sudetenland, without a war, but as what he had really wanted included a quick war, he felt that Chamberlain had outwitted him.

The applause which greeted both Chamberlain and Daladier on their return from Munich was followed rapidly by disillusionment, as the Czechoslovakian state was torn apart within a few months. Daladier realised at the time how much France had given away and turned to stiffening French opinion towards the probable necessity of war with Germany. Chamberlain did not despair of an accommodation with Germany, but decided that the threat of war must play a greater part in securing it. Neither Britain nor France totally trusted each other, both fearing that their putative ally might seek a separate agreement with Germany, but in February 1939 talks began between their general staffs. After Hitler's entry into Prague and the end of the Czechoslovakian state on 15 March 1939, followed by the seizure by Germany of the Lithuanian town of Memel on 23 March, came the Anglo-French guarantee of Poland on 31 March.

The guarantee of Poland's independence, followed after Italy's invasion of Albania by further guarantees to Romania and Greece, and then by an Anglo-French-Turkish Treaty in May, has been seen as the great turning point in British policy. Public opinion was now against further appeasement of Hitler, while Chamberlain himself was disillusioned both by Hitler's failure to keep his word and by the fact that he had now incorporated non-German areas into the Reich. It would be a mistake, however, to think that the guarantees marked a complete change of Chamberlain's policy rather than of his tactics; the aim was the same, a European settlement, but the tactic was deterrence rather than concession.

Praised by some as a firm stand, the guarantee of Poland has been criticised by other historians. There was not a great deal the allies could do to defend Poland, or Romania for that matter. Czechoslovakia had appeared to have stouter defences and a more modern army. The most important dispute between Germany and Poland concerned Danzig, a German town given limited freedom from Polish control as a free city, and this seemed to be one of the less-defensible provisions of Versailles. Poland had taken the opportunity to seize Teschen from Czechoslovakia in October and thus could be seen as an aggressive state. Negotiations had been taking place between Germany and Poland and, although the Poles had turned down German offers of an alliance in return for concessions over Danzig and Poland's corridor to the sea through German territory, the guarantee could be seen as a strengthening of the Polish hand if such negotiations were resumed. Although it was 'Polish independence' that was guaranteed and not every square mile of Polish territory, it could be argued that Britain and France had placed their fates in the hands of a Poland always too ready to overestimate its strength. Poland was not a state that could be easily coerced for, unlike the Czechs who had a civic sense of nationhood, the Poles had a heroic and aristocratic national ethos; they were determined not to become satellites of either Germany or the USSR, and were prepared to fight for their independence without giving too much consideration to the odds. From the point of view of Poland, the choice of accepting Anglo-French protection and defying Germany was fateful. It can be argued that the best option for the Poles was to accept the loss of Danzig and ally their nation with Germany against the Soviet Union and that, indeed, there was a real possibility in 1939 that this could have occurred had the Poles not had a misplaced confidence in their army's ability to repel a German attack.[19]

Did the guarantees deter Hitler? Well, clearly not in September 1939, but by then the Hitler-Stalin Pact was in place and Germany was secure in the knowledge that the USSR would not only be a friendly neutral in a war between Germany and the Western powers, but would provide essential raw materials for the German war effort. It is true that on April 3 General Keitel instructed the German armed forces to prepare for an invasion of Poland at any time from 1 September; that Hitler ordered a diplomatic offensive to isolate Poland; and that the 'Pact of Steel' was signed by Germany and Italy on 22 May. Certainly Hitler intended to invade Poland if circumstances were propitious, but it is clear that he expected Britain and France to fail to support Poland in the event, and that he relied on Italy to declare war alongside Germany. By late August it seemed much less certain that Britain and France would fail to honour their guarantee and it was clear that Italian 'steel' was unreliable, but the new dimension was the agreement with the USSR and it was this which enabled him to summon up the nerve to invade.

The view that the possibility of alliance with the Soviet Union was the crucial factor for both the liberal-democracies and Germany during the summer of 1939 has much to recommend it. British and French military delegations were in Moscow during August but made no headway in their discussions with the Soviet delegation, largely because they could not agree to the entry of Soviet troops into Poland in the event of a German attack. Unknown to them, parallel negotiations between Germany and the USSR were under way and on 23 August Ribbentrop, the German foreign minister, and his Russian counter part, Molotov, signed a non-aggression pact.

Given Hitler's known antipathy to communism and his well-publicised desire for living space in eastern Europe, together with the anti-fascist and popular front policies trumpeted by the Comintern for the last four years, an entente between Germany and the USSR came as a great shock; even Communist Party members in Britain and France, supple in their ability to change policy at Soviet command, took a few days to adjust. There is, however, little to be said for the view that an earlier and more enthusiastic approach by Britain and France could have succeeded.

A cool glance at what the two suitors had to offer Stalin demonstrates that the Western powers could only have hoped for an alliance by ignoring and overriding Polish and Romanian interests, while they could not proffer the sacrifice of the independence of the Baltic states as Hitler could. The USSR was in no shape to fight a war, and, while Britain and France offered an alliance which might not avert one, agreement with Germany freed her from the threat of imminent major conflict. At the same time, the secret protocols of the pact enabled the USSR to regain most of what Russia had lost at the end of the First World War.

Daladier had been much more enthusiastic about an alliance with the USSR than Chamberlain, who always disliked the idea, and was conversely much less keen on the guarantee to Poland, suspecting rightly that the latter ruled out the former. Even with the agreement with the USSR in place, Hitler hesitated when he heard that Britain and Poland had signed an agreement for mutual assistance and that he could not expect Italian support, and called off the attack planned for 26 August. He launched the offensive on 1 September, still hoping that Britain and France would back down. 'What now?', he is supposed to have said to von Ribbentrop when he received Britain's declaration of war on 3 September.

Chapter 2: A European War

Germany's Victories

Britain and France went to war in September 1939 to prevent a German domination of Europe. Poland and its independence were the occasion rather than the cause of their intervention. The aim of the Allied powers was not the total defeat and surrender of Germany, but to achieve by war what diplomacy had failed to achieve, a European settlement. Such a settlement would leave intact the revisions to Versailles which had taken place, with the exception that the Czechoslovakian Republic, dismembered in the spring of 1939, would be re-established. Hitler had proved himself both aggressive and untrustworthy, and it was hoped that military pressure would result in his replacement by a new German leader with whom it would be possible to negotiate.

The Allies had gone to war with great reluctance. Public opinion in both countries had undergone a major change between the summers of 1938 and 1939, with large sections of society coming to accept that war might be necessary, though its terrors were realised and even, as with bombing, exaggerated. Daladier and Chamberlain had hoped to avoid war, but had come to accept that if the threat of military intervention proved insufficient to prevent further German expansion, then the threat must be translated into action. Yet they were aware of the enormous dangers to their economies, their empires, and to the very positions of Britain and France as great powers in the step they had taken. Not to have gone to war in September 1939 would have shaken Britain's and France's credibility as great powers, but going to war could shatter the remaining physical basis for their claim to that position.

There was little direct assistance that the Allies could give to Poland. That the Poles would be overrun by Germany was accepted by the British and French governments from the beginning. Like Serbia in the First World War, Poland would have to await a general Allied victory before it could re-emerge. It had, however, been hoped that the Polish army would put up a prolonged resistance, during which a British army could establish itself in France and Anglo-French military command structures and planning be coordinated. The Hitler-Stalin Pact was to ensure that Polish resistance would not be prolonged.

What then was allied strategy? It was to fight a defensive war which would wear Germany and her economy down while allied strength increased. Neither Britain nor France was prepared for an offensive and adventurous initiative. The French had promised the Poles that an invasion into the Rhineland would be launched within 15 days of the beginning of a war, but it is clear that General Gamelin, the French Commander-in-Chief, had no intention of honouring that promise. Secure as they considered themselves to be behind the fortifications of the Maginot Line, the French generals had a complementary respect for the German fortifications, the Westwall or 'Siegfried Line', and there was no more than a token French advance within the range of the protective guns of the Maginot Line.

There were, however, good reasons for Allied confidence that time was on their side and that a defensive war would see the balance of strength shift in their favour. That confidence has, naturally, been viewed with scepticism by historians. A lost war or a campaign looks, after the event, like one that was likely to be lost, and allied hopes in late 1939 looked foolish and complacent from the viewpoint of May 1940. The overwhelming German victory won in 1940 was not, however, the result of superior manpower or weaponry but came about because of the daring of German strategy and the superior performance of the German army. The relative abilities of armies are rarely apparent until they are put to the test, while daring strategies are only bold, rather than rash, when they prevail.

From the viewpoint of 1939, there was much to be said for the optimistic analysis of the Allies. British and French rearmament was overtaking German arms production and it was widely believed that war would place unacceptable strains upon the German economy. By September 1939 British and French production of tanks and aircraft exceeded that of Germany. British aircraft production had been planned in depth, with the emphasis on new production lines rather than the immediate production of planes, and 1940 was expected to see the fruits of this. The British Expeditionary Force might be tiny but conscription had been introduced in Britain earlier in the year and there were plans for a formidable British army. The French general staff had every confidence both in the security of the Maginot Line and the results of rearmament. In addition to French production, France was receiving 170 modern aircraft a month from the USA. Allied naval supremacy seemed assured, and the British and French navies would be able to protect supply routes and weaken the German economy by sinking German ships. A further factor in the Allies favour was that, the Indian Empire, Australia, New Zealand, Canada and, after a change of government, South Africa had all declared war on Germany. In a conflict of any duration their assistance was likely to be significant.

Another factor was not favourable to the Allies. While it had been expected, when Anglo-French staff talks had been held in the spring, that Italy would enter the war on Germany's side, it had been presumed that the Soviet Union, even if not prepared to intervene, would be hostile to a German attack on Poland. In the event, Mussolini's caution kept Italy neutral, but the Hitler-Stalin Pact meant that Hitler had no worries to the east and had a free hand in the west. Soviet supplies of oil, minerals and raw materials meant that the effectiveness of a blockade of Germany were much reduced.

There was, as we have seen, no Allied plan to give practical assistance to the Poles. But did the Polish government know that? Did they not rather expect that their role was to hold up the *Wehrmacht* for two weeks, after which there would be a French invasion of Germany across the Rhine? This was, after all, what they had been promised.

The commanding image of the German invasion of Poland is one of cavalry with lances against tanks, a hopeless, but gallant defence by an anachronistic army and an aristocratic nation. There are nuggets of truth in this image for the Poles did indeed have cavalry regiments, and the Polish army did indeed fight with great bravery and gallantry. But the Polish army was no comic-opera affair, but an efficient and well-commanded fighting force. Its problems with equipment reflected those of the lightly industrialised Polish economy. Poland just did not have the industry to produce modern tanks and aircraft, nor did the economy produce the money to buy them from abroad. In addition, geography had not blessed Poland with natural defences, a perennial flaw that had dogged Polish history. To add to these problems, the Polish army had had to prepare ever since the Treaty of Riga for a war against the Soviet Union. As the threat from Germany increased, that from the USSR did not diminish. In 1939 the nightmare scenario of an attack from both Poland's enemies became fact.

To add to their difficulties the Polish generals were hamstrung by political considerations. Prior to his invasion, Hitler's aim had been to provoke an incident which, however scantily, might clothe his aggression with some semblance of an excuse. The Polish aim was not to give him such an excuse and a Polish mobilisation might have done so. Britain and France advised against mobilisation, and it was essential that the Poles retained their support. Thus, the German invasion found the Poles in the midst of mobilising. Then there was the question of what strategy to adopt in the face of attack. The invader had the initiative and could choose where to launch his most effective divisions. The best military response would have been for the Poles to have kept the bulk of their army well back and concentrated, ready to engage the most powerful sections of the German forces. This would have meant leaving large areas of Poland without any real defence, and an army's duty is widely seen as to attempt to defend its whole country. For essentially political reasons therefore, the Polish army adopted a broad defensive strategy, which allowed the *Wehrmacht* to split it up and surround sections of it.

Whatever the strategy adopted, the Poles were not going to be able to defeat a German invasion. The best hope was to hold up the Germans and trust in a French attack on Germany. Hitler judged, correctly, that he need not fear a French invasion and concentrated upon subduing Poland quickly. Nearly two million German troops took part in the invasion, advancing in five armies from the south, from East Prussia and from Slovakia, against which the Poles were able to mobilise a million men. More importantly, the Germans had some 2000 tanks against the Poles' 180, and Germany had control of the air, its 2000 planes quickly sweeping the small Polish airforce from the sky. In a sense the Germans had two armies, one much like that of the Polish army consisting of infantry divisions, which marched on foot and were supported by horse-drawn transport and artillery, and the other, comprising 16 divisions, consisting of panzer heavy and medium tank divisions and motorised infantry divisions. It was these latter forces which were the key to the rapid German victory. The tank divisions raced ahead and, supported by dive-bombers, made deep incursions into the Polish defences, dividing the Polish armies into 'pockets'; the fast-moving motorised infantry consolidated the ground gained by the tank divisions; and the ordinary infantry divisions occupied territory and mopped up. Without armour or motorised transport, the Poles lacked the manoeuvrability to respond effectively. The Polish Command lost control of its forces as its communications were disrupted, and by 10 September, most of northern and western Poland was in German hands. By 14 September Warsaw was encircled.

This first example of what became known as *blitzkrieg* tactics testified to the formidable skill of the German forces, but the Polish army acquitted itself well against an enemy vastly superior in weaponry and mobility. The Poles had hoped to hold out until the promised French invasion across the Rhine should be launched. That invasion was not forthcoming, yet they managed to launch a counter-attack west of Warsaw that was not crushed until 17 September. On that date the Soviet Union, despite having a non-aggression treaty with Poland, invaded from the east, occupying territory assigned to it under the Nazi-Soviet Pact, while German units withdrew behind the prearranged partition line. Even then, Warsaw did not fall until 28 September and the last Polish combatants did not surrender until 6 October.

Not for the last time in the Second World War, the Poles had fought gallantly, been let down by their allies, and been crushed between the upper and nether millstones of Germany and the Soviet Union. There was little to choose between the savage cruelty of the German and Soviet occupations. Both Hitler and Stalin had a hatred of the very idea of an independent Poland and sought to ensure that one would never re-emerge, though the Germans' racialist policies were probably less effective in this respect than Stalin's policy of destroying the Polish upper and middle classes, of which the massacre of captured Polish officers at Katyn in the spring of 1940 is the most chilling example.

The Hitler-Stalin Pact had, said Stalin, been 'sealed with blood' and, along with partition of Poland, other provisions of the Pact were implemented. Latvia and Estonia, which had been assigned to the Soviet sphere of influence, were forced to sign pacts of mutual assistance allowing Soviet troops to be stationed in their countries. Lithuania had originally been assigned to the German sphere, but the Germans agreed to exchange it for central Poland, and Lithuania too was forced to sign a mutual assistance pact with the Soviet Union. Moscow began to apply pressure on other countries seen as within its sphere, Romania, Bulgaria and Turkey, and at the end of November attacked Finland when the Finnish government refused to make the territorial concessions demanded of it.

While east central Europe was being reshaped by Nazi-Soviet agreement, Hitler turned his attention to the west. Having never understood why Britain and France had gone to war for Poland, he was confident that peace could be made with them now Poland no longer existed. On 6 October he spoke to the Reichstag suggesting the Allies accept the new order in Eastern Europe and make peace.

That Hitler wanted peace, albeit on his own terms, is not in doubt. The question is rather whether he simply wanted time to prepare for an attack on the west, or was genuinely prepared to leave France alone and had a positive desire to preserve the British Empire. This, of course, takes us back to the contentious question of Hitler's long-term aims, though it is worth noting that, if Hitler wished to destroy Britain, he would surely have given a greater priority to the production of the submarines that would have enabled him to cut off British supplies from across the Atlantic. Britain and France had not, however, gone to war for Poland alone, but for the European balance of power and they had confidence in their defensive strategy. Clandestine negotiations continued (they almost always do), but so did links with factions in Germany known to be opposed to Hitler, and the allies had no inclination to come to an agreement which would mark their humiliation and defeat.

Hitler accordingly moved to a serious consideration of how to defeat the Allied armies and, even before France and Britain had rejected his peace offers, he issued a directive on 9 October for a Western offensive. His generals thought this a formidable task as the French army and its defences were highly regarded. As we have seen, there is much dispute as to the future plans behind German attempts to increase their armed strength. Had the German armaments programme reached a peak consistent with a reasonable standard of living for the population – or was Germany in the middle stages of preparation for total war? Even if the latter, Germany might still be in a position to defeat the allies since she was secure to the east and her economy was reinvigorated by conquests, while if the former, now was the moment to strike, before Britain and France had grown stronger. The generals argued for caution and plans for an attack on the west were postponed again and again. In the end, it was to be Hitler's confidence and will that carried the day, but not until May 1940, some six months after the initial planning.

The Allies did not spend these months well. Given their defensive strategy, a quiet war – even what became known as a 'phoney war' – was to be expected, but even the defensive preparations of the British and French were incompetent. No uniform command structure was agreed upon, while the timidity of the Dutch and Belgian governments made proper provision for the defence of Holland and Belgium impossible. Almost certainly, a German attack would come, as it had in 1914, through the Low Countries, except that this time Hitler's ruthlessness, and a grasp of the importance of Dutch ports in a continuing war with Britain, would involve a German invasion of Holland as well as Belgium. Both the Dutch and Belgian governments, however, clung to the hope that if they were circumspect, the

Germans might not attack them and they refused to have proper staff talks with those they trusted would secure them in the event of a German invasion.

The Anglo-French strategy was therefore unclear: should they simply aspire to defend France; should they keep armies on the Belgian frontier ready to advance to the aid of possible allies; or should they take the initiative and move troops into Belgium and Holland before the Germans invaded, even without the permission of the Belgium and Dutch governments? The first and last of these courses of action were the most sensible military options but were rejected on political grounds. Belgium and Holland couldn't be left to their fate, nor could they be protected against their will. As in Norway, the Allies would come to the aid of countries after they had been attacked, almost always the worst military option. Convinced that Germany's only viable strategy was to attack through Holland and Belgium, a conviction which was strengthened by the evidence of plans found on a German staff officer whose plane landed accidentally in Belgium, the Allied commands decided to commit their most effective forces to an advance into Belgium immediately after a German advance. Like a chess player who commits himself to a game plan on the basis of what he assumes his opponent will do, the allies were to lack any flexible response when their opponent produced an unexpected strategy. Any hopes of an effective alliance between the Dutch Army and its putative allies were destroyed by the Dutch plan to withdraw northwards, away from the planned Allied advance, while the Belgian army refused to co-ordinate its plans with the forces that hoped to protect the country.

The 'phoney war' is well named. The civilian populations of Germany, Britain and France braced themselves in September 1939 for the massive bombing raids that seemed inevitable. On the outskirts of London, warehouses were filled with cardboard coffins ready for the thousands that the bombs would kill, while a complex evacuation of city children to the countryside took place. In the event, both sides eschewed the bombing of civilian targets at this stage of the war in the west, partly to escape the obloquy that would fall upon the first to bomb cities, and partly for fear of retaliation. The RAF dropped leaflets rather than bombs on Germany in an expensive and vain attempt to get Germans to rise against their *Führer*. The main military action was at sea, with German surface raiders and a small number of U-boats active in the sinking of British shipping and achieving several major kills: the liner *Athenia*; the aircraft carrier *Courageous*; and the battleship *Royal Oak*, sunk at the fleet anchorage at Scapa Flow. The German pocket battleship, *Graf Spee*, was forced by British cruisers to take refuge in Montevideo harbour, where it was scuttled rather than face the British warships that awaited it, just about the only success for British arms in 1939.

The main fighting during the winter of 1939 occurred not between the forces of the powers fighting what the Soviet Union termed the 'imperialist war', but between the Soviet Union and Finland. This was a classic David and Goliath affair for Finland's armed forces were tiny in comparison to Russia's enormous armies, yet Finnish resistance to the aggressor was fierce and effective. French ministers favoured giving assistance to the Finns and bombing the Caucasian oilfields, which were supplying Germany, though the British government was more sceptical about the desirability of acquiring another enemy. A combination of the Finns' efficiency in an inhospitable terrain and the incompetence of the purged Soviet senior ranks meant that the 'Winter War' lasted from late November to early March, and cost the USSR 200,000 casualties. Soviet might could not be denied in the long run, however, and although an independent Finland survived, it had to give up the territory close to Murmansk and Leningrad that the Soviets had originally demanded.

Although Finland's defeat ruled out a British and French intervention, in the early months of 1940 the allies were looking northwards for an opportunity to weaken Germany. Swedish supplies of iron ore were seen as crucial to the German war effort and their disruption was seen as a major allied aim. It was proposed to lay mines along the Norwegian coast, blocking the route used by ships carrying Germany's iron ore supplies. If Germany reacted by invading Norway and Sweden, then British and French troops would move into the northern regions of both countries. Hitler, however, had his own plans to secure both his ore supplies and provide northern bases for the German navy. On 9 April the Germans launched a well co-ordinated invasion of Denmark and Norway which involved only 10 000 men. Denmark capitulated immediately and the Norwegian capital Oslo surrendered to a small force of paratroops, but the sea and airborne forces that landed elsewhere in Norway were opposed and Norwegian forces held out in the north, where they were joined by British, French and Polish troops.

The Norwegian campaign was characterised by German command of the air, the incompetence of British generals and British superiority at sea. The Germans suffered substantial naval losses: the cruiser *Blucher* was sunk by a Norwegian coastal battery and two other cruisers were damaged by British submarines; nine German destroyers were sunk at the cost of two British in an engagement in Narvik fjord;

while in the closing stages of the campaign, the German battleships *Scharnhorst* and *Gneisenau* were torpedoed and seriously damaged by British submarines after being needlessly exposed in operations off the Norwegian coast. However, German command of the air and the use of warships to transport troops had enabled them to establish positions even in northern Norway. The belated landings of Allied, mainly British troops were anything but the well co-ordinated affair the German invasion had been. French, British and Polish troops landed in central Norway around Trondheim, but were forced to evacuate or surrender by 3 May. Further north, Anglo-French forces took Narvik at the end of May after a stout defence by vastly outnumbered German units. Given British naval superiority, control of Narvik might have been put to good use, but allied forces were withdrawn a few days later, losing the aircraft carrier *Glorious* during the evacuation. The German offensive in the west was under way.

The caution and procrastination of the German generals, and then the distraction of the Norwegian campaign had resulted in the German attack in the west, ordered by Hitler in October 1939, being delayed time and again. The generals overestimated the ability and the strength of the French army, but they were not alone in this as international military opinion concurred that it was the strongest in the world. Hitler's adventurous policies had enjoyed enormous success and had brought territory without war and then territory with easy victories, but to take on the French army on home ground, backed by the British, was a different matter. The prospects of overwhelming success seemed dubious and another bogged-down and mutually debilitating war, like that of 1914–18, the most likely outcome.

Hitler had different views. He had little respect for France and the French armed forces; the power he feared and respected was Britain, but a British expeditionary force did not rank high in the reasons for this fear and respect. Essentially Hitler's military successes were based on a conjunction of his belief that morale, determination and a preparedness to take the adventurous and unexpected course, would win the day and the existence for a few years of a military balance that favoured a German army prepared to be daring and aggressive.

He was fortunate in that military thinking lagged behind military technology when it came to the possibilities of surprise and offensives and that, although few military thinkers realised this, some did and some of them were Germans. Some of them were British and some French, but they did not find a receptive audience; the German ones did. Generals von Manstein and Guderian were listened to by Hitler; de Gaulle and Captain Liddel-Hart were not listened to by their respective high commands and governments. Hitler, aggressive and impatient, was psychologically predisposed to adopt daring and mobile strategies. Germany's late rearmament enabled it to go for up-to-date weaponry and innovative military formations that those whose military assets and posture had been determined in an earlier period were naturally reluctant to embrace. The British army in 1918 had been perhaps the most efficient fighting machine in the world, but years of defence cuts in the twenties and early thirties, and a policy which was posited upon continued peace had favoured military conservatism. Neither the British nor French commands were prepared to envisage tank divisions without artillery cover, nor to consider that support from aircraft could enable tanks to range far ahead of infantry and artillery support. The Germans were, but the German army was, nevertheless, only partially motorised and the notion that it was prepared for what was coming to be known as *blitzkrieg* warfare involving racing panzer divisions supported by Stuka dive-bombers is something of a myth.

The initial plan for the Western offensive, Operation Yellow, drawn up by the German general staff and approved by Hitler was conventional enough. It had limited objectives: the occupation of Belgium and the Netherlands and north-eastern France, the defeat of as much of the French Army as possible, and the seizure of territory including Channel ports, which could provide a basis for a war by sea and air against Britain. The main German thrust would come across the plains of Belgium and into northern France. This was the sort of attack that the French and British generals were prepared for.

When plans for an attack fall into the hands of an enemy, it is usually to the enemy's advantage but, when the pilot of a German military aircraft was forced to land in Belgium because of fog and the Belgium police discovered the top secret German plans for the German attack in the West carried by the passenger, a German officer, the eventual outcome was to Germany's considerable advantage. The realisation that the allies knew of their plan and the success of General von Manstein in persuading Hitler there was an alternative resulted in it being changed. The Manstein plan was for a powerful push through the Ardennes, a hilly and wooded region between the Maginot Line and the main defences around Liege. Most senior German generals agreed with the Allied view that the Ardennes provided unsuitable terrain for major military movements involving tanks and motorised infantry, but Manstein's plan appealed to Hitler and it was adopted.

The Germans went ahead with part of their original plan, an invasion of the Netherlands and Belgium which would sweep west and south, and bring their armies deep into the invaded countries. The main German armour, however, was allotted to the central prong of *Sichelschnitt* (scythe sweep or sickle-cut), as the plan was called, which was Army Group A under the command of Field Marshal von Rundstedt. A much smaller army was left facing the Maginot Line. Von Rundstedt's task was a formidable one: to drive through the Ardennes, cross the Meuse River at Sedan, Montherme and Dinant, and then swing northwest and drive for the channel.

Sichelschnitt was a good plan, but it carried considerable risks. The most obvious of these was that the German armour could get bogged down and disorganised in the Ardennes. A second was that Army Group B, which had to attack 'Fortress Holland' where the Dutch army was committed to the defence of Amsterdam, Rotterdam and Utrecht, take on the quite formidable Belgian army, and cope with advancing British and French forces, was relatively weak, the best forces having been allocated to von Rundstedt. Another danger was that, even if the German armour did succeed in getting through the Ardennes and dividing the allied armies, a rapid reaction by the Allies could result in thrusts by these divided armies across the panzers' supply lines and cut off the cream of Army Group A. The scale of Germany's victory had much to do with the ambitious nature of *Sichelschnitt*, but that it was a victory at all was because it was well executed and incompetently opposed.

In terms of numbers and weaponry, the allied and German forces were evenly matched. The Germans had 136 divisions as compared to 138 allied divisions (94 French, 12 British, 22 Belgian and 9 Dutch), 2500 tanks as opposed to 3000 and 3200 aircraft as opposed to 1800. The Germans had the advantages of a unified command and superiority in the air. If many Allied divisions were inadequately equipped, the difference between the best 50 or so German divisions, which were motorised and had modern weapons and trained men, and the majority of their divisions, which had weak artillery, large numbers of untrained or over-age men and which were dependent on horse-drawn transport, was striking. Few Allied formations were pure tank divisions, while the Germans had grouped their tanks into ten panzer divisions. It was the crack divisions, the panzers and motorised infantry, covered and assisted by dive-bombers, which were to make the German victory possible, a victory by the motorised divisions of a largely un-motorised army.

The German attack began on 10 May 1940 with the bombing of Dutch, Belgian and French airbases, after which the German army crossed the Dutch, Belgian and Luxembourg frontiers, while paratroops seized canal crossings and airfields. The Dutch surrendered after five days of fighting, but not before Rotterdam had been largely destroyed by bombing. The Belgian army was believed to be a more formidable fighting force, but it met an early and serious reverse when the strategic fortress of Eben Emael surrendered after 70 German troops glided onto its roof.

According to plan, General Gamelin ordered about a third of the British and French forces, including most of the Allied tanks, to cross into Belgium to meet the German advance. Lieutenant-General Alan Brooke, who commanded a corps in the British Expeditionary Force, was one of the few Allied commanders to have pointed out the dangers of leaving prepared defences to engage in mobile warfare against an enemy who might be better prepared.[1] As some two fifths of the French army was left to defend the Maginot Line, the allied centre was thinly defended and when the main German thrust burst out of the Ardennes on 12 May, it quickly swept through the defending French divisions and crossed the River Meuse north of Sedan. The panzer divisions began to race westwards with spearheads reaching the sea on 20 May. In the very moment of German victory lay the greatest risk of defeat, for if the attack by British tanks from the north and French from the south, ordered by General Weygand who had replaced Gamelin as Commander-in-Chief, had succeeded, the panzer divisions, far in advance of the German infantry, could have been cut off from support. It failed and soon Guderian's tanks, having cut the allied armies in two, swung north to take the channel ports. It seemed likely that the British expeditionary force, along with the northern French forces, would be cut off in Belgium. Orders were still being issued for combined allied attacks from north and south when Lord Gort, the British commander, decided that evacuation was the only way of saving his army, and on 26 May the Admiralty gave the order for Operation Dynamo, the evacuation from Dunkirk.

Various reasons have been put forward for the success, indeed the 'miracle', of the Dunkirk evacuation which enabled 220,000 British and 120,000 French and Belgian soldiers to be taken off the Dunkirk beaches by a vast array of assorted vessels, warships, coastal steamers, and even pleasure boats and yachts. The suggestion that Hitler deliberately allowed the British army to escape because he hoped for peace with Britain can be discounted. Hitler did indeed wish for peace with Britain, but the more complete the German victory was, the greater his chances of achieving this were. The German tanks were halted on 24 May, on the orders of von Runstedt, because almost half of them had already broken down and the rest were urgently in need of maintenance after the many miles they had travelled. Their advance was not resumed, in part because both von Runstedt and Hitler believed the terrain around Dunkirk was unsuitable for tanks, but also because Goering was pressing the claim of the *Luftwaffe* to be allowed to finish the British off. This was the German Command's first serious tactical mistake; the RAF was able to protect the Allied troops from airfields in England and, despite heavy casualties, the evacuation was complete by 4 June.

The bulk of France was still in French hands, but the decisive campaign had been won by Germany. The Belgian army, putting up a stouter resistance than British sources gave it credit for, had been pushed back into the southwest of Belgium and on 27 May, King Leopold had surrendered. His decision to follow the Danish king's example and stay with his people, rather than, like the Norwegian and Dutch monarchs, leave for Britain, has been much criticised but, if hindsight reveals it as mistaken, it was just as, if not more, courageous in the circumstances of the moment as departure.

The German armies now turned south. Weygand's front along the Somme and Aisne was broken after a fierce five-day battle, and a stand on the Marne-Seine Line failed when the panzers penetrated east of Paris. On 11 June Paris was declared an open city and on 14 June it was occupied, almost symbolically on the same day that the Germans broke through the 'impregnable' Maginot Line. Mussolini finally mustered the courage to enter the war on 10 June, but the failure of the Italian army to make any progress when it invaded southern France only cast into relief the ability of the *Wehrmacht*. By the time an armistice was signed on 22 June, the Germans had taken all but the south of France having advanced close to Bordeaux and south of Lyons.

Germany had won an overwhelming victory but it was not the result of the Third Reich's military-industrial preparations: the high command had not envisaged a war with Britain and France; the initial hurried plans for an invasion of France had not involved a *blitzkrieg*, and the only partially motorised army was not designed for such warfare. It was the result of improvisation, daring, the concentration of maximum force at the enemy's weakest points, and the skill and superior morale, of the German army. Ironically, the supposedly authoritarian German army had a more flexible command structure which gave its junior officers and NCOs more initiative than any of the Allied armies. It was able to implement one of the most daring strategies in the history of modern warfare and to achieve in 42 days what its predecessor had failed to achieve in four years of debilitating war. German casualties were what would have been expected from a few days' combat in the First World War, yet Holland, Belgium and France had been defeated, and if the British expeditionary force had limped home, it had done so without its armour and equipment. The campaign puts the 'hopeless' resistance of Poland into perspective. The German army's success and the myth of the *blitzkrieg* gave it a reputation for invincibility, but disguised for Hitler and his generals, as much as Germany's opponents, its failure to be prepared for total war.

The battle for France was lost and the only decision remaining for the French government was whether to fight on from the French possessions overseas or to accept defeat. That the decision taken was to come to terms with defeat was hardly surprising, but it has been much misunderstood. Essentially, it marked a French recognition of German hegemony in Europe and a determination to get the best terms for France under such hegemony. Ever since 1870, French governments and the French nation had struggled to elude, deny and defy the ineluctable facts of German economic strength and population increase. The year 1940 was the year of recognition. The German victory was not, as we have seen, just the result of overwhelming strength, for the contingent factors of good generals and good soldiers had played a great part in it, but it did confirm a long-term German superiority. France had been bled white to deny that superiority in a previous war and the hard-won victory had failed to be permanent, due in part, so the French believed, to Anglo-American perfidy.

France accepted defeat, not with any denial of French greatness – the choice of the aged Marshal Pétain, hero of the First World War, as head of state bore witness to that – but the French surrender was an acceptance that she was no longer Europe's leading power and must, henceforth, be allied with Germany within Europe. Both ideology and the subsequent course of the Second World War have obscured this watershed in French consciousness.

It must be emphasised that the French surrender was the act of the legal government of France. The prime minister, Reynaud, was succeeded by Marshal Pétain and an armistice was signed on 22 June. When the French senators and deputies met at the spa town of Vichy on 10 July, they voted by an overwhelming majority to give full powers to Pétain. In the short term, the new Vichy regime found no dissent from the French communists bound to Moscow's policy of opposition to the war, while positive support extended far beyond conservative and right-wing opinion. The great body of moderate support came from a broad cross-section of society, which was both reluctant for further sacrifice and convinced that defeat had to a large extent come from the corruption and divisions of pre-war politics. As one authority has put it: 'Pétain was widely seen as a leader for all of the French and not just for those of the right.'[2] Charles de Gaulle led a small minority of French officers to London but the significance of this has been greatly exaggerated and he commanded little support in France. France was eventually to be liberated by US and British forces, while the nature of post-war France was to be decided within France and by the changing pattern of collaboration and resistance.

The German terms seemed better at the time of the armistice than they did a few months later. Although the Germans occupied a much larger section of France than had been expected, the whole of the north and west of the country and the entire Atlantic coast, this area was supposed to be under the civilian administration of the French government at Vichy, while no mention was made of an annexation of Alsace-Lorraine. In practice, however, the control of the Vichy government over occupied France was nominal, while Alsace-Lorraine was quickly incorporated into the German Reich. The Vichy government was, nevertheless, to enjoy widespread assent until at least the end of 1942.

Our Finest Hour?

The speed and scale of the German victory left Britain stunned and Hitler at once triumphant and undecided as to how to use his triumph. He had not expected a war with the Western powers and had never desired war with Britain. Although he ordered plans for an invasion across the Channel on 2 July, he made a speech in the Reichstag on 19 July offering peace terms to Britain. Hitler's talk of peace was couched in vague terms but it seems likely that what was on offer was that, in return for British recognition of Germany's hegemony in Europe, Britain would be allowed, even encouraged, to maintain her empire and her navy. Whether he would have insisted on limits to the size of the British army and airforce is less clear.

That the rejection of Hitler's terms was axiomatic, and that Britain was correct to continue the war, has for generations of historians been unquestionable. Dunkirk itself, the Battle of Britain and the Blitz have been seen not just as stages in a war that few dispassionate observers at the time believed Britain was likely to win, but as 'Britain's finest hour', the culmination and expression of her greatness. This it may well have been, but the cost was a heavy one. From the vantage point of the twenty-first century, it is clear that not only did the continuation of the war exhaust Britain, but that the war was only to be won by a Grand Alliance, which would reduce Britain to a junior partner and lead to the end of her position as a great power. Only recently have some historians dared to question whether it was wise to rule out an acceptance of Hitler's peace offer.[3]

If Chamberlain had remained prime minister, there is little doubt that the arguments for a compromise peace would have been considered more carefully. The strategy of containing Germany and wearing her down had clearly failed. The possibility of an invasion of the continent by British forces was non-existent and there was not even a sphere where German forces could be engaged on land. Italy's intervention did offer the opportunity to engage an enemy in the Mediterranean, a mixed blessing in the light of Italy's supposed naval strength, but the plans of early 1939 to defeat Germany's weaker partner before defeating the main enemy looked far less feasible in the light of the French surrender. A blockade of Germany was unlikely to produce dividends when Germany controlled the resources of western Europe and had a seemingly firm understanding with the Soviet Union which ensured supplies from the east. The only optimistic scenario was to count upon Germany and the Soviet Union falling out or, what seemed even more optimistic, upon the USA deciding to enter the war on Britain's side. Both possibilities had their down side: only the 'my enemy's enemy is my friend' argument could justify alliance with a power committed to world communism and with a regime just as ruthless and evil as Hitler's, while United States' intervention was unlikely to assist the long-term interests of the British Empire.

It was not Chamberlain who was prime minister, however, but Churchill. The failure of the Norwegian campaign had resulted in a vote of confidence, which the Chamberlain government had won, but some Conservatives had voted against the government and there had been a substantial number of abstentions. Chamberlain resigned and Churchill, who, ironically, bore much responsibility for the Norwegian campaign, became head of a coalition government which included Labour ministers. Churchill had been the most vocal campaigner for rearmament before the war and was widely considered to be the politician most determined on the war's effective prosecution.

Churchill's replacement of Chamberlain was to have momentous implications not only for the British war effort, but also for Britain's future position in the world and for her domestic policies. Both men came from political dynasties but, whereas Chamberlain, who had spent his early life in the family business, had a practical and businesslike approach to politics, believing in compromise and consolidation when necessary, Churchill was a romantic who saw politics and international affairs as great drama and a succession of heroic causes. Both were dedicated to the preservation of British interests and Britain's position as a great power, but their analyses of Britain's problems were very different. Chamberlain realised how vulnerable Britain really was, whereas Churchill never faced up to the mismatch between British resources and her commitments. A perennial optimist, Churchill looked to national spirit and ethos and to historical parallels rather than to a cool appraisal of the national interest. Chamberlain had hoped to preserve as much of British power and influence as possible, but had realised that some decline was inevitable. Churchill hardly recognised the problem or, when he was forced to, thought it could be resolved by will power.

The view that the cabinet brushed aside the possibility of peace with Germany can no longer be substantiated. There were cabinet discussions and contacts with the Germans via Swedish diplomats. Lord Halifax and R. A. Butler were both in favour of exploring Hitler's terms. Churchill was not yet in a position to impose his views upon the cabinet and Chamberlain remained leader of the Conservative majority in the Commons. In the war cabinet of five, Halifax argued consistently for negotiations and was opposed by Churchill, who, nevertheless, did not rule out a consideration of any terms Hitler offered. Churchill was supported by the Labour ministers Clement Attlee and Arthur Greenwood, but the decisive voice was Chamberlain's for it is unlikely that Churchill could have prevailed against both Halifax and Chamberlain. The ex-prime minister's attitude seems to have been that Britain should continue to fight, if only for better terms rather than the hope of victory, but he also felt that he had a duty to support Churchill.

In view of Britain's position, it would surely have been irresponsible for the government not to have given German proposals some consideration. That such matters were only discussed in private is hardly surprising, for to openly air the possibility of peace would have risked weakening the resolve of the public. It is clear, however, that Churchill continually insisted that any proposals from Hitler should be found unacceptable and he was determined to prejudice them; by a mixture of bullying, rhetoric and cunning, he ensured that no prolonged or serious thought was formally given to an agreement with Germany.[4]

The attractions of a peace, however humiliating, would have been greater had so many troops not been taken off the Dunkirk beaches, but it seems unlikely that Hitler, in the first flush of his victory in France, would have offered terms that were compatible with Britain's sovereignty and self-respect. Late in 1940, after Britain had won the Battle of Britain, British morale had withstood the early months of 'the Blitz', and when Hitler was beginning to get seriously worried about Soviet intentions in eastern-central Europe, more generous terms might have been forthcoming. By then, however, Churchill's position was more secure, Chamberlain was dead and Halifax was no longer foreign secretary.

The day after Hitler ordered preparations to be made for the invasion of Britain, Churchill signalled his determination to fight on by an exceptionally ruthless action. That the formidable French Navy might fall into German hands was a risk he felt Britain could not take even though the French government had promised that its ships would be scuttled rather than allow this to happen By Operation Catapult the Royal Navy was instructed to offer the French Navy the options of continuing to fight alongside Britain, sailing its ships to neutral ports, where they would be disarmed, or scuttling them; if the French refused their ships would be sunk. French ships at Portsmouth, Plymouth and Gibraltar were secured with only the death of one French sailor and at Alexandria Admiral Sir Andrew Cunningham persuaded the French commander to mothball his ships, but at Oran and Dakar the refusal of French commanders to comply with British ultimatums led to Royal Naval action against French warships. At Mers-el-Kebir, near Oran, Admiral Somerville's ships sank several French destroyers and sank or put out of action three capital ships; 1250 French sailors were killed. There seemed little immediate danger of this fleet falling into German hands and the action was to scar Anglo-French relations for a generation. It did much, however, to convince the USA of Britain's determination to continue the war and this may, at least in part, have been its purpose. A recent study has seen this action as beginning 'England's Last War with France'.[5] It deepened French animosity to Britain and Vichy forces were to put up fierce resistance when British forces sought to take control of Dakar, Syria and Madagascar.

Was this drastic action necessary? Ironically, when the Germans took over Vichy France in 1942, the French Navy scuttled its ships at Toulon, thus honouring the promise made in 1940. There were, nevertheless, strategic arguments for the attack on a navy which had so recently worked closely with the Royal Navy. Britain's survival depended upon superiority at sea and, if a substantial portion of the powerful French fleet had fallen into German hands, British naval superiority would have disappeared, not just in the Mediterranean, for warships taken by the Germans could have been transferred to the Atlantic, the North Sea and even Channel ports. That Britain was able to maintain her air-defences was important but command of the seas was as crucial as during the Napoleonic Wars.

The summer of 1940 was to prove that Britain could not be subdued from the air and that a German invasion by sea would be a hazardous and costly affair with no guarantee of success. The German army was, with good reason, confident of conquering Britain if it could get its forces ashore intact, but the German navy was in no position to protect an invasion force from the Royal Navy. Air supremacy was therefore essential and the *Luftwaffe* was ordered to clear the sky of British aircraft as the first stage of Operation *Sealion*. From July mixed groups of German bombers escorted by fighters attacked.

Germany had enjoyed air superiority in the battles to date, but the *Luftwaffe*, though it enjoyed a considerable advantage in the total number of aircraft, 2500 as opposed to the RAF's 1000, was not well equipped for its new task. It had insufficient bombers with the range and bomb-load to inflict the damage necessary to put British airfields and aircraft factories out of action against the formidable opposition of the RAF's Fighter Command, while the German fighters lacked the range to operate over more than a corner of southern England. The RAF's main weakness was its shortage of trained pilots; 'The Few' was an accurate designation of Britain's fighter pilots. What Britain did have were fast monoplane fighters, the Hurricane and the Spitfire, which matched the German Messerschmitt 109s, and increasingly the capacity to produce them. Chamberlain's armaments programme had, since 1937, seen an emphasis upon the building of aircraft production lines and Lord Beaverbrook, Minister of Aircraft Production, was able to oversee an acceleration in productivity which the Germans could not match. The RAF had some 700 Hurricanes and Spitfires in June, but by the end of the year 400 a month were being completed, in comparison to the average of 200 fighters a month the *Luftwaffe* were receiving. As the air combats took place over Britain, the British had the advantage of being able to repair damaged planes and recover pilots. Britain also had radar, enabling RAF fighters to be airborne by the time German aircraft were over their airfields.

Despite the effectiveness of British fighters, a consistent German policy of targeting fighter airbases and radar stations might have succeeded had it been persevered with. 'Eagle Day', 13 August, saw the commencement of such a strategy and when, from 24 August, the *Luftwaffe* increased the proportion of fighters to bombers in their attacking formations in order to deal more effectively with the British fighters, the RAF was for two weeks losing more Hurricanes and Spitfires than it was able to replace, even though the Germans were experiencing an even greater deficit and losing too many of their most effective fighters, the Me 109s. At this critical moment, the *Luftwaffe* switched tactics and changed its targets to airfields further inland and to London. This was a major mistake and can only be explained by poor intelligence. Both sides exaggerated the number of aircraft they had shot down and the German Command were convinced that the fighter airfields in the southeast of England were virtually finished, destitute of aircraft, their runways inoperable and their command posts destroyed. That this was not so was to be revealed by the heavy losses the *Luftwaffe* suffered in the following weeks during daytime raids on London. In mid-September the *Luftwaffe*'s attempt to destroy Britain's air-defences was suspended and *Sealion* was postponed indefinitely. The Battle of Britain was won in the air by a small elite of 2945 RAF aircrew, of which a sixth were killed and about the same proportion wounded – modern knights on extremely expensive chargers – but it was also won on the ground in the factories which, just in time, produced the British fighter aircraft.

The Germans then switched to a heavy bombing offensive of night-time attacks against military and economic targets in major cities. These were the sort of air raids that had been expected in 1939, but although the Germans dropped 35,000 tons of bombs between September 1940 and May 1941, 19,000 tons of them on London, the widespread panic, even insanity, that had been foretold did not occur, while deaths, though considerable, were not on the anticipated scale.[6] The picture of a cheery and defiant London clearing up the debris after nights of heavy bombing with cockney good humour is one of the enduring images of Britain at war. It is, no doubt, part myth, a brilliant creation of wartime propaganda. National myths are usually romanticised fact, however, and the contemporary propaganda could not have worked if London had, in fact, witnessed widespread confusion and demoralisation.

The British reaction to bombing raids is, of course, crucial to the image of Britain at war. A major effort at debunking the 'spirit of the Blitz' has pointed to the panic of key local officials and the temporary breakdown of administration in Coventry after the major raid on the town in November 1940, and to other less than heroic episodes, and concludes that 'There has, in particular, been a massive, largely unconscious cover-up of the disagreeable facts of 1940–41.'[7] Perhaps it would be truer to say that reactions to the bombing raids were glamorised, but if make-up can disguise defects, it cannot create glamour without a basis to work on. The riposte that we should 'see the Blitz as a cultural phenomenon in its own right, an event to be explained rather than a lie to be uncovered'[8] has much to recommend it, but may push relativism too far. The Blitz and the reactions to it were real enough and, if any explanation must weigh bravery, endurance and defiance against panic and cowardice, there were enough of the former to make the 'cultural phenomenon' credible.

Bombing raids and potential invasion were not the only, nor perhaps even the most serious, threats Britain faced. Her ability to continue to feed her population, arm her troops and supply her ships, aircraft and tanks with fuel depended upon command of the sea and being able to keep her shipping lanes open. For centuries a great naval power, but only towards the end of long wars the possessor of a large army, Britain had traditionally relied for security on a combination of naval supremacy and a balance of power in Europe. Now France was defeated and Germany was supreme in western Europe, with the result that the enemy was in control of the Channel ports and the Atlantic coastline. Small though the German navy was, it was able to sink British shipping with surface raiders and submarines and Hitler belatedly ordered an intensive U-boat building programme, with a production target of 25 a month for 1941. Italy was a naval power and her navy presented a threat to British communications across the Mediterranean. To that naval threat was added the ability of planes to sink ships, a discovery that seems to have taken admirals all over the world by surprise; German bombers based in France and Norway were soon taking a heavy toll of British merchant shipping.

Surface raiders provided the most spectacular, but, given the Royal Navy's preponderance in warships, the least effective threat. Though they sank several hundred thousand tons of British shipping, the attrition rate of merchant ships converted into raiders was high, while during 1941 the German Navy suffered the loss of two of its few capital ships: in May the *Bismarck* was sunk and a month later the pocket-battleship *Lutzow* was sunk by a torpedo. The great threat came from aircraft and submarines, and during 1940 over 1000 British ships, a quarter of British merchant shipping, were sunk. By February 1941, shipping losses were so serious that Churchill had to order that priority be given to anti-submarine warfare. As he said the following month, Britain was fighting the 'battle of the Atlantic'.

An important factor in the war at sea and, indeed, a great advantage in most British and, later, allied operations was the ability of the British to decipher the German 'Enigma' code. Code-breakers at the special unit formed at Bletchley Park owed much to the Polish government, which had set up a cryptography group as early as 1928 and adapted the commercial version of the Enigma machine invented by Dr Arthur Scherbius so that they could crack German radio codes. After Poland's defeat the codebreakers and their machines were brought to Bletchley Park where a British team was set up. The intelligence gleaned from the interception of German communications was termed 'Ultra' and the Germans remained unaware that their system was insecure. Churchill called Ultra, 'the goose which lays the golden eggs', but, traditional methods of espionage,[9] including a system of double agents, also played a crucial role in giving Britain a decided advantage in intelligence, while deception, the deliberate misleading of the enemy, was also a sphere in which Britain excelled.

Such intelligence together with new technology and tactics was particularly important in the ruthless Battle of the Atlantic. The information gathered from interpreted German signals enabled convoys to be diverted during 1941 from the known position of U-boats but, despite Ultra, the British merchant fleet continued to suffer severe losses and when, in February 1942, the Germans made their code more complicated, the tonnage of shipping lost rapidly increased. The contest between convoy protection and U-boats involved technical and tactical innovation: to counter British detection (sonar) equipment which only found submerged vessels, U-boats attacked at night when on the surface but high frequency radar sets able to detect surface craft could be mounted on escorting warships. U-boats started to work in 'wolf packs', mounting concentrated attacks on convoys. The balance of advantage between predator and prey shifted back and forth with these developments, but no decisive answer was found to the U-boat menace. With the obstacles in the way of a German invasion more apparent than ever after the success of the RAF in denying the enemy air supremacy, the Atlantic was the most promising arena for a German victory.

By May 1941 when Hitler called off the intensive bombing, it was clear that, provided the Atlantic sea routes were kept open, Britain was not in immediate danger of defeat. By October the British government knew, because the German code had been broken, that *Sealion* had been called off. The long-term outlook, however, was grim. Given time, with the resources of most of Europe at its disposal, the German economy would be able to produce more bombers and fighters than the British and, perhaps more ominously, the submarines that could sever the Atlantic lifelines. Even if Britain could hope to survive – without new allies she could not hope to win.

Britain did not stand alone, the British Empire did. The Empire was both potent and vulnerable. The dominions and the Indian Empire provided troops, both for Britain's defence and for what military initiatives were possible in North Africa and the Mediterranean, as well as food supplies and raw materials. In too many British accounts of the war, the role of the armies and navies of the empire are underrated. Canada, in particular, made an enormous contribution to Britain's war effort. If German troops had invaded Britain in 1940 they would have been met by Canadian units, the Canadian Navy was, at one stage of the war, the third largest in the world, and the Canadian contribution to D-Day is well, if not well enough, known.[10] At the same time, the worries that had long haunted Chamberlain and the War Office as to the weakness of imperial defences in the Far East in the event of Japanese aggression increased.

That Churchill proved to be an inspiring leader, whose personality and charisma became permanently linked with Britain's defiance of Germany's ambitions in 1940, and was a great wartime leader who managed to capture and enthuse a nation in its 'darkest hour', is undeniable. Whether he was the able military expert and strategist he considered himself to be is debateable. His relationships with his Chiefs-of-Staff, especially those with General Alan Brooke and Admiral Sir Andrew Cunningham, were strained, and he perennially considered his generals and admirals too cautious, displaying a penchant for rash initiatives and a liking for dashing, glamorous or eccentric commanders, such as Lord Mountbatten or Orde Wingate. His strength was his determination and optimism, his weakness the obverse, a failure to recognise Britain's military limitations and the need to husband resources and keep the fleet in being.

Only two limited options were open to Britain in 1940. The first option was to counter and then reverse the offensives Mussolini had launched in Africa and Greece. Here considerable success was enjoyed and during the winter of 1940–1, the Italian possessions in East Africa were taken, the Italian army driven out of Egypt and the Sudan, and all but expelled from Libya, while Greek forces drove the invading Italians back into Albania, and in November Royal Navy carrier-borne aircraft inflicted heavy damage on an Italian fleet in Taranto harbour, while in the surface battle at Cape Matapan in March 1941 a British fleet sank three Italian heavy cruisers and two destroyers. The other option was to bomb Germany and a limited bombing offensive was begun. The damage inflicted on the German war effort was slight, but it did remind the German population that Britain was still in the war and laid the foundations of the great bombing offensives of future years.

Little, not even Churchill's inspiring rhetoric, could disguise the fact that, if Germany had not defeated Britain, there was no possibility of Britain defeating Germany. What sustained Churchill was a serene confidence that the USA would come into the war. His confidence was not well founded. President Roosevelt did not, it is true, wish to see Britain defeated, but there is little evidence that he was preparing to enter the war and much evidence that he would not have had the support of Congress for any plans to do so. A much-lauded agreement of September 1940 gave Britain 50 First World War destroyers in return for which the Americans demanded bases in British West Indian colonies and at Newfoundland.

By the end of 1940, Britain was virtually out of dollars and yet dependent on US imports. Roosevelt, though committed to economic aid for Britain, fought the 1940 presidential election campaign on a platform of keeping America out of foreign wars. After his re-election, US support for Britain became more overt. The Lend Lease agreement of March 1941 maintained the flow of supplies, but the price was to be the high one of client status and compromised independence.

The United States' neutrality was, by the summer of 1941, heavily qualified: American troops had taken over from a British garrison in Iceland and US warships were escorting convoys bound for Britain half the way across the Atlantic. There seems little reason to believe, however, that the USA was about to come into the war. Churchill placed great faith in his personal relationship with Roosevelt, first established by letters and, so he believed, sealed when the two met on HMS *Prince of Wales* off the Newfoundland coast in August and signed the Atlantic Charter. Churchill, however, was never less than sanguine as to the effects of his personality and his ability to establish special relationships, while the Atlantic Charter, a joint declaration of principles as to the basis of any post-war settlement was a worthy, but vague document to which even Stalin was to be able to sign up at a later date.

The other possibility for an end to Britain's isolation lay in her finding a new 'continental sword' to replace France. Despite his anti-Bolshevik record, the idea of an alliance with Russia appealed to Churchill's sense of history, while he assiduously wooed Turkey, to little avail, throughout much of the war. But the Soviet-Nazi Pact still held, even though strains were becoming evident, while Turkey was determined to remain avariciously neutral whatever glittering prizes Churchill held out to it in the Middle East.

Churchill's policy of continuing the war whatever the price was to be vindicated, not by his foresight, but by two decisions of Adolf Hitler's: his decision to invade the Soviet Union when Britain was not defeated and when Italy had opened up new fronts in the Balkans; and his declaration of war against the USA after the Japanese attack on Pearl Harbor.

Operation *Barbarossa*

Why did Hitler, leaving Britain severely wounded but undefeated, turn on the Soviet Union in June 1941? To what is perhaps a majority of historians, the answer is obvious: he was fulfilling the missions he had clearly spelled out in *Mein Kampf* and which had, at least since the early twenties, been his fundamental aims, the destruction of Bolshevism and the creation of living space in eastern Europe for the German people. As a major history of the Second World War has put it:

> The whole project of crushing France and England had, after all, been undertaken only as a necessary preliminary, in Hitler's eye, to the attack in the East which would enable Germany to take the living space, the *Lebensraum*, he believed she needed.[11]

To those who do not share the view that Hitler's aims were so firmly set or so consistent over time, the answer is not so obvious. They argue that he had choices in the period between the defeat of France and the decision to invade Russia, a decision which was made late in 1940.[12] This disagreement goes to the very heart of the debate about Hitler. Was he a man with a programme, a mission even, which he pursued relentlessly and ruthlessly throughout his career or was he, like most political leaders, someone who changed his preoccupations and plans throughout his career as opportunities offered and problems arose?

Recent work has to some degree de-demonised Hitler in that, although he was devilish enough morally – like several other twentieth-century leaders – it is clear he had no demonic mastery of events, and not even the mortal iron grip over party and people enjoyed by Stalin. During the latter part of 1940, he was uncertain as to his next moves and reacted to Soviet initiatives in Eastern Europe. It has been widely assumed that the nature of the Nazi regime and Hitler's personality combined to make it impossible for Germany to rest content with the victories of 1940. However, Hitler stated on 25 June '[n]ow: 'Now we have our hands full for years to come to digest and to consolidate what we have obtained in Europe.'[13] It can be argued that what impelled his attack upon the Soviet Union the following

year was not a programme planned years previously, but the combination of Britain's refusal to make peace and the expansionist aims of
the Soviet Union.

Over many centuries Britain had, in several wars, found a 'continental sword' in a European ally, while she relied upon her maritime
supremacy and the support of her empire. By mid 1940 she had lost
one continental ally, France, and only the Soviet Union had the weight
to properly replace her. Hitler's analysis of Britain's position was that an
Anglo-Soviet agreement would pose a formidable threat to Germany.
Churchill's despatch of Sir Stafford Cripps as envoy extraordinary to
Moscow in May 1940 was viewed with alarm in Berlin. Two options
were open to Germany, a continental alliance with the Soviet Union
as a major partner against Britain or an attack on the Soviet Union
to destroy Britain's putative ally. In hesitating between these options,
Hitler did not brood alone, but considered the advice of his foreign
minister. He had also to take into account the rather different advice
of his generals.

The role of Joachim von Ribbentrop, Germany's foreign minister,
who was for long dismissed as a lightweight and mere creature of
Hitler's, has been revised by some historians.[14] They have seen him as
putting forward an alternative analysis to world politics and German
interests to that conventionally ascribed to Hitler, the enduring ambition to achieve the destruction of Russia. Von Ribbentrop, more
anti-British than Hitler, more aware of American power and more
opportunistic, favoured an alliance of the 'hungry powers', Germany,
Italy, Japan and the Soviet Union, against the British Empire and
the USA. For the German foreign minister, the pact with the Soviet
Union was no temporary expedient, but contained the possibility
of a permanent understanding. Hitler considered von Ribbentrop's
proposals but the advocates of a long-term alliance with the Soviet
Union were never in a majority in Berlin.

Less Eurocentric than Hitler, von Ribbentrop worked ceaselessly
to achieve a Russo-Japanese *rapprochement* and an agreement as
to spheres of influence between Germany and the Soviet Union.
Hitler's fondness for the British Empire was due, at least in part, to
the fact that he couldn't conceive what a world without it would look
like. Von Ribbentrop could. He conceived of a world map in which
Japan was allowed to be dominant in East Asia, Russia in the rest of
Asia, where Italy could find her empire in northern Africa and the
Mediterranean, while Germany would preside over most of Europe
and possibly central Africa. Ribbentrop's ambitious global strategy was
probably never really practical. It relied too much on an acceptance

by Japan, Italy and the Soviet Union of Germany's role as the conductor, while they played the parts assigned them. Ribbentrop's strategy did, however, have the merit of identifying the USA as a primary obstacle to any new global world order and of bringing Japan into play as a counter to America but Hitler never seems to have taken the Japanese alliance seriously and grossly underestimated the potential military strength of the United States.

It is easy, with the advantage of hindsight and an elevation of *Mein Kampf* into a programme, to see war between the Soviet Union and Germany as inevitable, but Operation *Barbarossa* must be seen in the context of Soviet actions as well as German. Soviet-German co-operation had gone smoothly until the spring of 1940, but then the German General Staff became worried by a build up of Soviet forces on Russia's western frontiers. It has been suggested that from late June and without consulting Hitler, the General Staff started to make plans for a Russian campaign. At the same time, Soviet expansionism began to exceed the terms of the Nazi-Soviet Pact. This Pact had proved advantageous for Germany and Russia alike, but although it provided broad lines of demarcation for the expansionist aims of the two powers, there were sensitive areas along those lines. Germany needed nickel supplies from Finland, iron ore from Sweden and, above all, oil from the Romanian oilfields. In the spring of 1940, Stalin had reminded Hitler that he had not been given a blank cheque when, worried about German ambitions in Scandinavia after Hitler's invasion of Norway and Denmark, he had temporarily halted supplies of grain and oil to Germany. In June he began to cash in his share of the Pact's provisions, incorporating the Baltic states into the USSR and forcing Romania to give up Bessarabia and northern Bukovina.

Romania was the last time bomb left by Versailles. On the winning side in the First World War, she had been rewarded beyond her own long-term advantage and was surrounded by states with claims on her swollen territory, those of Bulgaria and Hungary, as well as the Soviet Union. Disturbed as Hitler was by the consolidation of Soviet power in the Baltic, an area of great economic importance to Germany, it was Romania that was the crucial obstacle to continued Russo-German understanding since neither power was prepared to see it within the other's sphere of influence.

From June to late November, Hitler wavered between the options open to him, the Ribbentrop path of the great Eurasian alliance, or an attack on Russia. This was not the trouble-free period he might have expected after the great German victories: the attempt to destroy

British air-defences failed, *Sealion* was postponed, even what should have been mere client states, Spain and Vichy France, proved reluctant to enter into firm alliances against Britain, while not only the USSR, but Japan also proved reluctant to play the parts assigned to them, and Mussolini demonstrated an irritating tendency to go off and have his own unsuccessful adventures. A number of German initiatives can be seen as preparatory to an offensive against the Soviet Union: the agreement with Finland for the transit of German troops to and from Norway, the settlement of Romania's border disputes with Bulgaria and Hungary, followed by the guarantee of the new Romanian borders, and above all, the Tripartite Pact of September 1940 with Italy and Japan, which appeared to update the Anti-Comintern Pact and to be similarly anti-Soviet. Yet, if the right hand played one tune, the left hand played another: Japan was encouraged to settle her central Asian disputes with Russia, while it was suggested to Stalin and his foreign minister, Molotov, that the existing Pact with the USSR still stood and that the USSR itself could perhaps join an Eurasian alliance.

From September to late November, German policy was engaged in a last effort to establish whether long-term co-operation with the USSR was possible, and it was not until after two sessions of talks between Molotov and Hitler in November that Hitler decided that Soviet ambitions in eastern Europe were irreconcilable with Germany's, and that Stalin could not be persuaded to change them for opportunities in Asia.

Although Molotov seemed uncooperative, impatient with Hitler's broad-brush scenarios for future divisions of the world and determined to concentrate upon present differences over Romania, Finland and Bulgaria, he had taken back to Stalin Ribbentrop's proposal for bringing the Soviet Union into the Tripartite Pact, a proposal which involved secret protocols defining the spheres of interest of the four powers. Stalin seemed to be attracted by the concept of a sphere of influence which would include Persia and the Persian Gulf, and on 25 November replied accepting, provided Hitler agreed to certain conditions, including the withdrawal of all German troops from Finland, a Russo-Bulgarian Treaty, and a Soviet base on the Bosphorus which would give the Soviet union control of the Black Sea Straits. The impasse was Stalin's refusal to give up Soviet interests in eastern Europe in return for dazzling, but uncertain gains in Asia and the Middle East. No German reply was ever sent to the Russian note. Instead, in Directive Number 21 of 18 December, Hitler ordered his generals to prepare for an invasion of Russia.

Hitler now cast aside thoughts of a reconciliation of German-Soviet differences, as if the Nazi-Soviet Pact and more than two years of co-operation with Stalin had never been, or had at the least been forced upon him by circumstances. He was to write to Mussolini on the day before he launched his attack on Russia: 'I again feel spiritu-ally free. The partnership with the Soviet Union ... seemed to me to be a break with my whole origin, my concepts and my former obligations'.[15] A return to his life's mission, from which only tactics had diverted him? Or was this just another justification of a change of policy by a devious pragmatist? If Hitler's purpose had all along been the destruction of Russia, the Slavs, Bolshevism (Jewish or other-wise), and the provision of *Lebensraum* for the *Herrenvolk*, then he had followed a circuitous path and, ironically, it was only the circuit that brought him success. If on the contrary he, like other states-men, acted and reacted 'within the context of the changing political constellation',[16] this was a return to the language and sentiments of the twenties, a return born of his failure to knock out Britain, and Soviet obduracy over eastern Europe. Whatever explanation is accepted, Hitler either diverted or wavered from a consistent anti-Soviet strategy not only in 1939, but throughout 1940. This wavering of German policy was to be fraught with catastrophic consequences for Hitler. By going too far down the Ribbentrop path, Germany persuaded Japan to settle her differences with Russia, thus losing a probable ally for *Barbarossa*. Japan was persuaded that her future lay in Pacific conquests and this resulted in Pearl Harbor and US entry into the war. Hitler underestimated Soviet strength and, more seri-ously, Japan's possible value in a war against Russia.

The decision to launch Operation *Barbarossa* was undoubtedly congenial to Hitler because of his dislike of communism and atavistic contempt for the Slavs, but his mingled respect for and fear of Britain had as much, perhaps more, to do with it than a concern with the danger from Russia itself. He was convinced that Britain continued to fight because it was making progress with negotiations with the Soviet Union, as well as hoping for the eventual intervention of the USA. Britain would find its continental sword in the Soviet Union. To generations of historians brought up in the world of the Cold War when the USSR was a super-power and Britain a mere satellite of the USA, and with the knowledge of the major role the Red Army played in Germany's defeat, Hitler's analysis seemed inconceivable. To rate the Soviet Union as a secondary threat compared to Britain would have been to look through the wrong end of a telescope, surely his actions could only be explained by a long-term plan to go east.

But Hitler was a man of his time: he had lived all his life in a period when Britain was a great power and he had seen Russia defeated by Germany in the First World War and yet Germany defeated in the west; and he shared the very reasonable and widespread view of the Soviet Union as an inefficient tyranny with a demoralised army. Russia was only dangerous as a British ally. From the vantage point of the twenty-first century, when the Soviet Union has dissolved, Hitler's error becomes more comprehensible.

The factors that finally determined Hitler's decision to attack the Soviet Union have been the subject of much debate. An underestimate of Russia's military potential and a realisation that Stalin was not prepared to compromise over Eastern Europe were of immediate importance. Another reason was his conviction that time was not on Germany's side due to the USA's increasing support to Britain. His attitude to the USA was ambiguous. It has been claimed that from early in his career he saw that America with its enormous potential was bound to dominate Europe and that only bold action by Germany could prevent this.[17] On the other hand, it can be argued that, purblind in economic matters, he did not appreciate that the USA's economic strength could rapidly be converted to military strength and thought America a degenerate society which could not be a great military power. He did worry about the possibility of US intervention, which he considered might come about in 1942, but thought of this as more of an extra post-colonial sword for Britain than as coming of age of a great military power that it proved to be. A fundamental divide is between historians who see *Barbarossa* as the result of ideological considerations and a determination to crush Bolshevism, eradicate the Jews and create a new German empire in the shape of a *lebensraum*,[18] variously seen as Germany's substitute for India or the American frontier, and those who see ideological factors as ancillary, not the primary determinant of the attack, 'But they gave it its indelible colouring, its sense not just of war, but of crusade'.[19]

The German army needed time to prepare and an offensive would not be practical until after the spring of 1941. Diplomacy had secured most east and central European states as allies, but Mussolini's initiatives had gone badly and Hitler was forced to rescue the Italians from the consequences. Mussolini's attack on Greece had resulted in a crushing defeat for the Italians, while the British were enjoying a succession of victories over the Italian army in North Africa. Hitler, worried at the implications of British air bases in Greece, prepared for Operation *Marita*, the invasion of Greece and, in January 1941, despatched an army to North Africa under General Rommel to help the Italians in Libya. Mirroring the German moves, the British diverted a substantial force of three divisions (two Australian and one New Zealand) and an armoured brigade from North Africa and sent it to Greece.

To Churchill Greece offered opportunity, but the decision to weaken General Wavell's army in North Africa and to help the Greeks were two interlocking mistakes. The opportunity of expelling the Italians from North Africa was lost and Rommel was soon making good use of the base they retained, and would continue to threaten Egypt for another two years. To expect to hold Greece against the land and air forces the Germans could concentrate there was to invite disaster. It duly came.

The intervention in Greece has often been seen as one more in the long sequence of military disasters that Churchill was responsible for throughout his career. It seems likely, however, that Churchill, having initially favoured sending forces to Greece, would, by March 1941, have liked to call off the expedition and that it was the formal agreement Eden reached with the Greek government on 4 March which led to the landing of British troops in Greece. Churchill cannot be exonerated, however, for as one historian has put it: 'all along, Churchill had been attracted by the variety of different arguments for intervention, which were not superseded by the one strong argument against: the near certainty of military defeat'.[20]

Once again the *Wehrmacht* demonstrated an unnerving ability even though, on the eve of the launch of *Marita*, the British engineered a coup in Yugoslavia on 27 March, overthrowing the government of the Regent, Prince Paul, which had just joined the Tripartite Pact. Yugoslavia, like Romania, Bulgaria and Hungary was in an invidious position as was demonstrated when the Germans, having stationed forces in Bulgaria some weeks earlier, were able to invade both Greece and Yugoslavia which they did on the same day, 6 April. The Royal Yugoslavian Army held out for a week but, after its surrender, Yugoslavia was divided into German and Italian zones together with an independent Croatian Republic. On 27 April Athens was taken, and three days later the British expeditionary force was evacuated from the mainland. It moved to Crete which Churchill wished to keep as an airbase. The fall of Crete, when German paratroops took the island from overwhelmingly numerically superior British, New Zealand and Greek forces, was a major humiliation for Britain.

It has often been claimed that the need to invade Yugoslavia held up *Barbarossa* and that, perhaps, the delay was fatal to any chances for the success of the enterprise. The evidence for this is not very convincing. This was hardly the first time a German attack had been postponed and the inclement spring of 1941 might have been reason enough for delay in itself. In any case the Germans were convinced that the war would be short, some three months should be sufficient. Hitler had made his mind up and the attack began on 22 June. Historians have found Stalin's policy during this period difficult to explain. So long as the assumption is made that he had no immediate intention of attacking Germany, this is understandable. Germany's victories in the west cannot, have pleased him, for he had hoped for a long war between the 'capitalist powers' that would wear them all out. Now he had a much more powerful Germany on his hands, and hesitated between conciliating and annoying it. He obviously had expansionist aims, whether these were based on some notion of the advance of communism or simply a desire to protect Russia and get back the old Tsarist frontiers. He realised the qualitative weakness of his armed forces as a match for Germany's, but considered that their numbers, Russia's size and potential economic strength would deter any ambition of Germany's to destroy the Soviet Union. He vacillated between defiance and co-operation, making territorial demands one day and assuring Hitler that essential supplies would continue the next. A natural bully, he found it hard to conciliate; however fearful, he couldn't resist making threats. Whether he knew it or not, he invited *Barbarossa*.

It has, however, been suggested that Stalin was intending to attack and hoped to take Germany by surprise. The results of the pact with Germany had been to give Germany and the Soviet Union common frontiers, thus greatly facilitating a surprise attack by either side. His desire to deny Germany control of Romania, and thus of the Romanian oil fields at Ploesti, was only a dimension of a greater plan to destroy Germany and conquer western Europe. The seizure of Bessarabia alerted Hitler to this dire threat and Germany launched *Barbarossa* just before Stalin intended to launch its equivalent. This is the interpretation of the ex-Soviet General Staff officer Viktor Suvarov.[21] It is also the excuse for launching *Barbarossa* that Hitler gave to the German people on 22 June 1941 when he said that Germany had attacked because Russia was about to strike. Probably there were Soviet plans for an offensive war and, if Stalin had thought the time and circumstances right, he might well have launched one, but there is little evidence that he was contemplating such an attack in the spring or early summer of 1941.

The ease with which German forces brushed aside the defending Soviet troops and the lack of Soviet defensive preparations has been used by proponents of the traditional, and still dominant, view that Stalin trusted Hitler as proof of their thesis. The disarray of the Soviet defences and the fact that major Soviet troop concentrations were close to the borders, in the worst possible position for defensive operations, can be used in support of the alternative interpretation that Stalin himself was planning to attack. According to Victor Suvorov, the reason Stalin dismissed rumours of an imminent German invasion was that the Russians themselves were in the last stages of deploying 183 divisions on Russia's western frontier, a move which could only have been in preparation for an attack. Were the two powers both seeking the right moment to launch their attacks, making their troop movements and reacting to each other's movements?[22] Certainly the task of the Germans in the early days of the invasion was made easier than it might have been by the Soviet dispositions, which resulted in Soviet aircraft in forward airbases becoming sitting targets for the *Luftwaffe*, while frontier cordons had been withdrawn, and roads and bridges been repaired to facilitate the passage of heavy traffic. Yet the weight of historical opinion is still against such an interpretation, which lacks firm documentary support, and holds to the view that Stalin had no plan to attack Germany.[23] The evidence remains conflicting and even further information from Soviet sources may not settle the matter. Stalin's daughter, Svetlana, has depicted him in later life as repeating: 'Ech, together with the Germans we would have been invincible.'[24] On the other hand, the combination of the disposition of Soviet forces on the eve of *Barbarossa* and the demolition of previously installed Soviet defence lines does require explanation. Stalin was not a trusting sort of man.

It is clear, nevertheless that Stalin and the Soviet army were taken completely by surprise. Molotov's tough line with the Germans during the discussions of the previous November and the lack of a response from Hitler to the Soviet offer, with many pre-conditions, to join the Tripartite Pact should have warned Stalin of German hostility. Nazi-Soviet relations had become troubled and the problems had not been resolved. Stalin, however, had come to a new economic agreement with Germany in January and seems to have assumed that Hitler would not want a war on two fronts, so long as supplies of grain and war materials were forthcoming.

The German plan to attack Russia was not the best kept of secrets and the British and the Americans had given Stalin warnings. Probably, he thought these were designed to drive him towards an alliance with Britain which he had no intention of entering into, but he also ignored the warnings of his own intelligence service and only the wilfully blind could have misread the significance of massive German troop movements. Right up to the day of the invasion, he continued to send supplies to Germany and to turn savagely on any advisers who dared to suggest that the Soviet Union was about to be attacked. Was this because he was blind to the threat from Germany or because he was preoccupied with his own plans for attack?

Barbarossa set the Wehrmacht a monumental task, which it was to ultimately to fail. It was, in its professionalism, the best army in the contemporary world, and one of the best the world had ever seen, an army which, whether it was advancing or retreating, consistently inflicted greater casualties on its opponents, than it suffered itself. Hitler had, however, asked it to conquer a vast state with a much larger population than Germany. It failed, but the failure was far from pre-ordained. Arguments that Hitler should have learned from history – from Napoleon's fate – and not attacked Russia are too simplistic. Victory would have been possible had he not underestimated his opponent and had he put a larger army with a better prepared strategy into the field. Hitler knew his European history, the vastness of Russian territory, the difficulty of the terrain and the bleakness of the Russian winter. He placed too much confidence in the ability of the excellent German army to overcome such obstacles, and under-estimated the capacity of Stalin's regime and its ability to organise a defence after initial defeats and retreats. He had not prepared for a winter war, in retrospect an enormous mistake, because he and his generals expected victory by the autumn. A German victory was possible, but German preparations had not maximised the chances of success. The army was not large enough for the task allotted it and it lacked sufficient tanks, motor vehicles and artillery, while the *Luftwaffe* had not the planes to maintain that command of the air which had been integral to earlier German victories.

German victories, hitherto, had been won by a combination of Hitler's daring and the capacity of the *Wehrmacht* to fulfil those dares. However, the German economy was not an efficient war economy and the German armed forces did not reflect the nation's potential strength. Germany had set the armaments pace of the thirties *vis-à-vis* the West and, because it was a sophisticated society and economy, its new weaponry was 'state of the art' *circa* 1938, but there was not enough of it and Germany relied upon the professionalism of its officer class and the well-educated NCOs and soldiers to make it count. In short wars over modest distances it had counted brilliantly, though the exhaustion of the panzers before Dunkirk and the lack of replace-ment tanks should have been heeded. Germany put 146 divisions into the attack, including 17 panzer and 12 motorised divisions, but there were not in total many more planes and tanks available than had been used in the battle for France. This was simply not enough for the gigantic and complex task.

It has been argued that the Wehrmacht was simply not up to the demands placed upon it because the 'incomplete industrial and economic development of Germany' was not capable of supporting a fully motorised army, while shortages of fuel and rubber were chronic problems.[25] As a result, three-quarters of the army that invaded the Soviet Union moved on foot and relied upon horses, more than 600,000 of them. There is weight in this argument, but Germany could have put a larger army behind *Barbarossa* and, whatever the limitations of its economy, a more total mobilisation for war could have increased its degree of mechanisation. A German victory depended upon a speedy and comprehensive defeat of Soviet forces within months and its failure to achieve this was at least as much the result of planning errors, strategic mistakes, and the unexpected resilience of the Soviet state.

Germany did, of course, have allies. As well as Italy, Hungary, Romania, and, less firmly, Bulgaria had all signed the Tripartite Pact by March 1941 and Hungary and Romania joined in the attack on the Soviet Union. Western historians have, on the whole, not been kind to those nations, placed between two tyrannies and with complex relations with their immediate neighbours, which, after endeavouring for years not to have to choose between Germany and the Soviet Union, were eventually forced to align themselves with the former. They should, it is tacitly suggested, have put the interests of Britain and her allies before their own. Until late in 1940, it had been in Germany's interests for the Balkan states and Hungary to be neutral but now they were with various degrees of willingness, strong-armed into an anti-Soviet war. The advantage Germany was to gain from the equivocal and unreliable support from states whose economies could only provide armies without heavy weaponry was marginal, while for those states the war would be a disaster.

Accounts depict Stalin as suffering some sort of breakdown as the reality of a full-scale German invasion dawned on him and as staying secluded at his *dacha*, dazed and silent, for several days. Whether he had been planning to attack Hitler and been out-manoeuvred or had simply trusted that Germany would not dare to invade, he had miscalculated badly. The view of a supine and shaken Stalin, having to be sought out at his *dacha* by the Politburo and, at first half-believing they had come to arrest him, being persuaded to take up command again, scarcely fits in with his tough and ruthless reputation. Edvard Radzinsky's theory is that Stalin was following the example of his hero, Ivan the Terrible, whose 'favorite trick was to pretend that he was dying, watch how the hapless boyars behaved, then rise from his sick-bed and cruelly punish them, to discourage all the others'.[26] Deeply shocked as he was, Stalin never relaxed his grip on power.

His position was, nevertheless, not an enviable one for he was in a position better than most to know the weaknesses of the Soviet army, still recovering from the purge of senior officers at the end of the thirties. The Red Army was large enough, having as many men in its western regions as the Germans could muster, organised in some 170 or 183 divisions according to different estimates, while there were further divisions in the interior and the East, but its morale was low, its command structure unwieldy and communications poor. The Germans' estimate of the efficiency of the Soviet army was not far wrong, though they had insufficiently appreciated how good its newer tanks of the T34 and KV classes were. What they had failed to realise was the strength of Stalin's fearful regime and the productive potential of the cumbersome state, but these factors only began to count after *Barbarossa* had already failed. The Germans needed a quick and complete victory and, though they gained spectacular tactical victories and captured huge areas of territory, an overall victory eluded them. *Barbarossa* failed in that its objective, the conquest of Russia west of the Ural Mountains within six months, was beyond the capacity of the German armies devoted to it.

The German forces were divided into three army groups, North, Centre and South: North was to attack towards the Baltic States and Leningrad; Centre to drive to and take Moscow; and South to advance into the Ukraine and from thence to the Caucasus. It was hoped to defeat the main Soviet forces in the first few weeks, encircling them as the panzer divisions moved rapidly forward and leaving their destruction or capture to the infantry. Although great advances were made in the first weeks, and the encirclement strategy went according to plan resulting in the defeat of whole Russian armies, the shortcomings of the attacking force were beginning to become apparent. One major problem was the inability of much of the infantry to keep up with the rapid advance of the panzers. It is noteworthy in this respect that if the Germans and their allies had put 3.5 million men into the invasion, they had also put 600,000 horses into it and troops advancing at the speed of the horse were bound to find it impossible to keep up with motorised divisions. A further factor was that even when the infantry did catch up, its numbers were insufficient to deal quickly with pockets of resistance, the surrender of Russian divisions or the effective occupation of territory. The tank force itself was too small and lacked reserves meaning that as tanks broke down on the dreadful Russian roads they could not be replaced so that, within the first month of the war, the tank strength of the German divisions dropped by half.

If the major reasons for the failure of *Barbarossa* have to do with the inadequacy of the German forces for their formidable task, Russian resistance was also important. Such was the superiority of the *Wehrmacht* that, given the command of the air which it had in these months, it could with more men, more tanks and more mechanised infantry have prevailed, even against stout Soviet resistance. In the absence of sufficient German strength, the conduct of Soviet forces became crucial. Many, including some senior Soviet officers, had had doubts whether the troops would fight at all; one commander telegraphed Moscow with the news: 'Soviet troops are fighting.'[27] Despite its early disarray, the Soviet army's resistance became fiercer the further the Germans advanced; both the Soviet armed forces and the regime itself were more formidable than Hitler had calculated. Stalin, after his lapse into an impotent state of shock in the first days of the invasion, recovered his will and took over as 'People's Commissar for Defence'. Inspired by a mixture of patriotism and fear, the Red Army did not collapse.

By September the German advance, though behind schedule, continued remorselessly: Army Group South, which had encountered the stiffest resistance, had broken through into the Ukraine and the Crimea, while Army Group Centre, having been held up by a strong Soviet resistance at Smolensk, was diverted from giving the taking of Moscow priority and ordered to assist Army Group North which in conjunction with Army Group South trapped a large Soviet army around Kiev. Hitler's directive, of 6 September, ordered Groups North and South to continue towards Leningrad and Rostow, while Centre, now reinforced, was to take Moscow. A division of opinion between Hitler and the Army High Command had become increasingly overt with Hitler giving priority to the northern and southern prongs of the German advance with the aims of securing the Baltic, taking Leningrad and conquering the Ukraine, while the generals gave priority to the prize of Moscow. Kiev fell on 19 September and more than half a million prisoners and vast quantities of ammunition fell into German hands but to General Halder, Chief of the General Staff, the concentration on Kiev at the expense of Moscow was a major mistake.

At this stage, the Germans should have been content with their gains, recognised that complete victory was unattainable in 1941, and consolidated their positions until after the spring of 1942. It was obvious that the Red Army had an unexpected fighting spirit and tenacity, that German intelligence had underestimated the number of existing Soviet divisions and never imagined the speed at which new ones could be formed. In a rare moment of rational calculation Hitler at the end of July had begun to realise that he might not be able to achieve victory in 1941 and by August was even considering the possibility of a negotiated peace. That he decided to press on is understandable, for it seemed that one last effort might finish the war. The German forces, however, were in need of reinforcement and replenishment, the autumn rains were due and Stalin, now there was little threat from Japan, was able to call upon both new divisions from the interior and fresh, battle-hardened divisions from the East. The German attack was blunted by a combination of the following factors: these new divisions which, because of the constant danger of war with Japan, had been largely spared from Stalin's purges; the effectiveness of General Zhukov (put in command of the defence of Moscow); better Soviet communications (for the railways from the east to Moscow were undamaged); German exhaustion; and the weather, which made advances by German tanks difficult. As the German offensive ground to a halt outside Moscow, a Soviet counter-offensive, begun in early December, enjoyed relative success. Hitler refused to permit tactical withdrawals. At the end of 1941 it was clear that, although the Germans still had the advantage, the USSR was undefeated.

Barbarossa, nevertheless, came close to success with German armies at the gates of Moscow in late 1941, while the offensive of 1942 was to take the *Wehrmacht* into the Volga and the Caucasus. Nor was this just a German invasion for Germany was assisted by numerous allies, such as Hungary, Romania and Finland, and even the traditionally most pro-Russian of the east European states, Bulgaria, gave assistance though stopping short of declaring war on the Soviet Union; in addition to regional allies, Italian, Spanish and French brigades fought on Germany's side. Such support was of variable effectiveness militarily but meant that the composite force launched against the Soviet Union bore some similarity to that led by Napoleon against Russia in 1812. Too often the war in Eastern Europe is seen purely as a titanic struggle between Germany and the Soviet Union – it was that of course, but it pulled into its vortex, willingly or unwillingly, contingents from far afield and all the states and peoples of the region. Neutrality was impossible and, in the fluid situation, states and peoples took their chances and pursued their ambitions, aligning themselves with the likely victors.

Britain found her continental sword in her enemy's enemy, rushing with indecent haste to find virtues in Stalin's tyranny and quickly declared war on Finland, which she had considered supporting against the Soviet Union in 1940, and became equivocal as to the interests of the exiled Polish government.

With hindsight, it can be argued that, by the end of 1941, Barbarossa had failed. The aim had been to defeat the Soviet Union by the end of the year but, if the German invasion had penetrated deep into Russia, the *Wehrmacht* had met reverses and the difficulties of supply over great distances were becoming apparent. Above all the Germans had underestimated the strength of the Soviet regime and its ability to withstand huge losses of men and weaponry. The army assembled for *Barbarossa,* some 410 divisions, had just not been big enough for the task. General Halder bewailed in early August that, although the strength of the Soviet army had been estimated at 200 divisions, 'Now we have already counted 360'. This too was a great underestimate and by the end of 1941 the Red Army had fielded 600 divisions.[28] No doubt, with an accelerated armaments programme and a better judgement of enemy strength, Hitler could have assembled a larger invasion force which might have made victory in a short war more likely but it was now clear that this was not to be a short war. Were Germany's population and economy sufficient to provide the necessary forces for a long war against such an enemy, especially as Britain was undefeated and the USA was now in the wider war? Hitler had always realised that time was not on his side. Nevertheless, to most contemporaries Hitler still seemed to have the upper hand and 1942 was to see further advances. Hitler remained determined to win the European civil war.

Chapter 3: A World War?

The Origins of the Far Eastern War

What gives the Second World War its claim to have been a world war in a more complete sense than the First World War is the involvement of Japan. The Japanese attack upon the US fleet at Pearl Harbor can be seen to have made a European war a world war. There are, however, a number of problems with this essentially Eurocentric perspective.

From an American point of view, the Second World War can be seen as beginning in December 1941, while from an East Asian, especially a Chinese, viewpoint, that date marked merely an extension of a Sino-Japanese war that had been going on since at least 1937. Even the terms 'World War II' or 'Second World War' are not always used. Americans usually refer to 'the Pacific War', though often to 'World War II in the Pacific', but this puts the emphasis upon the war between the USA and Japan, thus neglecting the fighting in East Asia and particularly China. The Japanese referred during the war to 'the Greater East-Asian War' while the term 'the Far Eastern War' has recently found favour among British historians.[1]

Such terminological controversy raises the fundamental question as to how far the war in the Far East and the Pacific was linked to the war in Europe, and to what extent it should be considered a separate conflict. For the British Empire and the USA the links are obvious, their armed forces fought both in the European war and against Japan. For the Dutch and the French there were at least parallels for, just as they were defeated and occupied by Germany, so their headless colonies were overrun by the Japanese. For the Axis powers there was an alliance and plans for co-operation, but little harmonisation of strategy or practical mutual assistance. The Soviet Union, which had clashed with Japan in 1938 and 1939, enjoyed a wary neutrality in the

86

war between Japan and the Western allies until its opportunist declaration of war upon Japan in 1945. In many ways we can conceive of
two wars, bridged by the participation in each of Britain and the US.

Those who see the war in Asia and the Pacific as essentially one war
can find some common causal factors in the decline in international
stability in the 1930s, in the erosion of the authority of the League of
Nations, in the worldwide economic depression, and in the common
problems of Britain and France faced with the need to safeguard
colonial possessions in the Far East as well as prepare for a possible
war in Europe. The overarching explanation of a global clash between
the powers representing the 'old order' and those demanding a 'new
order', an idea which, as we have seen, lay behind von Ribbentrop's
plans for an alliance embracing Germany, Italy, Japan and the Soviet
Union, can also be employed,[2] but the immediate causes of the war in
Europe and that in the Far East were very different, while the Soviet
Union, hardly an old order power, ended up allied to the US and
Britain in the European War and stayed out of the Far Eastern War until
near its end. As one authority on the European War has written, 'Once
the Soviet Union had established a durable truce with the Japanese (on
15 September 1939), no further link remained between the European
and Pacific theatres of the Second World War'.[3]

The origins of the war in the Far East are to be found both in the
specific context of that region and in a world context. In the former
category come the weakness of China, the declining strength of the
colonial powers, American and Soviet interests, the impact of the
inter-war depression, and above all, the nature and ambitions of
the Japanese Empire. It was, however, the war in Europe between
1939 and 1941 which made the European empires such tempting
targets for Japan, while Nazi-Soviet relations gave Japan opportunities
and posed choices.

Japan had, of course, been a belligerent on the Allied side in the
First World War, but the Asian and Pacific aspects of that war had
been a mere echo of the war in Europe, involving only the seizure of
minor German colonies and threats to allied shipping from German
surface raiders. The war, nevertheless, seemed to the Japanese to
confirm the great-power status and the equality with the Western
powers that she eagerly sought, but the post-war world seemed to
thwart such ambitions.

The rapid emergence of Japan as both a modern industrial economy and a major military power has no parallel. It can be compared
with the several centuries during which Russia attempted to match
the economic and military progress of the western European powers,

with the many efforts of the Ottoman Empire to do the same during the nineteenth century, and with China's successive failures to westernise its armies, institutions and economy. The Western stereotype of the ability of the Japanese to adapt to European and American culture and technology as based on copying and mimicry is, at best, a half-truth. Japan had a long history of cultural and technological importing, having taken so much from Chinese civilisation, but the phrase 'Chinese [or western] ways, Japanese spirit' sums up both the empirical nature of such borrowings and the continuity of Japanese identity. In addition, recent research has shown that Japan had already become a sophisticated economy before it was opened to Western influence in the mid-nineteenth century. The rapidity of Japanese westernisation did, however, leave psychological scars and its instantaneous success, most graphically illustrated by its victory over Russia in 1905, mixed heady ambition with a sensitivity that could not easily reconcile the nation to setbacks. Japan's very economic development made it necessarily a power dedicated to growth, whether by trade or conquest, for its modest raw material resources meant that there could be no return of its rising population to the introverted economy of the early nineteenth century. Japan required either a healthy international trading economy or an empire, preferably both. In this it resembled Britain. Military ethos and national pride combined with the impact of world depression to make Japan a hungry and expansionist power in the 1930s.

Was Japan an honorary Western power, content to trade in an international market and take her place with the United States and the colonial powers in the prevailing Anglo-American order, or was she rather a 'have not' power, which could lead Asia in the establishment of a new post-colonial order? Essentially the inter-war period saw Japan move from the former to the latter posture, a move which interacted with internal changes within Japanese politics. The Versailles Treaty failed to contain the clauses against racial discrimination that the Japanese had hoped for, the end of the Anglo-Japanese Alliance took away an anchor of security, and naval opinion in Japan was frustrated by the Washington Naval Treaty of 1921. Japan's aims in China were increasingly thwarted by the USA and even by Britain, which hoped to buttress its position in the Treaty Ports by more pro-Chinese policies. Rather like Italy in respect of Abyssinia, Japan felt that the western powers, having carved out dominant positions for themselves in Asia generally and China in particular, were now seeking to change the rules so as to deny Japan the expansion that her economic and military strength entitled her to. A combination of diplomatic reverses and economic difficulties unseated the pro-western and liberal factions in Japan which had managed Meiji Japan's entry into a Western dominated world. There had always been a degree of atavistic opposition to Japan's economic modernisation and acceptance of Western mores. Japan's success and the alliance with Britain had not only stifled such opposition, but obscured the eclecticism of Japan's borrowings from the West: a navy and economy modelled on the British, an army modelled on that of Germany, and an administration that resembled that of France. Divisions were not so much between westernisers and traditionalists, but between those who wished to persevere with a liberal and established Anglo-American path and those who argued that more authoritarian Western models were more compatible with Japan's traditions and interests. With the accession of Emperor Hirohito, but not because of his own views, there came a strong reaction against many of the manifestations of westernisation imported from Britain and the USA; free trade and the liberal economic ethic encountered opposition not only from socialists and communists, but also from traditionalists who saw them as destructive of hierarchy and collective values.

The depression in the world economy initiated by the Wall Street crash came at a time when the Japanese government was deflating the economy by cutting public spending in order to raise the value of the yen. The effect of world depression was to push the Japanese economy into a severe downward spiral at a time when rice farmers were feeling the effect of cheaper imports from Korea and Formosa (Taiwan). High unemployment and declining real wages and incomes discredited free-trade and liberal economics. Japanese society which was remarkably racially and culturally homogeneous, was ill-equipped to face deep social discontent and the alienation of an agricultural sector that still accounted for some 50 per cent of the population, while the military reacted angrily to cuts in army and navy budgets. Some saw a better Western model for Japan with the rise of fascism and Nazism, and their corporatist and protectionist economic policies. These domestic problems interacted with Japan's quarrels over China with the League of Nations – and with Britain and the US – to produce a sea change in Japan's perception of its place and interests in the world.

Those who see Japan in the thirties as engaging in a top-down fascism are contradicted by historians who see Japanese militarism as a particular phenomenon which if it, like Mussolini's Italy and Hitler's Germany, glorified force and was torn between modernism and traditionalism, had no charismatic leader and no dynamic political party.

What made the Japanese militarist state such a strange entity was the lack of strong leadership. Japan moved slowly and ineluctably towards a new internal order, and towards a radical position in international affairs with an establishment riven by faction and with no clear mechanism for decision making. There was no revolution or successful *coup d'état*: existing institutions, the Diet, ministries, the Privy Council, all continued, but rather than a clear system for the exercise of authority and power, there was competition for the control of decision making between various parts of the government machine. The military gained increasing power and influence, but was riddled with divisions: senior against middle-ranking officers and the army against the navy. Paradoxes abounded: a cult of duty and authority leavened by rebellion, devotion to the emperor along with disobedience to his ministers, and consensus and conformity modified by assassination.

There were parallels between the ethos that became dominant in Japan during the thirties and Italian fascism and German Nazism: extreme nationalism and an admiration of violence and force are the obvious common denominators, while Japanese nationalism shared with Nazism an ambivalence towards modernity reflected in the divisions between two army factions: the Control faction, which sought to speed up the modernisation of military structure and equipment; and the Imperial Way faction, which emphasised morale and traditional fighting spirit. Japanese militarism shared with fascism and National Socialism, a hatred of both socialism and liberal capitalism, the one because, in putting class against class, it threatened national cohesion, and the other because its individualism did the same thing; as regards the economy, Japan, like the other Axis states, favoured protectionism and corporatism and sought to make economics subservient to politics. Yet such similarities are probably less important than the differences: the distinct nature of Japanese history and tradition; and the position of Japan as an Asian power torn between her erstwhile role as an ally of the established order and the attraction of heading a post-colonial new order.

The great characteristic of what has been derivatively called Japanese fascism was that no one was really in charge and there was no great political party or cohesive movement, but rather a spirit fanned by patriotic societies. Some historians have seen the Emperor's influence as important and even blamed him for leading Japan to war but, it seems more likely that factions in Japan claimed his authority and used it as a cloak, rather than that he took crucial decisions himself.[4] The Imperial Rule Association, founded in 1940, was too broad an umbrella organisation ever to wield effective influence. General Tojo Hideki, Japan's principal war leader, was no Hitler, nor even a Mussolini, but merely the most important of a succession of military politicians; he had no cult and only a shifting power base. Japan moved ineluctably towards expansionism and war and towards domestic authoritarianism, but it did so without decisive leadership and in a curiously pluralistic, even chaotic, manner.[5]

By 1941 Japan had in China been engaged for a decade in what recent Japanese school textbooks have described as a 'forward policy'. In the eyes of Japanese nationalists this was not empire building, but rather a recognition that only under Japanese leadership could a weak China assist Japan to resist Western dominance in east Asia. China was not given a choice and from 1931, Japan moved from exercising its influence through its political and economic rights in Manchuria and the Treaty Ports to an outright occupation of Manchuria, thinly disguised by the sponsored state of Manchukuo. The Chinese government of Chiang Kai Chek,[6] originally more concerned with the threat from the Chinese communists, was forced to take a harder line against Japanese ambitions and, in 1937, war broke out between Japan and China. Japanese leaders declared an Asian New Order and set out to conquer China's Pacific provinces.

The Japanese assault on China was not the result of any long-term plan. The Japanese army had been preparing for war with Russia, not China, and the incident which led to the Sino-Japanese War was a confused skirmish. In early July 1937 Japanese troops were on manoeuvres near Peking (Beijing) when, close to the Marco Polo Bridge, they were, or believed they were, fired on and what was initially a skirmish escalated, both sides called up reinforcements, and there was soon a full-scale war. The Japanese took Peking and Chiang Kai Chek then extended the war by attacking the Japanese garrison at Shanghai thus opening up a new front in central China. The Japanese, now determined on decisive action, co-ordinated their command via an Imperial General Headquarters, and took the Chinese Republic's capital, Nanking, where Japanese troops murdered men and raped women in what became known as the Nanking massacre. The Nationalists retreated to a new capital, Wuhan, but this fell to the Japanese in October 1938. An incident had led to full-scale, if undeclared, war in which the Japanese army found itself fighting across great swathes of Chinese territory. Despite the Japanese army's spectacular advance, which saw it controlling China's major ports and its most economically productive regions, with the Nationalist government confined to remote Sichuan, the Japanese found themselves conducting a difficult and expensive war which they could not conclude by a decisive battle.

Japan's ruthlessness and comparative success in her incursions into China brought her tangible, but limited, economic rewards, assuring food imports and some 15 per cent of the industrial materials she required. Japanese military operations were until 1944 never on a sufficient scale to crush Chinese resistance; it is indeed doubtful if there was a considered policy in Tokyo as to what exactly Japan's ultimate aims in China were. The results of Japan's incursions, however, were considerable: a deterioration of relations with the Western powers, followed by a push towards further expansionist policies in order to cut off military aid to China, followed by embargoes on trade, which in turn propelled Japan to desperate and wider aggression and expansion.

Relations with the USA, which saw itself as the defender of Chinese interests, went into steep decline. Anglo-Japanese relations also deteriorated though there were attempts at *rapprochement*. A realisation of the weakness of Britain's military position in the Far East and what has been termed the 'afterglow' of the Anglo-Japanese Alliance made influential sections of opinion in the government, the treasury and the military favour either co-operation with Japan or at least the avoidance of open quarrels.[7] It is possible to argue that a realistic and hard-headed assessment of British interests and resources demanded co-operation with, rather than opposition to, Japan. Contrary to the rewriting of history by some post-war Australian politicians, the Australian government and senior military figures were well aware of the weakness of the British military position in the Far East and favoured a policy of compromise with Japan.[8] The British Foreign Office appears, however, to have seen any significant improvement in relations with Japan as likely to strain relations with the United States and rejected the overtures of the Japanese ambassador in London. The inability of governments in Tokyo to control the actions of often anti-British army officers in China further exacerbated relations, while liberal and internationalist sections of British public opinion was implacably opposed to Japanese aggression in China. A far greater obstacle to Anglo-Japanese agreement came from the Japanese Imperial Navy, which became committed to a policy of expansion in south and central China, and increasingly saw Britain as its principal enemy. A progressive but gradual alienation between Britain and Japan during the 1930s was the result.

The deterioration of the USA's relations with Japan was more predictable. Critics of US foreign policy have pointed to the mixture of liberal idealism and self-interest which has characterised it, while more severe critics have seen the former as a mere cloak for the latter. In the specific instance of Japanese-US relations, America's curious relationship with China was the determining factor. The USA had important economic interests in China, as did Britain and Japan and had been as determined as either to exact the maximum profit, via its 'open door' to trade policies. Was, indeed, the United States an imperial power without many colonies, which rather like Britain in the mid-nineteenth century pursued its economic interests via free trade and protected them with a powerful navy?

At the same time, however, important sections of US opinion had 'adopted' China as an Asian child, spared from the evils of incorporation into a Western colonial empire, which could be brought up in an American way and become a liberal, modern, and even Christian adolescent. American missionaries, both religious and secular, had invested much in China and small American towns, colleges and churches had special interests in China's future. A benevolent myopia towards China, and particularly towards Chiang Kai Chek's Nationalists, was the result. Thus American detestation of Japan's incursion into China combined with antipathetic Japanese and American economic interests and naval rivalry in the Pacific to make the USA a resolute opponent of Japanese expansionism.

If Japan was to embark upon a policy of military expansion, there were two possible options open to her: a move south to gain supplies of rubber, oil and other essential materials, with the certainty of war with Britain and the other colonial powers, and probably the USA; or a move northwards against the Soviet Union. The northwards move was in accordance with previous Japanese policies and was favoured by the army, while the majority of naval commanders favoured the southern option. Two factors militated against the northwards move at the beginning of the European war in 1939. One was the successive defeats suffered by Japan in fierce clashes on the Manchurian and Outer Mongolian border in 1938 and 1939, which convinced the Japanese that the Soviet Union was a formidable military power. The other was the Nazi-Soviet Pact, a diplomatic rebuff to Japan in that her partner in the Anti-Comintern had not consulted her, but which, nevertheless, presented the Japanese with the opportunity of using their friendship with Germany to improve their relations with the Soviet Union. With their backs secured against a Soviet attack, the Japanese could consider the possibilities of a southward advance while Britain and France were fighting a war in Europe.

The decisive decision of the Second World War was the Japanese decision to attack the USA and the British Empire instead of the USSR. Had Japan attacked Russia at the same time as Hitler launched *Barbarossa*, it is difficult to conceive of the Soviet Union surviving, while

US entry into the war would not have been precipitated. The path to that decision was tortuous, with Japanese governments influenced by German actions, but for long ignorant of German intentions. Just as the Japanese government heard of the Nazi-Soviet Pact after the event, so the signatory to the Tripartite Pact was told nothing of the plans for *Barbarossa*. When the Japanese foreign minister, Matsuoka Yosuke, was in Berlin in April 1941 nothing was said of plans to attack Russia and Matsuoka, supposing Russo-German relations to be on a cooperative footing, went on to Moscow and signed a neutrality pact with Stalin. The affronted Matsuoka said to the Japanese cabinet in June: 'I concluded a neutrality pact because I thought that German and Russia could not go to war. If I had thought they would go to war … I would not have concluded the Neutrality Pact.'[9]

A combination of Hitler's confidence in his ability to flatten the Soviet Union within weeks and reluctance to share his victory with the Japanese, together with his belief that Britain remained his most dangerous and implacable enemy, caused him to discourage a Japanese assault on Russia and to encourage a Japanese thrust to the south against Britain and the USA. At the same time, Japan's moves to prevent supplies to Chiang Kai Chek through Burma and Indo-China ineluctably brought war with Britain and America closer.

Few states were less suited to the policies of protectionism and autarchy favoured by the totalitarian powers than was Japan. Like Britain, with whom she shared a maritime history and an incapacity to feed her population and provide raw materials for her industry without imports, she was a trading power or she was nothing. The paradox that Japan needed American oil in order to go to war with America sums up her problems. The logic of an expansion southwards was that Japan could secure an empire or co-prosperity area by such expansion, which would give her the oil of the Dutch East Indies, the rubber of Malaya and other essential raw materials. Such a strategy depended not only on the feasibility of conquest but on the maintenance of conquests in a long war. The Japanese leadership seems never to have faced up to the difficulty of protecting shipments of oil and rubber from conquered territories back to the homeland.

Although US policy was to secure a Japanese withdrawal from China, there was disagreement among Roosevelt's advisers as to whether to take firm actions which might result in a war the USA was, as yet, ill-prepared to fight, or to exercise restraint. A strong argument for the latter course was that US naval rearmament meant that in a couple of years America would have the larger navy. From July 1940, however, Roosevelt adopted the policies of his more hard-line advisers and placed economic sanctions upon Japan by limiting shipments of scrap metal and oil. US policy may have been meant to deter but in practice it provoked and the combination of economic sanctions, which Roosevelt ratcheted up in August by restricting the export of aviation fuel to states outside the western hemisphere, and America's Naval Expansion Pact of June 1940 were factors in Japan's decision to sign the Tripartite Pact with Germany and Italy in September which provided for mutual assistance if any of the three powers were attacked by a nation not involved in the European war.

The defeat of France and the Netherlands left their Pacific colonies a tempting target which the Japanese were unable to resist and in September 1940, Japan sent troops into northern Indo-China with the reluctant acquiescence of the Vichy government, and then into southern Indo China in July 1941. This was a decisive step towards war as it brought Japanese air power within striking range of Thailand, the Philippines, the Dutch East Indies and Malaya.

Once Hitler had launched his attack on the Soviet Union, the Japanese leadership gave a final consideration to the northern strategy. Matsuoka argued that *Barbarossa* changed everything, that Japan should join in the attack on Russia and only after victory in the north should she turn south. Battles between Japan and the Soviet Union along the Manchuko-Siberian-Korean borders in 1938 and 1939 had, however, cost the lives of 185,000 Japanese troops and revealed that a victory in the north would be no easy task, while conquests to the north would not yield the raw materials, primarily oil and rubber that Japan needed. The southern strategy was confirmed and perhaps, as Rear Admiral Ugaki Matome wrote in his diary on the eve of Pearl Harbor, the die had already been cast: 'When we concluded the Tripartite Alliance and moved into Indo-China, we had already burned our bridges behind us in our march towards the anticipated war with the United States and Great Britain.'[10] Neither Japan's path to war nor her first act of war, the attack on Pearl Harbor, can be seen as part of a coherent strategy. The steps taken were not intended to lead to the next step, but rather were subsequently discovered to necessitate it. Once Japanese actions in French Indo-China, its demands on the British in Burma and on the Dutch in the East Indies had resulted in ever-tightening US embargoes on essential Japanese supplies, then an oil-starved Japan had either to go to war or give up the possibility of going to war. Roosevelt did not intend a complete oil embargo on Japan when he imposed sanctions, in the late summer of 1941, after the Japanese had browbeaten the Vichy authorities in Indo-China into allowing them to set up bases, but through a number of accidents, this was the result and the President felt it would be weak to reverse the decision. The embargo not only put a time limit on Japanese options for a wider war but threatened their operation of the war they were already fighting in China.

Given that they were not to join Hitler in an attack on Russia, the Japanese still had a number of options: they could 'wait and see' at the cost of a deteriorating position in oil reserves; they could attempt to compromise with the USA; they could launch an attack upon British and Dutch possessions, hoping that this would not bring the USA into the war; or they could throw caution to the wind and attack all the Western powers. Whether Japan could have moved south without a war with the USA, attacking British, French and Dutch colonies, but not US bases, is doubtful. Such a course of action would have involved the risk of leaving the Philippines – with their US bases – within the Japanese perimeter. However, the attack upon Pearl Harbor did not just mean war with the USA, but ensured that the United States public opinion would demand the pursuit of war until Japan was defeated. There could be no compromise peace, leaving Japan with most if not all of her conquests, as many Japanese ministers, generals and admirals seem to have optimistically expected, after Pearl Harbor.

Japan moved towards war amidst purposeful confusion as factions competed for influence. There can be little doubt, however, that Roosevelt's actions brought war closer: they brought home to the Japanese the vulnerability of their oil supplies and the fact that they had only a limited amount of time in which to take action. Nevertheless, negotiations between Japan and the USA took place during the autumn and early winter of 1941. There are those who see the Japanese negotiations with Washington as a mere charade, save that the negotiators, or some of them at least, didn't know the real agenda, while others contend that a possible US-Japanese compromise was open until late in November, but that those who advocated peace were simply overruled. Whether either side was seriously looking for a compromise is doubtful. Was there ever any chance that the final US terms, which involved withdrawal from Indo-China in return for a resumption of American oil sales would be accepted? The evidence that the Japanese military had already committed themselves to war, but that many in the government did not realise this, seems convincing.

Japan Attacks

Japan's first blows in her advance south seemed stunningly effective. The attack on the US naval base at Pearl Harbor in Hawaii by aircraft from six Japanese aircraft carriers, operating 4000 miles from their bases, on Sunday 7 December, resulted in eight battleships being sunk or extensively damaged, and a large number of aircraft destroyed on the ground. Simultaneous raids on Wake, Guam, Midway, the Philippines and Hong Kong were also effective, and a few days later the British battleship, HMS *Prince of Wales*, and the battle-cruiser, HMS *Repulse*, were sunk by Japanese aircraft off the Malayan coast.

The attack on Pearl Harbor has been seen as brilliant tactically but as poor strategy in that it ensured that America would fight till Japan surrendered, and it has also been criticised in terms of its effectiveness. The bombardment from the planes of the Japanese carriers did not destroy the port facilities, the arsenal or the oil supplies of the US fleet; most of the sunken battleships were raised from the shallow water, repaired and fought again; while, above all, no American aircraft carriers were in harbour at the time of the assault. It can be argued that, nevertheless, the attack delayed the capacity of the USA to mount a major naval offensive for two years.

The facts that the United States forces on Hawaii were taken by surprise and that no US aircraft carriers were in harbour gave birth to conspiracy theories. Did Roosevelt, determined to bring the US into the war against Germany, but prevented from this by opposition in Congress and by Hitler's refusal to react with a declaration of war to America's increasingly overt support for Britain, deliberately turn a blind eye to Japanese preparations for an attack on the US Pacific fleet?[11] American code-breakers had succeeded in breaking the Japanese Purple Code and were providing the results, known as 'Magic', of listening in to Japanese diplomatic radio traffic to government and military authorities. Did Roosevelt fail to inform Admiral Husband Kimmel and General Walter Short, the two commanders at Hawaii, both subsequently dismissed from their services, of an imminent Japanese attack? Mistakes, incompetence and an underestimation of Japanese capability, rather than a conspiracy seem to explain why the American forces were taken by surprise. Roosevelt may well have been intent on provoking Japan into war but it is inconceivable that he and his senior military officers would have deliberately sacrificed US servicemen, or that such a dark conspiracy could have been kept secret.

Pearl Harbor represented a switch of Japanese naval strategy from the defensive to the offensive. Highly successful in its own right, its main fault was to instil the Imperial Navy with a passion for the offensive. The mainstream of Japanese naval thinking had, since early in the century, assumed the possibility of war with the USA, taken account of US naval superiority in numbers and tonnage, and planned in the event of war to go on the defensive and then lure the US battle-fleet into a great set-piece battle in the western Pacific. Admiral Yamamoto Isoruku, appointed Commander-in-Chief of the Combined Fleet in September 1939, was only too well aware of the strength of the US Navy and was dubious as to Japan's ability to win with an exclusively defensive strategy. The attack on Pearl Harbor was designed not to protect the Japanese flank as its forces moved south, but to even up the relative strengths of the Japanese and US navies so that any American plan to move towards Japan in full naval force would be held up and weakened. The attack gave Japan a breathing space. Yamamoto had promised in April 1941 that the Japanese navy could give a 'wild show for six months to a year, but if the war drags on to two and three years I cannot be confident of the outcome'.[12] He was, of course right, but the wild show was to include the conquest of the Philippines, Malaya, the Dutch East Indies and Burma, and to bring Japanese forces to the approaches to Australia and across the Indian frontier.

The wisdom of the Japanese attack on Pearl Harbor can be criticised on the grounds that if Japan had attacked British and Dutch possessions but not American territories, the USA might well have not intervened militarily. The Japanese attack, which, like that on the Russians at Port Arthur a half century earlier, had taken place without a declaration of war, had the immediate effect of uniting American opinion behind a war with Japan and, after Hitler's declaration of war on the USA, with Germany and Italy. If there had to be a war with the USA, however, Yamamoto's daring raid gave Japan the best possible start. Japan's strategy was to conquer a large economically self-sufficient empire in South-East Asia and the southwest Pacific and then go on the defensive. In view of the potential strength of the United States and the effect of Pearl Harbor on American public opinion, this, in itself, was a desperate strategy, but given war with the USA, it was the best available. Its success depended on two things, a rapid conquest of the targeted territories and subsequent success in defending the perimeter of the conquests. Other factors, which might determine success or failure, were out of the hands of the Japanese and largely depended upon the progress of the war in Europe, but in the fluid world of 1942, Japan could hope for the success of her Axis allies.

The support of those allies was immediately made manifest with the declarations of war on the US by Germany and Italy. These declarations appeared to link the fortunes of the Axis partners and to turn a European and a Far Eastern war into a world war. Yet little thought had been given in Berlin and Tokyo as to how the Axis powers might co-operate and co-ordinate their strategies. The war in Europe and the war in the Far East were to remain largely separate, connected only by the active involvement of Britain and the USA in both.

Why Germany declared war on the most powerful economy, and potentially the most powerful military state in the world, has long puzzled historians. Germany had, after all, previously ignored America's increasingly overt support for Britain and been careful to avoid provocation. Many have concluded that Hitler had simply abandoned the degree of caution that had qualified his daring prior to *Barbarossa*, finally stepping out of the mind-set of political opportunism into a dream of world conquest into which practical considerations did not enter. He may have simply concluded that America was bound to come into the war against Germany in any case, failing to understand the US system of government and the power of Congress to prevent this. Roosevelt might, of course, without a German declaration of war, have been able to persuade Congress that America should enter the war in Europe, but this was by no means certain. Opposition in the United States to entry into a European war, when the country had the pressing task of avenging defeats in the Pacific and reversing Japan's expansion, would have been strong.

The reasons for Hitler's extraordinary decision are to be found in his previous vacillations between Ribbentrop's vision of a great alliance of the totalitarian and 'hungry' powers against Britain and the USA and his own, and much of the German military command's, distrust and hatred of Russia. Overconfidence as to the outcome of *Barbarossa* had made him spurn Japanese support in his war with Russia, while a fatal underestimation of US military potential led to the worst possible combination for Germany, a war with Britain, the United States and the Soviet Union, without Japanese assistance so far as the latter was concerned. With the support of the Soviet Union, a world war against the 'Anglo-Saxon' powers might have had a chance of success: as Japan advanced in the Pacific, a consolidation of the Mediterranean and a push into North Africa and the Middle East by the Germans would have held out the hope of gaining the Middle Eastern oil supplies and linking up German and Japanese forces in the Middle East and Indian Ocean. Alternatively, co-operation with Japan in an attack on the Soviet Union would have made Soviet resistance much more difficult. As it was, the war with Russia was to take up the greater part of Germany's military resources, making impossible any serious effort to advance from the Mediterranean towards the Indian Ocean and enabling Britain to defend her Middle East interests until America was able to enter actively the war in Europe.

Hitler, having successfully neutralised the Soviet Union while he achieved his victories in western Europe in 1940, had allowed his impatience with his inability to finish Britain off quickly to override caution and propel him into a war on two fronts. The declaration of war on the USA immeasurably strengthened the forces against Germany. The residual effects of the dalliance with Ribbentrop's strategy had now led to a war against both Russia and the 'Anglo-Saxon' powers, while the Japanese had signed a neutrality pact with Russia, which would enable Stalin to withdraw troops from the Manchurian border and use them against Germany. It was, from a Germano-centric viewpoint, a war of the centre against the periphery. This was a war that Germany was ill-equipped to fight and nor was her ally, Japan, an adequate partner for a long war in which industrial strength would be as important as military *élan*.

Japan's major goals were quickly achieved after the major prerequisite, a temporary command of the seas by the Imperial Japanese Navy, had been won. Dutch, French and British colonies, the US administered Philippines and US bases, together with neutral Thailand, were taken or occupied within four months. Hong Kong, Wake Island, Guam, Singapore, Manila and Batavia (Jakarta) were taken successively. By the end of April, the last American redoubt on the Bataan Peninsular of the Philippines had surrendered and the British been driven from Burma across the Indian frontier.

The Japanese victories were due to their command of the sea, the poor air defences of the colonial powers and the USA, and not least, to the superior performance of the Japanese army. The land forces ranged against the Japanese were numerically formidable: 89,000 troops under British command in Malaya (including 37,000 Indian, 19,000 British and 15,000 Australian); 35,000 Dutch regular troops in the East Indies; and 31000 American troops in the Philippines. The resistance was uneven: the forces defending Hong Kong put up a stout but futile defence, while a numerically superior, but poorly trained and inappropriately deployed Commonwealth army was hustled through Malaya by a Japanese force half its size and forced to surrender on 15 February 1942; the Dutch colonies were taken with ease; but, although Guam was quickly overrun, Wake Island's small garrison put up a legendary defence and American resistance in the Bataan Peninsular and Corregidor Island set back the Japanese timetable for the conquest of the Philippines by four months. The end result, none the less, was the same in each instance, Japanese victory, and if the surrender of Singapore was a humiliation and that of Bataan and

Corregidor brave defeats, the number of troops killed or surrendering in the Philippines was much the same as in Malaya and Singapore.

The defeat of the British and Commonwealth armies in the Malay Peninsular and the surrender at Singapore were important, not just for the course of the Pacific War but for British prestige in the Far East. The fall of Singapore has been regarded as symbolic of the end of the colonial era. The debacle revealed the degree to which Britain's commitments had for long been beyond its economic and military power, but they also demonstrated the shortcomings of British strategy, the incompetence of much of the senior command and the poor training and low morale of both British and Australian troops. To Churchill, who bore some responsibility from his time as Chancellor of the Exchequer in the 1920s for the inadequacy of Singapore's defences, the idea of a 100,000 strong army of forces of the British Empire surrendering to a Japanese force it outnumbered was inconceivable. So, unfortunately, was the idea of two powerful capital ships being sunk by aircraft, though the Admiralty shared that view, as did Admiral Phillips, who paid for it with his life as he was one of the 900 men who died when the *Prince of Wales* and the *Repulse* were sunk. It also demonstrated Churchill's shortcomings as a war leader who took an intimate concern in military decisions. The loss of the two capital ships deprived Singapore of the protection of any effective naval forces but General Percival's forces outnumbered the invasion force commanded by General Yamashita which nevertheless rapidly made its way down the Malay Peninsular towards Singapore where, thanks to Percival's poor tactics, it bypassed British forces in forward positions and cut off Singapore's water supply. Once the battle for the Malay Peninsular had been lost, it is probably true that Singapore could not be effectively defended, especially as the Japanese had command of the air, while the fate of the city's 900,000 civilians had to be considered but that Percival and 80,000 British, Australian and Indian troops surrendered after little resistance made for an ignominious defeat. As Churchill saw it in retrospect, 'Defeat is one thing, disgrace is another.'[13]

Japan had achieved great victories but it was still bogged down in a war with China it seemed unable to finish. It now had to decide whether to concentrate on defending the wide perimeter of its new conquests or to continue on the offensive while its enemies were still reeling from their defeats. The Imperial Japanese Navy was in a far better position to take on the might of the US and Royal navies than its commanders in the 1920s and 1930s could ever have imagined, but time was not on its side, especially in view of the resources of the United States with its ability to launch new warships. Japan had a powerful ally in Germany, but how could it benefit from that alliance when no plans for cooperation had been made? Defeats had left the British Empire demoralised and the loyalty of its Asian subjects shaken, while the colonies of the other European empires had been occupied, but could Asian nationalisms be harnessed under the Rising Sun? A German victory in Europe would immeasurably improve Japan's position but a Soviet victory over Germany would revive old threats from the north. Above all, Japan's prospects were limited, not by the determination or ability of its army and navy, but by the productive power of its economy.

The Japanese Empire had not gone purposefully to war, nor been led into it by a strong and dynamic leader. Now, after heady success, important decisions and choices had to be made.

Chapter 4:   Behind the Lines

The Balance of Strength

Despite the successes of the Japanese, the humiliations of the British and the defeats of the Americans, and despite the great swathe of Soviet territory conquered by Germany, it could be argued, from a British point of view, that, with the entry of the USSR and the USA into the war, ultimate victory was secure. As Churchill wrote in his memoirs: 'We had won the war. England would live.' His optimism that, if Britain could hold out long enough, the USSR and the USA would be drawn into the war, had been justified, even though their entry had been determined by the aggression of Germany and Japan rather than by their own volition.

It has become accepted by most historians that the balance of power between the Allies and the Axis powers was indeed such that, in the long run, the latter could not prevail and that the views of those contemporaries, who considered in 1942 that, though there might be further setbacks, the tide would turn, were correct. R. A. C. Parker is representative of this analysis, writing that

> Together, the United States, the British Empire and the Soviet Union were certain to defeat Germany provided all of them went on fighting long enough. The defeat of Japan would be a lesser problem once they had disposed of Germany, especially if the Soviet Union then joined the British and Americans against Japan. The allies must win if they stayed together. The effort and length of time needed for victory was fixed principally by the proportion of the world that Germany and Japan could conquer before they were halted. Three great campaigns determined the result: the amphibious operations of Japan in the Pacific and south Asia, the German

land offensive against Russia, and the submarine campaign against Britain.[1]

This is a powerful argument and the concept of the certainty of allied victory in 1942 is, of course, supported by the fact of allied victory in 1945. It is worth remembering, however, that the weight of contemporary opinion in 1939 had considered the combined military and economic strength of France and Britain, backed by the resources of their empires, as bound to result in the ultimate defeat of Germany. The advantages enjoyed by France and Britain had, however, been outweighed by the superiority of the German army and the daring of German generals.

The concept of the inevitability of Allied victory in the circumstances of 1942 is essentially based on an elevation of economic strength and resources over military decisions and the outcome of battles. It has been challenged by Richard Overy in his assessment, *Why the Allies Won*.[2] In Overy's view we need to consider, not just the resources of the home economies of the combatants, but the potential and the use made of the economies of conquered territories, the decisions of high commands, the performances of armed forces, and the choices made as to the development and production of weaponry. The reasons for allied victory lay in the mistakes of the Axis powers, as well as in the strengths of the Allies. Those mistakes included the failure of Japan to exploit the economic fruits of her victories in the East Indies and of Germany to fulfil both her own productive potential and that of her European conquests, together with errors in the development of aircraft, tanks and submarines, as well as the strategic and tactical choices of Hitler and the German and Japanese Commands.

We need to consider in turn the factors making for allied success.

The Sinews of War

The great strength of the inevitability-of-victory argument lies in the potential of the US economy, a potential amply proven by its wartime performance. The following table by Paul Kennedy demonstrates the way that the American economy was able to move, seemingly effortlessly, towards armaments production that put it in a different league to other powers.

Armaments Production of the Powers, 1940–3[3]

(billions of 1944 dollars)

	1940–1	1941–2	1942–3
Britain	3.5	6.5	11.1
USSR	(5.0)	8.5	13.9
USA	(1.5)	4.5	37.5
Combined Allied total	**3.5**	**19.5**	**62.5**
Germany	6.0	6.0	13.8
Japan	(1.0)	2.0	4.5
Italy	0.75	1.0	–
Combined Axis total	**6.75**	**9.0**	**18.3**

Take away America's contribution, and the enormous number of tanks, planes, ships and guns that it represented, and the Axis was still at a disadvantage, but one that could be made up by superior strategy, better generals and more efficient armies. Retain it and the force of the argument – that what was remarkable was how long it took the allies to win – becomes apparent.

The productive potential of the USA was well recognised at the beginning of 1942, but its capacity to adapt rapidly to armaments production and to expand its fighting services was less apparent. America harnessed capitalism for war. Almost overnight, General Motors and Ford came to be amongst the biggest arms manufacturers in the world; automobile production stopped and planes and tanks rolled off production lines. A single firm, General Motors, came to supply one tenth of America's war production. It was found that even ships were capable of being produced by mass-production techniques, when Henry Kaiser began to build a standardised cargo ship, the Liberty ship, by using standardised parts produced in different places, some far from any port. The Ford Motor Company built the giant Willow Run complex and turned out the B-24 Liberator bomber on assembly-line principles, while the Chrysler corporation built an even bigger plant for the manufacture of Oerlikon anti-aircraft guns.[4] By 1943–4 the US was producing 'one ship a day and one aircraft every five minutes'.[5] This was no 'New Deal' war effort, but rather government and the military giving orders and leaving private enterprise, and especially America's giant corporations, to get on with the job. The productive potential that had been held back by years of depression was unleashed.

The Soviet economy and its war effort stood in direct contrast to those of the United States. In war, as in peace, the USSR had a command economy, where the 'orders' that came from above were in the military rather than the commercial sense of the word. Instead of profits for manufacturers and high wages for workers, there were draconian penalties for managers and workers alike if they failed to deliver, and subsistence and below subsistence living standards for workers. There was also, the land of the GULag, the USSR's archipelago of concentration camps, where 'up to 10 per cent of the population were slave labourers'.[6]

Yet the Soviet achievement was remarkable. Vast areas of the Union were overrun, yet, in 1942 the factories were able to increase production of arms and munitions. This was despite the fact that the territory occupied by the Germans by November 1941 was where 40 per cent of the pre-war population had lived and had provided some 60 per cent of such crucial materials as coal, steel, pig-iron and aluminium. The most spectacular and extraordinary development was the way in which factories, about to be overrun and taken by the Germans, were 'packed up' and transferred to the eastern regions of the state. This was neither a planned nor a smooth process, but amidst chaos and disorder, it was accomplished; the managers of individual plants salvaging their machinery and supervising the transport of it and their workers to new sites. Beyond the Volga River and the Ural mountains, they found that little had been prepared for them and they had to build their factories and living quarters on frozen ground. The one advantage was that before the war started the coal and steel industries of the East had been developed, providing the basic resources for renewed armaments production. If central planning still dictated the demand for production, the supply of that demand was dependent at factory level on the initiative of managers and workers, who squeezed production from machines that were damaged, improvised or put together with cannibalised parts, while shortages of supplies necessitated an *ad hoc* self-sufficiency.

Such efforts staved off a collapse of the Soviet armaments industry and therefore of Soviet resistance to the advancing Germans. Helped by the fact that the Soviets had only a small number of different types of weapon, two main models of tank and five of aircraft, mass production was able to maximise output even in desperate conditions. Even in 1941 and 1942 Russian armaments production exceeded that of Germany. It was, nevertheless, a close run thing, for there was a real danger that the concentration on arms production at all costs would run down the supporting economy to the degree that arms production itself would become impossible. Although built upon the back of the suffering of a half-starved work force, the creation of a new war economy in the Ural region, symbolised by the giant Magnitogorsk steel works, which employed 45,000 people, was one of the wonders of the war. It was by its own efforts that the Soviet Union held off the German attack and supplied its armies. After 1942, however, US aid was to become important for supplies of high quality steel, food and, crucially, transport. The Red Army that advanced westward from 1943 did so in American jeeps and trucks, while much of the technology which enabled the Soviet Union to produce aircraft capable of seizing command of the air from the Germans came from the Western allies.

It has been said that 'England and Russia achieved the greatest subordination of economy and society to the war effort'.[7] The experience of the First World War had prepared public and business opinion in Britain for such subordination, and the necessary legislation and planning machinery were ready in 1939. Among centre and left political circles 'planning' had for long been credited with miracle-working powers and the formation of the Coalition government gave influence to factions of the Conservative Party, who favoured corporatist policies, and to Labour ministers. Much power on the 'Home Front' went to Ernest Bevin at the Ministry of Labour, Herbert Morrison at the Home Office and, later, Hugh Dalton at the Board of Trade. Residual opposition to increased government direction of the economy was silenced by the desperate situation the country was in: Britain was fighting for survival. The direction and allocation of labour was pushed as far as the trades unions would stand, while the coal mines, shipping and the railways came under government control. More and more of the population were working for the state in one way or another – 49 per cent by 1941 – and more of them were women as the government implemented conscription of the female population.

This siege economy was in part supported by high taxation and a high level of personal savings, but above all, it was based on the sale of Britain's dollar assets and aid from the USA. Even before the end of 1941, Britain enjoyed not only military, but also economic assistance from the Commonwealth and lend lease from the USA. The downside of American aid before and after the USA's entry into the war was not just the political price to be exacted by the Americans, but was the degree to which the British economic war effort gradually came to depend upon a US life-support system.

The achievements of the British war economy may well have been overestimated. It has been claimed that, although Britain produced some specialised developments such as high speed cameras, radar and

Rolls Royce engines, and saw major advances in the chemicals industry, she was found wanting in almost every branch of second-generation industrial technology.[8] If Britain forced her production from an aged and inefficient industrial structure, her record in armaments production was, nevertheless, impressive. In 1940 Britain produced more tanks and planes than Germany and, though tank production thereafter lagged well behind Germany's, the lead in aircraft production was retained in every year but for 1944. However, the 1944 figures are instructive, Britain producing 5000 tanks and 26,461 aircraft against Germany's 17,800 tanks and 39,807 aircraft.[9] Even with US aid, Britain could not compete with a German economy moving belatedly into top gear. It must be remembered, however, that by this time, it was Germany which was fighting for survival and the scale of American war production allowed Britain to relax. The verdict that 'British productive performance was close to a realistic optimum', given a commitment to maintain reasonable living standards and the co-operation of workers and industry, seems just.[10]

The failure of the Third Reich to fulfil its economic potential and fully to mobilise its economy for war until 1942 has, as we have seen, occasioned considerable debate among historians. However, that debate has been about the reasons for failure and not about the fact of it, and as one authority has put it: 'There can be no doubt that throughout the war the German economy produced far fewer weapons than its raw resources of materials manpower, scientific skill and factory floorspace could have made possible.'[11]

Germany's advantages as a war economy lay in the high standard of education and the skills of its population, which were reflected in the strength of its engineering industry. The Germany of 1939 was, though, dependent to a dangerous degree on the import of raw materials: iron ore, copper, bauxite, nickel, and above all, oil. Such materials could, of course, be seized along with conquered territories, but success in a long war would depend not only on the speed of such seizure, but on the successful integration of the conquered territories into the greater German economy.

Hitler's attitude to the war economy epitomised the ambivalent Nazi attitude to modernity and a belief that the main factors making for victory were will, dynamism, aggression and daring rather then the productive achievements of factories. This contrasts with Stalin's view that modern wars were won in factories rather than on the battlefield. Factors making for Germany's poor performance as an armaments producer include the chaotic nature of Nazi decision making – an acute concern for the morale of German workers, which prevented the full direction of the population towards the war effort – and the interference of the military with production. If the skill of German workers and the strength of the machine tool industry gave Germany an advantage, they may in themselves have made for a prejudice against the mass production of serviceable, but less refined and highly finished weaponry. A singular mistake was the failure to adapt the civilian motor industry to war production. Neither the Volkswagen works nor that of the General Motors subsidiary, Opel, were fully utilised for the production of military vehicles.

A successful mobilisation of the German economy for total war only came with the appointment of Albert Speer as minister of munitions and armaments in February 1942 and the realisation of Germany's desperate position after the *Wehrmacht* had failed to knock out the Soviet Union with a decisive blow, and in addition, the US had entered the war. Speer established a centralised machinery of control, the Central Planning Board, and by 1943 he had complete control of the economy. The production of armaments and munitions soared: production of aircraft went from 11,800 in 1941 to 24,800 in 1943 and nearly 40,000 in 1944, while tank production went from 500 a month in 1942 to 2000 per month in 1943. This first German economic miracle was based on a combination of centralised planning and a belated embargo on non-essential consumer products, together with the intensified exploitation of occupied territories, the plundering of their raw materials and the conscription of their labour. Despite British and American concentration on destroying Germany's productive capacity by bombing, Germany attained its highest levels of munitions production in August 1944, of aircraft in September 1944, and of weapons production in December 1944.[12] This great effort came too late. Whether this was because of a tardy recognition of the need for full mobilisation or because of the inefficiency and inappropriate timing of plans for such a mobilisation is less important.

A major disadvantage to the Axis forces was that only Germany had a real capacity for the production of modern weapons on a scale to match the USSR and Britain, much less the USA. About the only index which matched Italy's ambition to be a great power was the size of her population, which exceeded that of France. Italy's record of industrial production during the war was lamentable. Italy had peaked in terms of war production before her entry into the war. In the years 1933–9, 11.8 per cent of her national income had gone on preparations for war, and although this was pushed up to 18.4 per cent in 1939–40, this proved unsustainable, and both war production and industrial economy as a whole fell back after 1940.[13] Like Germany and Japan, Italy had problems with raw materials. She also had endemic difficulties born of the north-south divide and the weak administrative structure of the Italian state, but the failings of the fascist leadership to make good their boasts of a transformed Italy, and even to equal the record of Italy in the First World War, became quickly apparent.

The failings of the Italian army were real enough, but even when it fought with determination, its weaponry put it at a disadvantage against the British, Americans or Russians. The record of the Italian navy was better than is usually supposed. It was relatively successful in protecting convoys across the Mediterranean and its battle-fleet continued to present a threat to the Royal Navy. Italy, however, lacked the industrial base to replace ships that were lost quickly enough. Other German allies, Romania and Hungary, had much the same weaknesses as Italy; however well they fought, their lack of effective medium-weight tanks put them at a great disadvantage when facing Soviet forces.

Japan, as we have seen, had very basic disadvantages when it came to her war economy. Her chronic shortage of raw materials and the inadequacy of her pre-war industrial base made it difficult for her to produce in sufficient numbers the necessary modern weapons that could make success in a long war possible. That Japan lacked effective tanks was not a great problem given the nature of the Pacific War, but her inability to build aircraft carriers and planes in sufficient numbers, or even to replace those she lost in 1942, was crucial to the course of the war in the Far East. 'In absolute terms Japan's success in expanding its industrial output was considerable. 'Between 1937 and 1934, Japan achieved a 24% increase in manufacturing, and 46% in steel production',[14] but, viewed alongside the vast increase in productivity of the US, they were insubstantial.

Tactics and weaponry

Production in itself was not the only factor since it was important both to produce the right weaponry and for armies to make the best use of it. The German armed forces won their sweeping victories in the early stages of the war because the weaponry used by their cutting edge, their mechanised divisions, was up to date and appropriate to the task, while it was assisted by dominance in the air, and by daring strategy and superior tactics. Allied victories after 1941 were to be won not just because of the increasing quantitative advantage of the allies, but also because German weapons ceased to be qualitatively superior and Allied tactics improved.

Throughout the Second World War the German army was a magnificent fighting force and, when not heavily outnumbered or outgunned, tended to prevail. As Paul Kennedy has written, military historians are virtually unanimous as to the reasons for German effectiveness:

> German operational doctrine, emphasising flexibility and decentralized decision-making at the *battlefield* level, proved far superior to the cautious, set-piece tactics of the British, the bloody, full-frontal assaults of the Russians, and the enthusiastic but unprofessional forward rushes of the Americans.[15]

Such decentralised decision making requires junior officers and NCOs of the highest calibre and the professional tradition of the German army, its training system, and the educational level of much of the German population combined to ensure that, even in the last year of the war, the quality of middle and lower levels of command remained high.

The overwhelming superiority of the German forces, demonstrated in the early years of the war, was however, to erode. In 1939, 1940 and 1941, the Germans had not only good soldiers, but also superior weaponry and command of the air, while their use of mechanised units represented almost a new method of warfare. By 1944 the latter advantages were no longer with them. They had lost their command of the air and their tanks were not only outmatched in numbers, they no longer had a qualitative superiority. The Allied powers had also improved their tactical use of tanks and aircraft. Why did Germany fail to maintain its early superiority in weapons and their use?

With the development and the utilisation of weapons of war, as with consumer goods, it is always easier to catch up than to innovate. The USSR and Britain caught up, while the USA turned the dynamic spirit of its free-market economy to the military field. But this still does not explain Germany's failure to build on its lead and develop new and effective second-generation tanks and planes. The reasons for this are complex and various. As we have seen, Germany was until 1942 unprepared for a long war; there was too little co-ordinated planning as to which weapons should be given priority, even when under Speer's guidance, Germany developed a real war economy; and the demands of the military too often resulted in too many projects, too many different designs, and piecemeal production of a diverse number of weapons. As Overy has shown there were at one point in the war: '425 different aircraft models and variants in production. By the middle of the war the German army was equipped with 151 different makes of lorry, and 150 different motor-cycles'.[16] To the problems of a diverse and fragmented production of war materials were added the demands of generals for finely engineered and sophisticated weapons that were produced at the expense of quantity and standardisation. German scientists pioneered the weapons of the post-war world – missiles and jet-aircraft – but failed to develop effective successors to the tanks and planes that had brought victory in 1940. Above all the *Wehrmacht* did not progress from what it had been in 1940, a horse-drawn army with specialised mechanised units, into a fully mechanised army. What it did develop might have been sufficient to hold, if not to defeat, the Russians had it not been that the Soviet Union was able to benefit from the troop-carrying vehicles and jeeps which American industry provided for the Soviet army, giving it a new mobility from 1943.

The Germans produced in the Tiger and Panther a new generation of tanks to replace the Panzer II, III and IV, but although they had considerable firepower, they were heavy and cumbersome, and required an army of mechanics to maintain them, faults which were even more pronounced in the King Tiger and the Mouse. The Russians produced only two types of tank at any one time, the very successful T-34, only equalled by the American Sherman as a medium tank, and the heavier KV-1 (replaced by the Josef Stalin 15-2 in 1943). Both were turned out in numbers the Germans failed to match, and because of the concentration on two models, repair and maintenance were simplified. German success in the first years of the war was based on tank and motorised infantry divisions providing the spearhead of an otherwise unmechanised army. The next step was a move to fully mechanised and motorised armies, a step which only the Americans and the British fully made, but to which the Russians, with American aid, were able to come close. Instead of using tank divisions as the decisive offensive force, the Americans fused tanks, artillery and infantry together in every unit; there remained a distinction between armoured divisions and infantry divisions, but this was a matter of the preponderance of tanks in the armoured divisions.

The balance of air power followed a similar cycle, save that Germany's position deteriorated more rapidly in the air than on land and the *Luftwaffe* was to be virtually eliminated by 1944. As was so often the case with Nazi Germany, a man chosen for inappropriate reasons presided over a confused and inefficient empire in which there were too many competing projects. Ernst Udet, the choice of Goering, was responsible for a series of aircraft which were failures and had to be dropped after much investment of time, money and materials. Only one fighter, the Focke-Wulf 190, was a success, and earlier models had to be modified and put back into production. Germany had lost the opportunity for creating a second generation of aircraft and of acquiring a long-range bombing capacity; even more seriously, the production of the models the *Luftwaffe* was stuck with had been held up and the time lost was never to be made up. That a state which had purposively prepared for war and which was renowned for its scientific and engineering ability should have so easily lost one of the keys to modern military success, air superiority, is astonishing. Just as surprising is the achievement of the Soviet Union, its airforce driven from the skies in 1941, in managing to develop and put into large-scale production fighters, the Yak-9, Lagg-3 and LA-5, which by 1944 could outperform the German ME-109. Once lost, German air superiority could not be regained: losses on the Russian front occurred as Anglo-American bombing raids both interfered with the production of aircraft and forced planes to be withdrawn from the Russian front to defend the home economy. A downward spiral was set in motion which was to result in the German army fighting the last years of the war largely without air support.

One other dimension of warfare followed a similar pattern of early German superiority being reversed in the war's latter stages. Intelligence gathering, counter-intelligence and the dissemination of false information reached a high degree of sophistication during the war. The traditional techniques of using spies and interrogating captured prisoners played their part. Perhaps the most effective spy was Richard Sorge, a Soviet spy in Tokyo. His warnings of a German invasion may not have been heeded by Stalin, but his assurances that there were, in the autumn of 1941, no Japanese preparations for an attack on Russia enabled the Soviet High Command to move vital reinforcements to the west. By and large, however, the most successful espionage was conducted by the Soviet Union, but at the expense of its allies rather than the Germans or Japanese. Communists and 'fellow travellers' within US and British intelligence and the scientific establishments provided a steady flow of secrets to their ideological homeland. What was far more important for the outcome of the war was signals' intelligence. Germany in 1940 enjoyed a considerable advantage in the battles for Norway and for France in the ability to read the enemy's signals, but thereafter the British enjoyed greater success.

As we have seen, the success of British intelligence in decrypting the German 'Enigma' or 'Ultra' codes was to make an important contribution to the war effort, as did the work on Japanese codes of the American 'Magic' code-breaking centre at Honolulu, but there were intelligence successes on the Axis side too. In the war at sea, the intelligence battle in the Atlantic went backwards and forwards, each side for a time having the advantage in both breaking the other's codes and maintaining the integrity of their own. The Japanese had an accurate perception of the weakness of the British position in the Far East, thanks to their German allies who, after the surrender of the British merchant ship, SS *Automedon*, to a surface raider, passed on to them the top secret information, including minutes of Cabinet and Chiefs-of Staff meetings, unwisely trusted to a mail bag on a merchant ship. Losses of code and cipher material from the *Automedon* and from a British MTB sunk off Crete led to the insecurity of Royal Navy communications.[17] On the whole however, the Western allies seem to have had the best of the intelligence war. In the Far East the Americans were able to read Japanese signals from early in the war and broke the code by which merchant ships were directed in 1943. In North Africa the Germans for a while broke the Eighth Army's code, but the British ability to read the Enigma code used by Rommel's army assisted the British at both battles of El Alamein. By 1944 British ability in code breaking was established and was considerably to assist in both the D-day landings and the Normandy Campaign.

Occupied Europe and the New Order

An important question is whether Germany and Japan could have made better use of the territories they overran or which were within their spheres of influence. Could the expanded German hegemony established by late 1939 in central Europe, the 'new order' in western Europe which emerged in 1940, or the position in eastern Europe which Germany and her allies had secured by 1942 have been forged into effective economic units with a productive capacity that might have made up for Germany's disadvantage compared to her enemies? Could an orchestration of the concept of Europe rather than of Germany have secured the positive support of other nations and even enabled large armies to be raised to assist the German war effort?

There seems little doubt that, after 1945, a curtain was drawn over the degree of support Hitler's New Order enjoyed in western Europe from 1940 until 1943. Active collaborators were portrayed as small and unrepresentative cliques, passive collaborators as merely resigned, while the role of the resistance movements was exaggerated and trumpeted. The reasons for this development are obvious enough: it salvaged national self-respect; ensured that all but small segments of the populations could be on the winning side; enabled post-war reconstruction to employ the same technocrats, administrators and industrialists that had co-operated with the New Order; while it was a necessary fiction for national reconciliations. It has not only obscured the reality of Hitler's Europe, but many of the continuities of European history from the thirties to the present day.

It remains apparent that there was widespread dislike in western Europe of occupation by German troops and officials, combined until at least the middle of 1943 with an equally widespread feeling that it had to be accepted for the time being. What is less obvious is what was seen as the desirable long-term alternative. The defeat of Germany at the hands of the Allies was likely to mean being fought over once again; if, from mid-1941, Communists yearned for a Soviet victory, substantial numbers dreaded such an outcome, while Britain and the US were far from generally popular. Added to this was disillusionment with the pre-war order.

What the German 'New Order' had to build on was not merely resignation after military defeat, but a congruence of intellectual attitudes conducive to an acceptance of a Europe under German leadership. The experience of the thirties had led to a widespread disillusionment with capitalism and liberalism, which were seen as having brought about mass unemployment, and with their demands for modernisation on market terms, led to the destruction of the small businesses of the self-employed middle classes and independent artisans, and to an erosion of the living standards of peasant farmers. This tuned in with an atavistic hostility in Catholic Europe to the impact of usurious market forces on traditional trades, communities and cultures. Parliamentary government was widely discredited as corrupt, divisive and incapable of organising economies in the service of communities. Added to this was a pessimistic view of Europe's future while national states quarrelled and divided the continent and Europe continued to decline. If world communism and the Soviet Union were seen as one threat to European values and traditions, then the 'Anglo-Saxon' powers of the US and Britain – the archetypal liberal-capitalist states, the one extra-European and the other only loosely attached to Europe – constituted another.

Such attitudes could lead to different political paths, but not to a liberal-capitalist one, though they did provide opportunities for Germany and for fascists to gain adherents for a European unity programme. As we have seen, although fascists used nationalism, many went beyond it towards Europeanism and a policy of modernising and uniting Europe into an economically efficient, welfare state that would also protect European culture against Americanisation. This had a potent appeal to many who were not fascists. Opponents of the European Union have pointed to structural similarities between western Europe under Hitler's hegemony and the European Union. Economic agreements between Germany, France and Italy between 1940 and 1943 foreshadowed not only the European Coal and Steel Agreement of 1951, but also other aspects of the later development of the European Union: close links between the economies and a centrist and corporatist direction to them, while there were plans for a common agricultural policy, regional policies by-passing national governments, and a common currency. As a Nazi plan for European integration put it:

> The solution of economic problems with a view to immunity from blockade, the regulation of trade on the basis of European prefer-ence *vis-à-vis* the rest of the world, with the eventual object of a European customs union and a free European market, a European central clearing system and stable exchange rates in Europe, looking towards a European currency union. Objectives would include the standardisation and improvement of conditions of employment and social security, as well as long-term production planning in the field of industry, agriculture and forestry.[18]

Such Europeanist sentiments were briefly allied to a general acqui-escence in the new German-dominated *status quo*, which for a time found an enthusiastic response not just from fascists, but from some, like François Mitterrand, who later became prominent in post-war politics.

Any possibility that occupied Europe could have been forged into a positive force under German and nominal Italian leadership was undermined by a number of factors. The German attack on the Soviet Union brought the Communist parties of Europe into outright oppo-sition, the progress of the war encouraged other opposition groups, hardships bred dissatisfaction, and above all, German rule demon-strated little respect for the interests of other European nations.

There is, indeed, little evidence to suggest that Hitler and the majority of National Socialist politicians in Germany had any belief in a fascist or corporatist Europe that was anything other than a facade for German domination. Hitler's strong anti-French bias dashed the hopes of those within the Vichy administration, who hoped in 1941 that France could wield some influence within Hitler's Europe, and confounded Hitler's overtures to Pétain. Germany might press for French support, but in successive negotiations with Pétain, Laval and Darlan, Hitler was not prepared to concede to France a strong position in Europe. In Belgium, the Netherlands, Norway and Denmark, propaganda that the occupation proffered a European partnership was belied by daily evidence that Germany offered not leadership but dominance.

Those fascists and Catholic conservatives who believed, for a while, that Hitler's western European 'new order' would usher in an era of European co-operation, which would protect European culture and society from Anglo-Saxon influence, were quickly to have their hopes confounded; a Nazi definition of German *kultur* and of German interests had little time for 'European civilisation' or for a general European interest that was not entirely subordinate to Germany. The various Spanish, French and Flemish groups who fought with the Germans were unappreciated by Hitler and nothing is more evocative of betrayed, if mistaken, hopes than that Hitler's last redoubt was defended at the end by the troops of the *Waffen* SS Charlemagne Division.

Much the same can be said of the technocrats, industrialists and politicians who sought a common European cause under Nazi leadership. That officials and businessmen in Vichy France saw opportunity for modernisation and stability in a corporatist Europe under Franco-German leadership is well proven, and if their trust in the Europe of 1940 was confounded, the same urge would distinguish post-war France. The corporatist organisations and structures set up by Otto Abetz, German ambassador to Paris in 1940, aimed at greater integration of the French and German economies, and they were also influential as a model in Belgium.

Certainly Germany never reaped the full potential of her expansion. It would have made better economic sense to have kept French workers in French factories than to transport them to German ones. It is striking, for instance, that while the French motor industry was kept going and provided Germany with thousands of trucks, the French aircraft industry was run down and produced only 1200 planes in 1943.[19] The main reason for this is that the Third Reich thought in terms of conquest, plundering and exploiting, and rarely considered building up captured or subservient economies. A more subtle approach, involving some care for the standard of living of conquered territories and of harnessing rather than plundering their productive capacity, might have had some success. In Belgium, where the regime was comparatively mild between 1941 and 1943 and where there was considerable collaboration, production actually rose.

Nor did Germany treat its allies in east and central Europe with respect. Slovakia, Serbia and Croatia were simply client states with regimes that were only the facade of independence, while, as the tide of war turned, the governments of Romania and Hungary were overthrown by Germany and replaced by puppet regimes in 1944.In Eastern Europe the Nazi approach was to plunder, loot and enslave rather than to strive for support. The German war economy undoubtedly benefited enormously from foreign and slave labour, which also enabled the German work force to be protected for a long time from the austere consequences of the war, but it is arguable that Germany could have gained more from policies which gave some profit to factories in occupied areas and some benefits to their workers. Even more carelessly in the East than the West, Germany, by its ruthless and callous disregard for the interests of the population, threw away both economic advantage and the possibility of dispensing with repression and gaining positive support. Of course, the Soviet forces pursued a scorched-earth policy which denied the Germans any immediate fruits of victory, but any possibility of revitalising local economies was negated by terror. The population of the Soviet Union was, in large part, to struggle with determination against the aggressor, but it is difficult to determine the degree to which this was born of patriotic loyalty or fear of the invaders; German conduct certainly ensured that there were plenty of grounds for the latter. The treatment of the Ukraine, where there was an initially favourable reaction to the German occupation, provides a spectacular instance of the maladroit policies of the Reich. Erich Koch, Gauleiter of East Prussia, was put in charge and, convinced that the peoples of the East respected only force, proceeded to stamp on Ukrainian culture and national self-respect. The German authorities arrogantly refused to make use of the ex-Soviet general, Vlasov, and his 'Free Russian Force'. Yet the Germans managed to raise numerous *Waffen* SS units in Eastern Europe, suggesting that with greater respect for other nationalities, they could have greatly strengthened the forces at their disposal.

As Norman Davies has commented:

[T]he Nazis' self styled 'Crusade for Civilisation' was able to attract considerable support. Large contingents were sent to the Eastern Front by Romania, Hungary and Italy. Romania took charge of Odessa and the district of 'Transistria'. General Franco's crack 'Blue Division' was sent from Spain. In the Baltic States, existing army and police units were transferred to German service. Recruits and volunteers flocked in from almost all the occupied countries.[20]

The opposite side of the coin was, of course, the Resistance. The French Resistance is the best known, though not the most effective, resistance movement. With Hitler's invasion of Russia, the French Communist Party began to organise a campaign of sabotage and killing aimed at weakening the German occupation. As the German military moved into all of France in November 1942, this both affected Vichy's claim to be the government of France and provoked a broader resistance involving elements of most shades of political opinion. General de Gaulle, leader of the Free French movement based in London, attempted via the Le Conseil National de la Resistance to control all factions, but it is clear that the communists had their own agenda and only co-operated with other resistance units when it suited their interests. The introduction of labour conscription in 1943 swelled the ranks of the Resistance, and by 1944, it was able to be of use both before and after the D-day landings. As the Germans retreated, the numbers of the *Maquis* grew until by the end of the year, almost everyone was claiming to be a member of the Resistance, including many, like François Mitterrand, who had been in the middle management of Vichy. John Keegan has concluded:

> Great honour is due to all who actively resisted in France; their armed numbers have been estimated as about 116,000 by June 6 1944. They ran terrible risks and were savagely punished whenever they fell into German hands. The truth is, however, that their numbers were greatly exceeded by those who prudently held aloof from opposing the occupation, the vast majority, and probably by those who collaborated.[21]

In general the Western Resistance movements shared common characteristics: they split into communist and anti-communist wings; they inconvenienced the Germans, but played little part in ensuring victory for the Allies; and they worked and jostled for influence after the Germans retreated. The most effective was the Italian Resistance, which came into substantial being in northern Italy once the Allies were in possession of the south and Mussolini's regime in the North could be seen as a mere German puppet.

To the East, resistance was a more dangerous threat to German control, and in Greece, Albania and Yugoslavia it is better described as 'partisan warfare'. Communist and non-communist partisans fought each other and the Germans with ferocity. In Poland, where there was almost a secret state working against the German occupiers, the Home Army was just that, an army, which was a branch of the Polish forces, fighting from exile and from underground in Poland, rather than a resistance or a partisan force. Poland epitomises the tragedy of non-communist opponents of Germany, fighting one ruthless enemy only to make occupation by another inevitable.

In general it can be said that the history of the areas occupied by Germany falls into two broad phases: during the first, lasting until late in 1943, German rule enjoyed the acquiescence of large sectors of the population and in many areas had opportunities for positive support which were largely squandered; in the second, majorities were increasingly passively unco-operative while minorities became actively mutinous. If the Germans were ineffective in utilising the productive potential of their widened frontiers, the Japanese also failed to take the maximum advantage of their conquests.

Like Germany, Japan had opportunities for enlisting support in the occupied territories and, like Germany, did not exploit them successfully. In Burma the Japanese set up a Burma National Army under Aung San and found a local nationalist politician, Ba Maw, who was given nominal authority under their aegis; they set up conferences attended by him and other figures, such as the Indian nationalist, Subhas Chandra Bose, attracted by the Greater East Asian Co-Prosperity Sphere. Rose was allowed to set up a government in exile in Singapore and then Rangoon. Nationalism had emerged as a force within the Asian possessions of the imperial powers. In 1941 it was a containable force and made its appeal to minorities, although often vocal and influential minorities, while colonial armies for the most part remained loyal to the ruling powers. Nevertheless, it is significant that many pro-Japanese figures went on to have post-war political careers; when the Philippines gained independence in 1949 the first president was Manuel Roxas, a prominent collaborator. The spectacular and rapid Japanese victories after Pearl Harbor had, dented the prestige of the Western powers and provided Japan with an opportunity to pose as a liberating power capable of reorganising eastern Asia under benign leadership but the arrogance and cruelty of their occupation largely destroyed their initial appeal.

If Japan's treatment of Korea and China had not already cast doubt enough on the possibility of her recognising the sovereignty of other states, her treatment of captured territories soon exposed her claim to benign leadership as false. The Greater East Asia Ministry, set up to exploit the resources of the expanded empire, was never more than a cipher, and in practice, the military organised conquered territory. There was never a coherent plan for the future of eastern Asia. Though Japanese propaganda made much of anti-imperialism, proposed an Asia Co-prosperity Sphere and sought to channel nationalism, it became clear that such talk merely disguised the reality of Japanese hegemony and that supposedly independent governments in the Philippines, or Burma, would be no more independent than the puppet regimes set up in China.

The Japanese home economy was unable to benefit from the oil and rubber of the Dutch East Indies and Malaya for long because, by the end of 1942, Japan had lost command of the sea. The merchant marine was unable, faced with determined allied submarines, to transport these materials to the home islands. Even food supplies grew short as communications with Manchuria became difficult.

The Holocaust

The most astonishing and horrific development within territory controlled by Germany was the organised murder of between four and six million Jews, a programme of genocide which did nothing to further, and much to impede, the German war effort.

The Holocaust, not the fact but the significance of it, remains the subject of intense controversy and debate. If only fools or liars deny that a systematic campaign of racial genocide took place, much about its significance, origins and timing is disputed. One major question is whether we should regard it as unique or as a very horrible instance of man's inhumanity to man, comparable to the Armenian massacres of the First World War, Stalin's attempt to wipe out the *Kulak* peasant proprietors, and Pol Pot's more recent assault on the urban population of Cambodia. Another is whether its origins lie in Christian hatred of Jews over many centuries or whether it should be seen as the Nazis applying to a race what the Bolsheviks had attempted to do to classes.[22] Was it the result of a long-nurtured plan that the Nazis had all along intended to put into practice or was it the result of the 'radicalisation' of Nazi policies by the war? To what extent should Hitler bear the main responsibility or should it be more widely shared by the Nazi Party, the German people, or even European civilisation as a whole?

European anti-Semitism, as it existed in the early nineteenth century, was widespread and had both ancient and modern origins. It manifested itself in a number of ways across the continent, from the vague social prejudice of the British 'not in our golf club' variety to the violent *pogroms* of Eastern Europe. The most common traditional reasons for it were: religious animosity, particularly marked in Catholic and Orthodox Europe; the unpopularity incurred by the role of Jews as money lenders; and the, fairly standard, suspicion about people who keep themselves apart. The modern reasons for it were very different and had to do with the very fact that Jews were, in large numbers, becoming secularised and were no longer keeping themselves apart. Secularised Judaism, releasing some of the energy and characteristics of Jewish religious and social practices on to a wider stage, played a major role in modern developments, economic, intellectual and political: Jews made good capitalists and entrepreneurs; their role in the development of science, psychology and the modernist movement in the arts scarcely needs emphasising; while, in political thought and practice, if there were conservative and liberal Jews, they seemed particularly prominent in socialist movements.

Why Germany, with a modest record of liberal treatment of its Jews, should have provided the context for the cold-blooded attempt to wipe out European Jewry has puzzled historians. It would seem most likely that it was in southern Germany and Austria that the conjuncture of the two streams of anti-Semitism came together virulently: a long-nurtured Catholic dislike and an anti-modernist hatred of Jews as capitalists and cosmopolitans threatening traditional society and its values. Germany's defeat in the First World War, for which Jews became one of many scapegoats, and Jewish ubiquity in attempted socialist revolutions at the end of the war provided a more immediate context for the anti-Semitism of the Nazi movement. The Jews were portrayed as anti-patriotic and cosmopolitan, while their supposed 'conspiracies' were at once, and paradoxically, in aid of international capitalism and world socialist revolution. The early Bolsheviks had included a disproportionate number of Jews, but at the same time, the Soviet Union provided the model for the view that whole sections of society which stood in the way of the future could be eliminated.

It does, however, seem that the anti-Semitism, so central to the early and later years of the Nazi movement, was sidelined from the late twenties until 1938. If most Germans were anti-Jewish, it was not a major preoccupation and provided no power base. Jews were progressively discriminated against, persecuted and encouraged to emigrate after 1933, but there was little that foreshadowed the Final Solution. As we have seen, historians almost always split into two camps over Hitler: those who see his intentions as clear from his early days, and those who see him as reacting to events and to the chaotic and fluid power structure of the Nazi Party. The former have argued that Hitler was merely biding his time and awaiting an opportune moment to put into action policies contained in *Mein Kampf*, for the latter, Hitler's words need not be taken too literally and his progressively anti-Semitic moves in the late thirties were responses to pressures from the party.

Despite a speech by Hitler in January 1939, prophesying that war could lead to the destruction of all Jews, it seems that the decision to initiate a 'Final Solution' to the Jewish problem was taken concurrently with the invasion of the Soviet Union. Whatever the ill treatment, the frequent murder and the ghettoisation of Jews in occupied Poland, the talk before 1941 was of resettlement (Eastern Poland was one proposed destination, Madagascar another) rather than extermination. Was Hitler merely dissembling over his intentions for the Jews in this period, just as many would claim he dissembled over his intentions towards the Soviet Union? It can be argued that, from June 1941, he happily returned to both his long-cherished ambitions and, after December, it was no longer necessary to worry about offending American opinion. The alternative view, as we have seen, is that there was no long-term plan for the liquidation of the Jews until the muddle of war exposed the impossibility of deportation and that *ad hoc* and conflicting initiatives by Nazi leaders led, in 1942, to a co-ordinated programme of extermination. As a German historian has argued, the liquidation of the Jews was 'a "way out" of a blind alley into which the National Socialists had manoeuvred themselves'.[23]

If, by the spring of 1942, well over a million Jews had been murdered by SS *Einsatzgruppen*, the one-day conference at Wannsee attended by sections of the Nazi leadership marked the real beginning of the Final Solution. The Jews within the Nazi area of control were to be killed, methods were decided upon and the organisation set up to implement them. A number of death camps were to be established, transportation of victims arranged, Zyklon B gas was to be the method of killing and the bodies were to be cremated. The process was efficient and inexorable. In 1942–3 the programme concentrated on the 3 million-strong Jewish population of Poland and then moved on to other sections of European Jewry: Jews from France, Belgium, Holland, Hungary and the Balkans. Most conscientious in their ghastly work, those working in the extermination programme continued their labours until the very moment of Germany's defeat.

One recent study of the economy of the Third Reich and of Hitler's ambitions has seen the 'Final Solution' as part of, if intrinsic to, the wider plan for *lebensraum*, a vast colonial project, seen by Hitler as analogous to America's frontier, its westward expansion and its settlement of new areas. At least 10 million Germans would be settled on the conquered territory which would provide a prosperous future for the German peasantry. This would involve not only the destruction of the Jews, but the majority Slav population of Eastern Europe. The land would have to be cleared of perhaps 45 million people; some would be put to work as slave labour to assist in the building of the infrastructure of the colony, some would starve as German invasion plans made no provision for feeding them, and many would have to be killed.[24] As we have seen, there is much controversy as to Hitler's wilder plans and his consistency and the secrecy the Nazi regime maintained as to its extermination programme still clouds the issue, while military defeats soon put an end to any chance of implementing a *lebensraum*. Yet, that the Reich's military expansion into Eastern Europe opened up the opportunity for, 'the wholesale racial reconstruction of all the inhabitants of Germany's eastern "living space"'[25] fits in with the thesis that the attack on Russia 'radicalised' Nazi aims. Nevertheless, though the treatment of the Slavs was callous and inhumane, the programme that was pursued relentlessly was the effort to exterminate the Jews along with some other groups such as Roma (or gypsies) of whom 40,000 perished in the death camps.

But who was responsible? The suggestion that there is little direct proof of Hitler's responsibility, no written orders or official mandate from him,[26] may well be technically true, but is also largely irrelevant The *Führer* can scarcely have been ignorant of the programme, nor could it have proceeded without his approval. A more important question is the degree to which responsibility should be shared, not just among the SS or the wider Nazi Party, but by the *Wehrmacht*, the German population as a whole, and even wide sections of French, Latvian and other European peoples.

Until quite recently, the dominant tendency was to blame ordinary Germans more for looking the other way, and pretending not to notice, than for actively participating in and willing the genocide. The responsibility belonged to the Nazi Party. Much recent work has argued that, not just every organ of the German state, including the *Wehrmacht*, was actively involved, but that broad sections of German society were 'willing executioners'.[27] The German elite in the army, the universities and the higher civil service were particularly culpable in that they allowed their own feelings – that Jews enjoyed a disproportionate influence in German society – to be used by the Nazis for their genocidal purposes.[28]

Nor can other European nations be exculpated for the genocide programme found enthusiastic administrators in Vichy France, from where over 100,000 Jews were transported to their death, and among the German allies in eastern Europe. The Danes refused to co-operate and subverted the programme, and the Italians were unenthusiastic, but if the major responsibility rested with Germany, there is evidence enough of a widespread European complicity.

The horrors of the death camps became known to the world as allied armies advanced, but were, in the immediate post-war years, seen as a ghastly aspect of the Nazi regime rather than almost defining it and were not, in the late 1940s and 1950s, given the centrality they would assume in later decades. It was not until the 1960s and 1970s, as the work of historians revealed all the horrific details of Nazi policy towards the Jews of Europe, that the term 'Holocaust' ('Complete destruction by fire') came into general usage. A number of contemporary factors came into play: the large number of Jews in the US had hitherto tended to internalise the grim fate of their parents' generation but now wished it to be memorialised; Germans became more prepared to confront their recent history; and the besieged nature of the Jewish homeland, Israel, and its victory in the Six Days War occasioned sympathy and support. Since then, literature and particularly cinema with films such as *Shoah* and *Schindler's List* have imprinted the Final Solution on the American and European consciousness. The Holocaust came to be seen as the greatest crime in history and, for many, almost synonymous with the Second World War.

Recent international developments have, however, complicated the picture. As tensions between the Islamic and Western worlds have mounted and the position of Israel become central to this divide, hostility to Israel has sometimes elided into hostility to Jews. Not only Muslims but Western sympathisers with the Palestinian cause have expressed an impatience with the view of the Holocaust as a unique crime.

Yet, even the briefest description of the extermination programme gives some glimpse of its horrors, and explain why it has been seen as the unique crime of history. Reasons for belief in the *Holocaust's* uniqueness include: that the crime was committed by a west European government; that it was done, unlike Tsarist pogroms, or massacres or 'ethnic cleansing' elsewhere in the world, systematically, cold-bloodedly and utilising scientific means; that the Jews were the victims; and that the regime which perpetrated the crime was totally defeated and overthrown for other reasons. There can be little doubt that in Western eyes, terrible crimes perpetrated by Western powers seem unnatural in a way that crimes perpetrated by Asians on Asians, or by Africans on Africans do not.[29] That Jews are successful and influential in many Western societies and are particularly important in the US has undoubtedly played a part in reinforcing the uniqueness thesis, while for some Jewish scholars the *Shoah*, the Hebrew term for the Holocaust, fits into Judaic theology and history – a unique fate for a unique people. That Hitler's regime was completely destroyed meant that there were no pragmatic reasons for glossing over the regime's great crime, whereas Stalin's Soviet Union, in which so many millions were murdered, was to last another 45 years until it disintegrated rather than was overthrown, while successor governments to that of Mao Tse-tung's, with as many millions of deaths at its door, are still in power. If numbers killed are the test, then the crimes of Stalin and the Soviet regime were the greater, though they took place over a longer time-scale. One estimate is that the Soviet Gulag was responsible for 22 million deaths up until 1945 and that such deaths were only a proportion of the deaths for which the Soviet regime was responsible.

If the Holocaust was unique, this is not because of numbers killed or the inhumanity involved. It was unique in the context of a modern Western world which considered itself, with some justice, to be more civilised than other cultures and than its own past, in ways that included humaneness, as well as ability in the arts and sciences. The Final Solution casts considerable doubt on that idea of moral progress.

Home Fronts

The term 'total war' is often used to describe the world wars of the twentieth century. The term applies not only to the scale of the conflicts and the ruthlessness with which they were waged, but also applies to the way in which the total resources and the populations of the combatants were mobilised for the war effort. If the 'home front' had become not only as important as the military front, but the two had in reality become one, both interactive parts of the machinery of war, then the dedication, morale and effectiveness of the civilian population would, in theory, have been as important as those of the fighting services.

The maintenance of civilian morale had both negative and positive aspects – the avoidance of defeatism and war-weariness, but also the inculcation of determination and enthusiasm. There can be little doubt that the European powers were very much aware of the importance of maintaining the loyalty and support of their populations. The lesson of the First World War, it was widely believed, was that failure to do so could lead to revolution, or at least, to such a deterioration in morale that a continued war effort could become impossible.

Hitler's care for the maintenance of the standard of living of German workers, even at the cost of the failure to totally mobilise the German economy for war, has to be seen in the light of the widespread belief that the German armed forces were 'stabbed in the back' by disaffected civilians in 1918.

Bombing raids, it had been widely believed before the war, would pose a dire threat to civilian morale. As we have seen, British morale survived the Blitz, as did the morale of the German and Japanese survive the intensive bombing that their cities were subjected to. Some historians have even argued that being bombed improved morale as it made people hate the enemy. The exception was Italy, where bombing seems to have made not the bombers, but the government and its ally Germany unpopular. Civilians were involved in the Second World War to a far greater extent than in the First World War and suffered even greater casualties than the armed forces, yet the victories and defeats of the war were military and not because of civilian unrest, while resistance movements made little difference to the outcome.

All states involved in the war made strenuous efforts to control, discipline, cajole and persuade their populations to stand firm. Even in Britain and the US, individual freedom was subordinated to the needs of war and the populace were conscripted and directed, their food and consumer goods rationed, their mobility limited, their access to information denied and their civil rights overridden. 'Don't you know there's a war on?' became the standard response in Britain to what, in peacetime, would have been a normal request for service or the desire to exercise a personal liberty. At the same time, governments held firmly to the belief that civilian morale depended on the careful rationing of information and the manipulation of opinion by utilising the media as propaganda. If the autocratic and would-be-totalitarian states had no great distance to move from their peacetime circumstances in these respects, Britain, and even the US, moved far away from liberal-democratic norms.

It would, no doubt, be encouraging if one could judge that democratic and liberal societies maintained a higher morale and endured hardship in a worthy cause better than the populations of authoritarian regimes did, but there seems little reason to believe this. The Russians withstood the rigours of war without turning on their unpleasant government, the Germans remained defiant to the end, while the Japanese endured extraordinary hardship in a cause they believed to be their Emperor's; on the other hand, French morale was bad from the beginning, the British grumbled but stoically put up with things, and the average American civilian didn't have much to grumble about. The fall of the Mussolini regime in 1943 is the only important instance of internal discontent bringing down a combatant government, but although Italian popular discontent with the state had mounted, it is noteworthy that it was not 'the people', but the elite which removed the government.

If the nature of societies at war was of pressing interest to all the governments of the states involved in the war, it has, retrospectively, engaged the attention of historians. The effects of war upon society, and in particular the effects of the Second World War upon social and political change, has been the subject of much historical debate. It has been forcefully argued that an effect of total war, involving as it does the mass participation of the population, is to test the institutions and social structures of participant states, and therefore that war can act as a catalyst of social change.[30] The support of disadvantaged or subordinate groups or classes has to be secured by rewarding them with improved or relatively improved living standards and war, it is argued, thus has a levelling or egalitarian effect. Claims have, for instance, been made that the Second World War made a fundamental difference to the position of women in society and led to welfare states. It has also been suggested that political orientations were changed by the experience and the test of war, and that in Britain, a new political consensus emerged with the Coalition government.

The image of Britain at war, the Britain that 'could take it', a people united and defiant, yet cheerful and confident, revelling in a new egalitarianism and mutual respect while they took in evacuees or swept away the rubble from last night's bombing raid, comforted by cups of tea and the occasional Spam sandwich, is virtually indestructible. This is partly because it contains a substantial degree of truth and partly because this was no retrospective myth, but an almost instantaneous invention – an image propounded by a gifted politician and cultivated by a skilful media – but taken to its heart by a people, the majority of whom were prepared to fight on. Britain's lone stand against Germany in 1940 and 1941 became immediately part of the collective imagination by which nation's exist.

If, however, we consider Britain at war closely, we find contradictions not just between image and 'reality', but within the image itself for, even as projected by wartime propaganda, there were internal contradictions in the way the nation at war was presented to itself, and to allies and neutrals. We have, on the one hand, the concept of the 'People's War', which portrayed a people united in a just war, but sloughing off class divisions and rejecting their recent past, while the fuglemen of the leftist intelligentsia in the media projected the thirties as years of waste and depression. We have, on the other hand, a depiction of a martial, island race sustained by its heritage and history. Contemporary films give us the 'all in it together' image of *London Can Take It* and the emphasis on the need for social change of *The Common Touch*, but also the depiction of gallantry of *Ships Have Wings* and *In Which We Serve*, in which rank and class seem naturally synonymous.

As we have seen, one incontestable result of the war was the expansion of government and government power and, even in a democracy like Britain, the suspension of norms in relation to civil society and civil liberty. It had been with great reluctance that the 'liberal England' of 1914 had gone down this path, but the Britain of 1939 had been prepared for total war and went to war with the assumptions of 1918, which were that civil liberties, private property and consumers' needs should be sacrificed to the war effort. The assumption was also made that the state had the right to control the media, not only to censor, but to use propaganda to reinforce morale. The powers taken by government were formidable: rationing, the registration of all citizens, exchange controls and conscription of labour. The Emergency Powers Act of May 1940 gave the government virtually unlimited powers, income tax was raised several times, and in 1941, conscription was extended to include women. Resident aliens were interned and Sir Oswald and Lady Moseley, along with other leading members of the British Union of Fascists, were imprisoned in disregard of the normal process of law.

To what extent the war had an impact upon long-term social and political change has been much debated, but there has been almost universal agreement that, in the short-term, it brought greater equality and a change of political direction that was to continue into the post-war world. When it comes to equality we must, however, distinguish between a degree of levelling down in living standards and in social attitudes. The degree to which the war broke down class divisions has been much exaggerated and romanticised. If two nations met in the forces or with evacuation, they didn't always like each other and, in general, kept their distance. When a large percentage of the population is in uniform, with ranks displayed on sleeves or shoulders, hierarchy can be seen to be well intact. A close scrutiny finds different sections of society, not just different classes, fighting their own separate, if parallel, wars: academics in the intelligence services; the leftist documentary film-makers of the thirties in the Crown Film Unit; country gentlemen in cavalry units; and workers in factories or the ranks of the infantry. There was nothing unusual or alarming in this for Britain was what has been called 'a mature class society'.[31] The monarchy played a unifying role throughout the war as a symbol of the nation above party, and almost above class, to which the enthusiastic receptions accorded the King and Queen in the bombed East End of London bear witness. Monarchies played an important role in the Second World War which has not been fully recognised. Those monarchs who had withdrawn from their countries after German invasion proved potent icons of resistance; the celebrations of the birthdays of the absent Queen and her Prince Consort in the Netherlands were, for instance, the focus for expressions of national loyalty. King Leopold of Belgium was heavily and rather unfairly criticised by the British for remaining in his German-dominated kingdom. King Christian of Denmark, who did the same, helped mitigate the results of occupation. It would undoubtedly have been more difficult for the Italians to oust Mussolini in 1943 had the King not provided a legitimacy for his dismissal.[32]

The needs of the war demanded the mobilisation of women as well as men: women were conscripted for war work, served in armed forces, and unmarried women were moved away from family and neighbourhood. Hitherto sacrosanct spheres, even the War Office, resounded to what one remarkable woman who served in Churchill's war-time HQ, called 'the provocative tattoo of high heels'.[33] Some historians have seen such changes as making for not only a new independence for women during the war, but as affecting their position in society in the post-war world. Many women undoubtedly found the experience of war work rewarding and liberating, while films of the period like, *The Gentle Sex* and *Millions Like Us*, encouraged such attitudes, but the majority of contemporaries, including most women, probably saw women's changed wartime role as necessary but temporary. The twentieth century has undoubtedly seen a major change in women's place in society and in the work-place, but whether the experience of war played a major role in such changes remains debateable, and the view that more long-term processes, particularly economic and technological developments, were the real engines of emancipation seems persuasive.

It is widely held that, in Britain, the conjunction of the war effort with the discrediting of the politicians, who had governed in the thirties and had attempted to appease Hitler, created a new political consensus that lasted for decades after the war.[34] The 'Guilty Men' thesis, cunningly expressed in the book of that name in 1940, indicted the domestic and foreign policies of the old Conservative leadership along with their handling of the war.[35] The Coalition government brought a shift to the left in domestic policy with the inclusion of Labour and more left-wing Conservative ministers. The new political consensus was essentially in favour of greater state welfare, on the back of a planned economy that would abolish unemployment. If Churchill had promised 'blood, sweat and tears', other voices were soon talking of rewards, a 'New Jerusalem' after the war with family allowances, a free health service and expanded national insurance. The Beveridge Report, published in 1942, talked of conquering the five giants of Want, Disease, Ignorance, Squalor and Idleness, while the theories of John Maynard Keynes suggested the economic mechanisms which could underpin that Jerusalem.

As is the case with the question of women's role in society, it is unwise to see the war as doing more than give opportunity and promotion to more long-term developments and ideas. Nor should the extent of a change in attitudes be exaggerated. Those who have seen the war as not only a 'People's War', but a war which radicalised the British people,[36] underestimated the strength and enduring nature of the existing society, which formed the basis of wartime cohesion. As one historian has put it:

> [Just as the British people] were not made into quivering jellies by the air raids, so they were not made into utopian idealists by the MoI [Ministry of Information] film unit … there was a meaningful shift in emphasis because of the new possibilities opened up by the war, but it would not do to overstate it.[37]

Despite Hitler's concern to maintain the morale of the German people, a people whose will to fight he always distrusted, morale presented little real problem for the German government in the early years of the war. Germany, after all, appeared to be winning, and a succession of victories held out hope not just of triumphant conquests, but also, and more importantly, of a victorious peace. As confidence in victory declined during and after 1943, and the population became more and more pessimistic, this was not translated into a deteriorating will to continue fighting; throughout the last year of the war, workers continued to produce and soldiers to fight, while no organised popular resistance to the regime made itself felt. Why was this?

The Third Reich was, of course, an autocratic state, even if the term 'disorganised autocracy' has been used to describe it, and in addition it was a police state. Very nasty penalties awaited those who opposed the regime, or even spread defeatism, but the resilience of the German war effort cannot be explained by oppression. The regime had built up a reservoir of good will among the population by its success in solving the problems of depression and unemployment before the war, while the 'reluctant loyalty' with which the nation had gone to war had been initially rewarded. Historians of Germany have reluctantly come to accept the degree to which Nazi Germany was both seen to be and was, to a considerable degree, a modernising force. Despite the elements of anti-industrialisation and anti-modernism in Nazi philosophy, National Socialism was, in practice, socially egalitarian and committed to a welfare state. Between 1933 and 1945 opportunities for social mobility increased in Germany, while welfare benefits were extended. Far from being a mirror image of wartime Britain, the Nazi state at war resembled Britain in the way it held out the promise of a prosperous and secure post-war society. The German Labour Front's proposals, of 1940, for a new health and insurance scheme can be seen as a Nazi equivalent of the Beveridge Report.

The Third Reich's organisation of the German work force was both timorous and inefficient, and for the greater part of the war, the German civilian population was handled with kid-gloves, its position softened by the importation of foreign workers, over whom Germans presided as a foremen class. The War Economy Decree of 1939 sought to cut wages and increase taxes, but match these measures with reduced prices. Faced with passive resistance by an outraged work force and opposition from Nazi officials, the regime backtracked and withdrew the measures. The Nazi approach both forswore the ruthlessness of the USSR's socialist approach and failed to allow the market to draw workers towards the armaments industry by permitting higher wages in that sector, as happened in the USA and, to some extent, Britain. The result was a supposedly directed economy vitiated by inefficiency. Foreign labour,[38] both nominally free and at the same time totally enslaved, made up for the loss of increasing numbers of the German work force to the *Wehrmacht*, enabled the remaining German workers to enjoy immunity from the worst jobs and conditions, and allowed the regime to eschew the effective conscription of German women.

Despite National Socialism's declared belief in women sticking to their roles as wives and mothers, there had actually been more employed females in Germany at the beginning of the war than in Britain, but no great effort was made to increase the female work force or direct more of it to the vital armaments industries.[39] In 1943 women were ordered to register at their local labour office, but only a small minority were directed to employment, and the profile of the female work force remained substantially unchanged with large numbers continuing to be employed in domestic service. If there was little pressure to propel women towards war work, there were few inducements for many married women because of the generous allowances given to the wives of servicemen.

Just how effective propaganda was in Germany, or, indeed, in other countries, we will never know. Certainly the Nazis invested heavily in propaganda and, like the British, set up bodies to monitor its effectiveness. In the early years of the war, German propaganda could act as a megaphone for the triumphalism of the Nazi leadership and drum up hatred for external enemies, as with *Ohm Kruger*, a 1941 film castigating Britain for its actions during the Boer war, or for internal enemies, as with the anti-Jewish film, *Der Ewige Jude* (1941). The crisis for Nazi propaganda came as the war turned against Germany, and the regime havered between covering up defeats and Goebbels's desire to adopt a more realistic tone. Too great a gap between optimistic propaganda and the knowledge that the war was going badly resulted in radio broadcasts and newsreels being widely derided. Once the desperate nature of the situation was accepted, however, Goebbels was to be highly successful in calling for resistance to eastern invaders and in appealing to Germans' sense of history. As in Britain, where the film, *Henry V* (1944) sought public support for the war by appealing to a glorious war in the past, so in Germany, even as allied armies approached, the *Wehrmacht* provided 186,000 troops as extras for the making of *Kolberg* (1945), a film depicting Prussia's victory in 1806.

Fear, not of the regime but of the enemy, not only brought the support of the disillusioned to the war effort, but prevented the growth of a credible opposition, even of an underground opposition. The Allied policy of unconditional surrender gave little help to the possible emergence of liberal or conservative opposition, while communism and socialism were tainted by association with an implacable enemy, the Soviet Union, likely to bring the dire fate of fire, pillage and rape to a defeated Germany. The only internal threat to the regime came from the civilised remnants of the aristocracy, still dominant in the *Wehrmacht*; not only did the Generals' Plot fail, but it was widely seen as treason.

Just as the move to a war economy required no essential change in Soviet economic practice, so it was hardly necessary for the state to tighten its grip on the lives of the population. As in Germany, fear both of the enemy and of the state played a part in silencing opposition and ensuring that the work force and the armed forces remained obedient. That in all areas that fell to the Germans there was significant collaboration suggests that fear of the state apparatus was important in holding the home front together, though the behaviour of the German occupiers soon proved that they were no liberators. Hitler's stance towards the eastern territories was, as one historian has written, 'so unappealing as to provide only a very weak test of the Soviet population's true loyalties and national feeling'.[40] The state, which claimed above all to be of the people, clearly did not trust large sections of the population. A huge network of labour camps operated throughout the war, as it had in peace for suspect citizens, while a distrust of minorities resulted in deportations on a massive scale. Even before Hitler's attack, large proportions of the populations of the incorporated Baltic republics had been moved into the Russian interior, while the Volga Germans were, unsurprisingly, early victims of the war, being dispersed to central Asia. A major wave of deportations took place after Soviet territory had been liberated. Karachayevs, Kalmyks, Chechens, Crimean Tartars and several other peoples were uprooted and sent to eastern areas of the Union. Since most Western journalists and politicians had never heard of such peoples, the regime's crimes were ignored by the Western Allies.

It would be wrong, however, to see the regime's repressive capabilities as the only, or even the most adhesive, glue binding the Soviet war effort together. National ethos was another factor, though here we can distinguish between Russia itself and the many republics of the Union. Even before the war, some examples of stirring evocations of the spirit of 'Mother Russia' defending herself against Teutonic invasion were to be found amidst all the calls to work for socialism, as with Sergei Eisenstein's film, *Alexander Nevsky* (1938). With its powerful evocation of Russia's defence of the motherland against the Teutonic Knights, it was to hand when, after *Barbarossa*, it could inspire resistance to Germany. Patriotism and the defence of the homeland became increasingly the theme of radio, newspapers and films. Eisenstein's *Ivan The Terrible* (1944) enlisted that unsympathetic Tsar, a favourite of Stalin's, to the war effort, while the portraits of Tsarist generals were to be found in public buildings. The war became a great patriotic war.

Socialist egalitarianism was found wanting as the ethos for military achievement, and in 1943, ranks were made more formal with the return of gold epaulettes for officers associated with the imperial army and the reinstitution of the very word *ofitser*. Stalin was, however, careful to put himself on top of the military hierarchy, swollen with newly promoted marshals, and became Marshal of the Soviet Union. A further echo of Tsarist days came with the temporary rehabilitation of the Orthodox Church; anti-religious propaganda stopped and Orthodox bishops were allowed to elect a patriarch. What Stalin attempted to achieve, and to considerable degree succeeded in achieving, was a synthesis between socialism and Russian patriotism, epitomised by his own central role as a socialist Tsar. The mass of the Soviet population continued to work and to fight with little food, long working hours and harsh discipline inspired by fear of authority, fear and hatred of the enemy, and in the cause of Russian patriotism. The government was also careful to ensure supplies of one consumer item, vodka, a contribution to morale which should not be underestimated; indeed, all combatant states seem to have realised that shortages of alcohol were to be avoided.

The concept that war has a socially levelling effect finds little support in the Soviet instance. Soviet society became more hierarchical and the privileges of elite groups increased. The greatest support for the regime came from technological and administrative echelons, who had benefited most from the unbalanced modernisation of pre-war industrial programmes and whose living standards continued to be protected during the war.

The view of war itself, rather than defeat in war, as making for social change appears confounded by the Japanese experience. The Japanese people endured a long war, for in practice, Japan was at war from 1937 and from early on there were food shortages and rationing. The National Mobilisation Law of 1938 gave the government wide powers over the economy and society, and in 1941, the education system was remodelled in the interests of the militarisation of society. It was only in 1944 that air raids became a serious problem and it was in the last months of the war that casualties reached horrendous levels. Conventional bombing killed almost the same number of people as the nuclear bombs which ended the war, with the two together causing some 300,000 deaths. Yet dragooned by the state, hungry, and with inadequate air raid precautions, the civilian population remained stoic.

The experience of American civilians was in direct contrast to that of the civilian populations of the other combatant powers. The war effort finally brought the Depression to an end and marked the beginning of a long period of full employment and rising living standards, while there were, of course, no bombing raids. American

Blacks moved in large numbers from the South, attracted by the job opportunities in the North and Mid-West, and although the US armed forces remained strictly segregated, the fact of this segregation became the subject of debate. As in Britain, women were encouraged to take on war work normally done by men, but the Soviet-style posters of rather muscular women brandishing spanners, which urged them to do this, belie the fact that few thought of such work as more than a temporary expedient. The armed forces were at first more reluctant than their British equivalents to utilise women, but the pressure of war prevailed, and by 1945, hundreds of thousands of women were serving in the army and navy.

In the end, the only generalisations about the home fronts that are incontrovertible are that everywhere the state increased its powers and individual freedom diminished while civil society shrunk, and that the effects of bombing on civilian morale were less than had been expected. Whether there were links between the experience of war and greater social equality will no doubt continue to be debated, but the difficulties of distinguishing between the effects of war itself, the outcome of war, and more long-term factors making for social change are too great to permit definite answers.

Chapter 5:   Roads to Victory 1943–4

The Tide Begins to Turn

By the spring of 1942, the Japanese conquests in the Pacific and the position of the German armies deep within the Soviet Union suggested that military advantage and strategic initiative lay with the Axis forces. There is, as we have seen, a powerful argument that Germany and Japan lacked the resources to ultimately prevail, but the potential power of the USA and the Soviet Union was not yet fully realised, and both powers were still reeling from the force of Japanese and German attacks.

The initiative was not, however, to rest with Germany and Japan for long. Even before the effects of the great military-industrial complex that the dynamic economy and society of the United States was transformed into by the needs of war could be brought to bear, and before the results of the brutal and crude but effective Soviet war economy had been properly transmitted to the front line, the Axis experienced its first intimations of eventual failure. The German army met a severe defeat at Stalingrad, the Imperial Japanese Navy suffered not only defeats, but also the loss of vital aircraft carriers and planes at the Battles of the Coral Sea and Midway, while Rommel's army was checked and then defeated at the two battles of El Alamein.

Many historians have played down the importance of the war in North Africa, the Mediterranean and the Middle East. At the time the hard-pressed Russians saw it as an ineffective apology for a Second Front. It is certainly true that the scale of the fighting in the Mediterranean sphere cannot be compared to the great land battles on the Eastern Front. The Mediterranean and the Middle East were, however, of crucial strategic importance. As we have already noted, it was only by controlling the region that Germany and Italy had any hope of linking up with their ally, Japan; in 1942 it was feared that German forces might enter Iran from the Caucasus and join up with the German army in North Africa for an assault, along with the Japanese, on India.

Churchill's foolhardiness in weakening British, or more properly British Empire, forces in North Africa in the spring of 1941 in order to assist Greece had resulted not merely in the loss of great numbers of men and equipment, together with valuable warships, in the doomed defence of Greece and Crete, but had prevented the expulsion of the Italians from Libya. When Hitler decided to send a German army under General Rommel to stiffen the resolve of the Italians, it thus had a base from which it would threaten the British in Egypt for another two years.

Once the Germans had taken over the direction of the North African campaign, the balance of advantage swung back and forth between the combatants for a year and a half. This balance depended upon a number of factors. The nature of desert warfare, which was mobile and enabled defensive positions to be outflanked, led to long tenuous supply lines – longer and more tenuous the further a force advanced – making offensives the more perilous the more they succeeded. The British could be supplied from the Indian Ocean, but the Germans and Italians required dominance in the Mediterranean to get supplies to their armies. Once Germany had invaded the Soviet Union, the progress of Rommel's army came to depend on how many divisions and how many planes the German Command was prepared to spare from the Eastern Front. Thus, when the *Luftwaffe* withdrew much of its Mediterranean force for the Russian campaign in mid 1941, German and Italian shipping losses mounted as British planes, submarines and surface ships were able to operate effectively from Malta and North African bases; when, in November, the *Luftwaffe* was reinforced and German submarines sent to the Mediterranean, supplies to Rommel got through and the British *Crusader* advance was reversed. The British victories of 1942 came against the background of a further withdrawal of German aircraft in June 1942 and General Rommel's bold gamble of a dash for Egypt, which brought his tanks to El Alamein only 45 miles from Alexandria, took place against the background of a deteriorating German supply position as Britain gained control of the air and sea.

The British needed every advantage to defeat Rommel. Not only was he, but his senior officers were also, superior to their British opposite numbers, who rarely managed to concentrate their forces effectively, while German weaponry, tanks, anti-tank guns and, until the arrival of the Spitfire Vs in the early summer of 1942, planes were also superior. Hitler made a serious error in failing to make a real commitment to the North African campaign. Only a few of the many divisions destroyed in the war with Russia could have resulted in a victory for Rommel with immense repercussions for the course of the war. Without reinforcements or supplies the opportunity for Germany was lost. By June, General Auchinleck had superiority in numbers, the advantage of regular oil supplies and new Sherman tanks, while he gained intelligence from the breaking of enemy codes. In July he was successful in holding Rommel at the Gazala-Bir-Hakheim line outside Alexandria, a battle sometimes known as the first battle of El Alamein.

Montgomery's victory in the second battle during late August was achieved with an army of 195,000 men with 1000 tanks, almost double the size of the German-Italian forces which were desperately short of fuel and ammunition. He used his great superiority in a sensible if unsubtle manner. After a thunderous artillery bombardment, infantry divisions moved to the assault and, after three days of fighting, the British armour was committed. Two corridors were opened up through the German-Italian lines and Montgomery continued to drive his tanks through them until the defence had been worn down. As Norman Stone has written: 'The same method was applied again and again, and Montgomery's casualties were actually higher, as a proportion of combatant strength, than Haig's had been on the Somme. But he won.'[1] Montgomery failed, however, to press home his advantage.

The two battles of El Alamein resulted, none the less, in a considerable victory for the Allies and together constituted the first substantial British victory of the war. From then on Germany was in retreat in North Africa and, in November, Anglo-American landings in Algiers and Morocco posed a threat to Rommel's rear. Early in 1943, he would be forced to retreat to Tunisia and, by May, the Axis forces would be out of North Africa. The British displayed considerable tenacity and a desperate ruthlessness in not only defending Egypt, but in acting promptly to counter German threats to their supremacy in the Middle East. A German inspired coup in Iraq was swiftly dealt with, the Vichy authorities in Syria and the Lebanon were overthrown, while, together with the Russians, Britain invaded Iran. The Middle East was secured against pro-German Arab nationalism and Germany, increasingly preoccupied with the Eastern Front, was unable to counter this.

A significant disadvantage for the Axis powers and for their hopes of victory was the lack of cooperation between Germany and Japan and their failure to coordinate their efforts in any sphere of the war. Anglo-American successes in the Mediterranean and the Middle East made any link up of German and Japanese forces, impossible, at least for the moment, while setbacks to Japan in the Pacific and Germany in Russia were to make it increasingly unlikely that a future opportunity would occur.

By mid-1942 the seemingly irresistible Japanese advance had been checked. Its high point came in the early summer, when the British were pushed out of Burma. Japanese superiority at sea and in the air was confirmed by the Battle of the Java Sea on 27–28 February, when a combined American, British, Dutch and Australian fleet lost 11 of its 14 ships without sinking a single Japanese vessel. Moving into the Indian Ocean, the Japanese Navy sank a British aircraft carrier, two cruisers, two destroyers and a corvette, while in air battles around Ceylon, planes from Japanese carriers destroyed 43 British aircraft for the loss of 17.

According to the strategy worked out by the Japanese Navy before the war, this should have been the point to go on the defensive. The Japanese position was much stronger than those who had planned the strategy could have hoped for, but the essential balance of strength was still against Japan. She was up against the two greatest naval powers in the world. If the Royal Navy had suffered massive blows and its resources were stretched all over the globe, the British fleet in the Indian Ocean was largely intact. Above all, the US carriers had not been destroyed. The Americans still had a powerful fleet in the Pacific to which they could transfer ships from the Atlantic. A strategy of conserving their naval strength and luring the main US fleet towards Japan, with the hope of destroying it in a great battle, remained Japan's best option.

That Japan did not go on the defensive after the success of the first half of 1942, but instead ventured on an ambitious and fragmented offensive, has been put down to 'Victory Disease': Japanese generals and admirals began to believe their forces were invincible, underestimating the degree to which those victories had been made possible by the war in Europe and failing to appreciate the Allies' potential for recovery. It may well be, however, that Admiral Yamamoto's reckless decisions were born out of pessimism rather than optimism and that, recognising the USA had been a 'sleeping giant', he had little confidence in Japan's ability to win a long defensive war or to secure a compromise peace; only a daring and ambitious onslaught on her enemies, while they were still shaken, might give Japan a slim chance of success.

Japan's tortuous path towards the navy's option of an attack to the south left some 1.75 million men – the major part of her powerful army – bogged down in China and garrisoning Manchuria, so that her full military strength was never dedicated to the Pacific War. Inter-service rivalries constantly prevented co-ordinated action, while within the navy there were competing factions. Japanese strategy has been likened to an octopus, the many tentacles of which prevented an effective concentration of ships and men.

If Japanese operations were to continue to be offensive, there were at least three possible plans: the navy could press forward into the Indian Ocean, while the army pushed into India, hoping for support from Indian nationalists; there could be a continued push to the south with a conquest of New Guinea, which might cut communications between the USA and Australia; and there was the possibility of tackling the most powerful enemy directly by thrusting through the central Pacific against Midway Island and Hawaii, which might goad the main US fleet into giving battle.

By early in the summer of 1942, the first option had already been tested with the brief incursion of the Japanese fleet into the Indian Ocean in April, but the army command's refusal to provide the troops for an invasion of India, or even the two battalions thought necessary to take Ceylon, placed it on the shelf. As in the Middle East, Britain acted with unaccustomed decisiveness in seizing Madagascar from the Vichy French in order to pre-empt a Japanese occupation. The Indian Ocean option was, of course, the only one which looked towards meaningful co-operation with Japan's ally, Germany, for a link up with German forces in the Middle East had been one of the alliance's more optimistic possibilities. That the Japanese now sought to follow both the second option (the taking of New Guinea) and the third (an attack in the central Pacific), and even added a fourth (a northern thrust to the American Aleutian Islands off Alaska), in large part accounts for their major setbacks in two great naval battles in May and June.

The battle of the Coral Sea was the first sea battle where the opposing fleets were never within each other's sight and the attacking was done entirely by aircraft. The Japanese fleet assigned to cover the landings at Fort Moresby, the capital of New Guinea, was not big enough for its task. It consisted of three carriers and six cruisers, against which the Americans were able to put two carriers and seven cruisers. The US Navy could concentrate on sinking enemy ships, while the Japanese had also to shield landings. Both sides lost one carrier, but the other two Japanese carriers had to be withdrawn from service for repairs, while the Japanese lost the greater number of aircraft. Most importantly the seaborne invasion of Port Moresby was called off. Japan had suffered a major reverse.

The battle of Midway, 4 June 1942, was the most decisive naval engagement of the war. The Japanese plan was ambitious. It involved the taking of Midway Island and several of the Aleutian Islands, but a more important aim was to lure the American fleet into a great and decisive battle that the Imperial Japanese Navy was confident it could win. Admiral Yamamoto was in overall command of a huge fleet that included battleships, aircraft carriers, cruisers, destroyers and submarines, the largest fleet the Japanese Navy had ever assembled. That the Japanese lost the Battle of Midway was in part due to superior US intelligence from 'Magic' for the Americans were now reading Japanese naval communications, but owed much to Admiral Yamamoto's decision to split his forces by detaching two carriers to cover an attack on the Aleutian Islands, while the main fleet supported an assault on Midway. These two carriers were, as a result, too far way to return to the main Japanese force when the decisive battle commenced.

Although enormously strong in battleships, cruisers and destroyers, Yamamoto, now had a slimmer superiority in carriers, having four fleet carriers and a light carrier. Against this force, the US assembled three fleet carriers, eight cruisers and 15 destroyers. Japanese superiority in carriers was not, however, reflected in superiority in aircraft, for their carriers were not up to strength in planes after losses in previous engagements, while the Americans could rely on support from planes based on Midway as well as on their carriers. Admiral Nimitz had split the US naval force into two, one under Rear Admiral Fletcher, which included the carrier *Yorktown*, and the other under Rear Admiral Spruance, which included the two carriers, *Hornet* and *Enterprise*, with orders to rendezvous north of Midway and await the Japanese attack.

The Japanese carriers under the command of Admiral Nagumo Chuichi headed for Midway, followed by a landing force, and on June 4 Japanese planes bombed the Midway airfields and were met by US land-based aircraft. As the damage to Midway's defences was deemed insufficient for the landings to go ahead, a second air strike was ordered and Japanese aircraft returned to their carriers for refuelling and rearming. At this point Nagumo received the first reports that US warships were in the area. The turning point in the battle, came when US carrier-based dive-bombers from Spruance's task force caught the Japanese carriers while their aircraft were refuelling and rearming. In the first disjointed attack little damage was done to the Japanese carriers and many US planes were shot down, but dive-bombers from the *Yorktown* and *Enterprise* then arrived and in five minutes, three Japanese carriers were on fire and out of action, and although the fourth carrier, the *Hiryu*, launched its planes and crippled the *Yorktown*, it was itself put out of action later in the day. Having lost four carriers, the Japanese broke off the battle. Midway marked the end of Japan's temporary naval supremacy in the Pacific and it also firmly established the decisive role of air supremacy in naval warfare. Admiral Yamamoto on his flagship the *Yamata*, the largest battleship in the world saw nothing of the action and the Americans resolutely refused to be drawn into battle with his battleships and heavy cruisers.

The battle of Midway is usually regarded as the turning point in the Pacific War, but although it blunted Japan's spectacular southern advance, the Japanese persevered with overland attempts to take Port Moresby, and it has been argued that it was the six-months-long battle of Guadalcanal in the Solomon Islands and the recapture of the islands that spelled the beginning of the end for Japan.[2] Guadalcanal, which began with American landings on 6 August 1942, was a bloody and long drawn out fight for an island few or none of those who died or survived on either side would ever have heard of before they were transported to it; as such it was an extreme test of the fighting spirit and discipline of both sides. It involved major naval engagements, in which the US navy lost more battles than it won and a long war of attrition on land. When the Japanese withdrew in December, it was clear both that Japan's advance had been reversed and that the Japanese would fight hard to retain every inch of territory they had conquered.

Although, as we have seen, there was little co-operation between the Axis forces in Asia and Europe, there was in 1942 always the possibility that they could have co-ordinated their efforts. The battle of Guadalcanal may have done something to prevent this. The Japanese had promised the Germans, triumphant in North Africa in June 1942, that they would mount an offensive in the Indian Ocean and had moved submarines there, with the intention of limiting supplies to the British in Egypt and India, and to the Russians who were getting supplies from the Americans via Persia. Gerhard L. Weinberg has commented:

> It was in this regard that the campaign in the Solomans proved decisive. Unable to drive the Americans out of Guadalcanal with the resources they were willing to commit to that struggle, and

unwilling to give up trying, the Japanese found themselves in a battle of attrition which precluded implementation of the Indian Ocean strategy they had promised to the Germans. What is more, they found that they could not even maintain the allocation of submarines to the western Indian Ocean but had to recall these for use in the South Pacific.[3]

At the end of June 1942, when the Germans seemed to be heading for total control of the Caucasus, the Japanese hoped that they would then head for the area between Suez and western Asia and there were plans for the Japanese fleet to attack targets in the Indian ocean and seize a huge area from Ceylon to Chagos, but a combination of German setbacks in Russia and the American attack on Guadalcanal, together with Japanese army's refusal to provide troops for an invasion of Ceylon rendered this plan still-born.

Midway and Guadalcanal together registered that Japan was now on the defensive against the world's premier industrial power. Within a few months its ally, Germany, was to lose the initiative in Eastern Europe. Japan's war was to be confined to the Far East and the Pacific, but its desperate gamble depended upon a German victory in the West for, without it Japan would face the consequences of 'assaulting powers vastly superior to itself in military and industrial potential'.[4]

The great land battles between Germany and the Soviet Union had thus a major determinant of the course of the war in the Far East and they were the major determinant of the outcome of the war in Europe in that they saw the defeat of the bulk of the German army. If the war had a 'centre of gravity', it has been argued, it was 'Byelorussia (now Belarus) and western Ukraine' for 'they provided the ground over which the war's two biggest campaigns – *Barbarossa* and Bagration [the Soviet advance of June 1944] were fought'.[5] But if the war had a psychological turning point, it was the German defeat at Stalingrad.

With hindsight it may well appear that Germany's chance of destroying the Soviet Union had been lost in the winter of 1941 with the successful Soviet defence of Moscow. With their numerical inferiority and shortage of tanks and mechanised divisions, German planning had banked on a short and decisive campaign, and a long war of attrition now seemed likely. A strategy of defending the conquered territory might well have been Germany's best military option, but Hitler and his generals were still convinced that a dynamic offensive could bring success. It was the Soviet forces, however, which launched the first major offensive of 1942 when Stalin, rejecting the option of concentrating on the battered German Army Group Centre which had been pushed back from Moscow, ordered an attack on several fronts. These offensives forced German withdrawals, but left the German armies substantially intact along a jagged front. Further offensives in the spring led to major Soviet defeats at Kharkov and in the Crimea.

In the expectation of a renewed attack on Moscow in the summer, Soviet forces were concentrated on the central front, but, with German forces checked in the centre and the north, where the siege of Leningrad, begun in 1941, was to last until January 1944, the German offensive came in the south. This offensive of the summer of 1942, which was finally halted at Stalingrad, had the aim of advancing to the Volga and then thrusting down to the Caucasus and the oilfields, thus seizing the industrial and raw material resources that supplied the Soviet war effort. It met with initial success. By August von Manstein had cleared the Crimea of the Red Army, while the main German force, divided into army groups A and B, was with Group A advancing towards the Caucasus, while Group B was approaching the Volga and the city of Stalingrad. The intention was to cut off the whole of the Soviet Union to the south of the city. At this point, however, German weaknesses became apparent: once again supply lines were a problem with only a single bridge over the River Dnieper to supply the spearheads of the armies and the two groups were ceasing to support each other; there was a shortage of panzer divisions and less well-equipped Italian, Hungarian and Romanian divisions had to be brought up to protect Army Group B. The Russians managed to raise new armies to throw into the fray and the German 6th German Army under the command of von Paulus, although it had by late September taken most of Stalingrad, then found itself under ferocious attack by strong Red Army divisions. The scene was set for one of the most hard-fought battles of the war and a major defeat for Germany.

The battle for Stalingrad was to last from August to mid-November and saw some of the fiercest and most desperate fighting of the war, as the Russian troops defended the city house by house. The Germans had taken most of the city by October, but had been fighting an infantry battle of attrition against inferior, but resolute forces in which their tanks could not be used, while Zhukov, assembling an enormous force of a million men, 900 tanks and over 1000 aircraft, prepared for a counter-attack. On 12 November the Russian offensive began and quickly encircled the 200,000 men of Field Marshal von Paulus's army fighting at Stalingrad, but Hitler refused to allow von Paulus to attempt to break out and withdraw. His refusal has been much criticised, and was indeed to result in disaster, but it was not just based on obstinacy and foolish pride. There was some logic to it because the fortunes of Army Group A in the Caucasus depended upon the German position at Stalingrad and it could well be cut off if von Paulus did not hold out. The fate of the army at Stalingrad depended now on a relief attack organised by Manstein and the degree to which it could be sent supplies by air. Manstein failed to break through and Goering's promises about the *Luftwaffe's* ability to deliver supplies proved false.

The doomed army of von Paulus fought bravely and defiantly, its 91,000 survivors surrendering only on 31 January 1943 when their food and ammunition were gone. Von Paulus, promoted to field marshal and then vilified by Hitler within a matter of weeks, was taken prisoner with his men. That he had held out for so long did, however, enable the German army in the south to make a relatively orderly withdrawal from the Caucasus. German armies were still deep inside the Soviet Union, but the German advances of 1942 had largely been reversed and the *Wehrmacht's* reputation for invincibility destroyed.

Von Paulus did not surrender at Stalingrad until January 1943 but the cutting off of his army of 200,000 troops in November meant that the year 1942 had, with Midway and El Alamein, seen the first major defeats of the Axis forces on three fronts. The decisive year of the war, however, was 1943. The turning points were the success of Britain and the USA in the battle of the Atlantic in May and June, and the defeat of the German army at Kursk by the Soviet Union in July.

Allied Policies and Strategies

In January 1943 Churchill and Roosevelt met at Casablanca to review the progress of the war in all theatres and to decide on and co-ordinate policies and strategies. Theoretically, political leaders have policies or aims which, in time of war, they, in conjunction with their military commanders, attempt to further by their military strategies, while tactics are the means by which military commanders seek to ensure the success of strategies. In practice, things are rarely so straightforward and were certainly not so in regard to the war aims, the strategies and even the tactics favoured by the Western leaders, Churchill and Roosevelt, and their Commanders-in Chief, Generals Brooke and Marshall, during the Second World War.[6]

The prosecution of the war with the aim of defeating the Axis powers was the main and the only ostensible agenda at Casablanca,

but strategies and priorities were already affected by political considerations. The national interests of the USA and Britain would, as
eventual victory became more certain in the course of 1943, increasingly come to be seen as inseparable from the shape of the post-war
world. Eventual victory, however, was not yet assured, and as US forces
were not yet preponderant over British in the European theatre,
Churchill was able to play a more equal role in the discussions than
would be the case at later Allied conferences.

The decision to accept nothing less than the unconditional surrender of the Axis powers was probably inevitable in the circumstances:
the shadow of the end of the First World War, the peace settlement of
1919, and the resurgence of German expansionism played their part;
so did the effects of years of war upon the British, and the way Japan
had gone to war with the Americans; while the left, in both Britain and
America, was likely to complain at anything that hinted at the possibility of a compromise peace which might not suit the Soviet Union.[7]
It was, however, a momentous decision, and one with consequences.
In a sense, it marked a refusal to distinguish between enemy nations
and their governments. Britain had gone to war in 1939 hoping to
bring Germany, preferably with a new government, back to the peace
table. Unconditional surrender lessened the chances of a successful
coup against Hitler and made it more likely that Germany and Japan
would fight to the bitter end. Churchill attempted, unsuccessfully, to
exclude Italy from the decision, an initiative which might have facilitated a prompter peace with that combatant later in the year.

The policy of unconditional surrender also had implications for the
relations between the Western allies and the USSR. Britain and the
USA were always concerned to placate Stalin, aware that he was quite
capable of concluding a separate peace with Germany if it suited him,
but by placating him, they abandoned their influence over him.

The decision to give priority to the war against Germany was
confirmed at Casablanca; if it was welcomed by the British, it was also
Roosevelt's preference. The immediate question was not where to
fight, for the Western allies were already engaged in heavy fighting in
North Africa and it was clear that an assault on the French coast would
involve immense preparation. American and British forces had landed
in Morocco and Algeria in November 1942, anticipating that the
French authorities would quickly desert Vichy and come across to the
Allied side. Instead, the allies encountered a stiff French resistance,
which was only ended when the Commander-in-Chief of the allied
invasion force, General Dwight D. Eisenhower, came to an agreement
with erstwhile Vichy politician, Admiral François Darlan. Even Darlan's

influence was not sufficient to persuade the French in Tunisia to throw in their lot with the allies, and there was no French resistance when German troops moved in by sea and air. Despite the fact that Hitler had responded to the allied landings in French North Africa by occupying all of France, the forces of Vichy France were more prepared to fight the British and Americans than the Germans. Thus, at the time of the Casablanca conference, the Germans were still strongly entrenched in Tunisia, to which Rommel retired in the same month of January, and Axis resistance in North Africa would not end until May. The question remained as to what the Western allies should do, once the Germans and Italians had been expelled from North Africa.

Should Britain and America have seen their major task as the launching of a second front to give some relief to the Soviet Union, still fighting for survival? If so, was this because it made sense in terms of the interests of the Western allies or because it was a moral duty? If the answer to the first question was in the affirmative for either reason, then was an invasion of France, pressed for by the Soviets and favoured by the Americans, feasible? The second question almost seemed rhetorical in the propaganda-induced mind-set of the time, but deserves serious consideration.

It is still not quite politically correct to consider whether the Western powers owed the Soviet Union every assistance possible. The idea of 'our gallant ally' dies hard and the British public were, at the time, busy contributing to the 'Sword of Stalingrad'. But should Britain and America have really considered the interests of their ally of convenience, a power as implacably opposed to them as Hitler's Germany, the butcher, along with Germany, of Poland, the perpetrator of the Katyn massacre of Polish officers, the enslaver of the Baltic states, and the Goliath to Finland's David? In a sense the question is anachronistic for the circumstances of the time forbade it to be openly raised, but Churchill could hardly have been blamed had he secretly wished to conserve and husband Britain's declining power, and to safeguard British interests at the expense of the USSR. There were, of course, hard-headed arguments for providing maximum relief for the Soviet Union: without such relief, Hitler might still win on the Eastern Front; while a new agreement between Stalin and Hitler was by no means inconceivable, indeed, there were tentative contacts between Soviet and German representatives in the spring and summer of 1943.[8] For the moment there was, in reality, only one place that the Western allies could confront their European enemies and that was in and around the Mediterranean, but American enthusiasm and British reluctance for an invasion of France were marked.

Plans for an invasion of France in 1942 had never been realistic, but General Marshall, US Chief of Staff, was correct in his judgement that the effect of Roosevelt's agreement to Operation Torch, the invasion of North Africa, was the further postponement of landings in France. Furthermore, once involved in North Africa, the Americans found themselves increasingly drawn in to a Mediterranean perspective and had difficulty in extricating themselves from British plans for ventures in Italy, Greece and the Balkans. Marshall attempted at Casablanca to get agreement on a cross-Channel invasion in 1943 but Roosevelt sided with Churchill and Brooke. The outcome was a decision to take Sicily.

The Battle of the Atlantic

In fact, lack of troops and equipment ruled out a cross-Channel invasion, save as a desperate stratagem if the USSR were about to be defeated. The lack of troops and equipment was due to the grip of German U-boats on the sea lanes of the Atlantic. If successes in the war against the U-boats were to permit the gradual build up of US strength in Britain, Soviet victories were to ensure that there was little urgent need to take pressure off the eastern ally. Britain and the USA were above all naval powers. In desperation Britain and her empire could put a substantial army into the field, while the USA, when impelled by the needs of war, was able to raise, by dint of her vast population and economic might, an army capable of matching that of any power, but both depended on their navies for their security and without them could not even bring their armies into action.

Even before the USA was at war, Roosevelt had decided that in the event of hostilities with Japan and Germany, America would give priority to the war in Europe. Whether, without the American victories at the Coral Sea and Midway, the USA would have been able to persevere with such a strategy is debateable, but the destruction of vital Japanese aircraft carriers meant that Japan's offensive was blunted. The main obstacle to bringing US military power to bear in the European theatre was the ability of German submarines to sink the ships carrying American armies and equipment, while at the same time U-boats could starve Britain of supplies and interfere with allied aid to Russia.

In contrast to their relative failure in the wartime production of tanks and aircraft, one of the great German achievements of the war was their production of submarines. Not envisaging a long war against Great Britain, Hitler had given little encouragement to the building of U-boats, and in 1939, the German navy was unprepared to utilise a weapon that had proved so successful in the First World War and had only 18 boats ready for operations. Nevertheless, a handful of U-boats was able to inflict enormous damage on British shipping in 1940 and, as was quickly proven when the German navy was supplied with long range aircraft, planes were also effective in sinking ships. In 1941 1299 British merchant ships were lost.[9] From the spring of 1941, convoy protection was improved by the provision of better air cover and more destroyer escorts, while the partial breaking of the German naval code assisted a submarine tracking room in London in guiding convoys along safer routes. The merchant fleet was, nevertheless, in decline, while Germany was stepping up its production of U-boats.

The Battle of the Atlantic was to swing to and fro as tactics, intelligence and technology favoured either the U-boats or their prey. Admiral Doenitz, the commander of German submarines, estimated in 1942 that a monthly sinking of 700,000 tons of shipping would effectively prevent Allied operations in the European theatre. By then he had almost 300 submarines, with some 80 or 90 available at any time.[10] America's failure to establish a convoy system for ships sailing along their eastern seaboard or even to black out the lights of coastal cities gave the U-boats a 'happy time' for several months of 1942. Better-organised convoys with well-drilled escorts, equipped with radar capable of detecting submerged submarines, as well as with sonar, and armed with the multiple bomb projector, Hedgehog, assisted the Allied shipping. On the other hand, as we saw in Chapter 2, a change in the German code left the Allied navies without effective intelligence for most of 1942, and U-boats switched to the 'Black Gap', an area of the Atlantic that could not be patrolled by the long-range Liberator aircraft.

By the early months of 1943, the Battle of the Atlantic was still undecided. US mass production of merchant ships was helping to make good even huge shipping losses, while strong winter gales impeded U-boat activity, but Doenitz, now Commander-in-Chief of the German navy, had what he considered sufficient submarines. In Admiral Sir Max Horton, Commander-in-Chief of the Western Approaches, he had a formidable opponent. In March the U-boats had a successful month sinking 540,000 tons of shipping, forcing the suspension of convoys to Russia so that more escort vessels could be attached to Atlantic convoys. Horton utilised his extra ships to form support groups, ready to move in once the U-boats struck. At the end of April, the wolf packs, for Doenitz having decided that groups of U-boats were more effective, targeted a large slow-moving convoy, ONS 5, and striking in early May, sank 12 ships for the loss of two U-boats. Support groups and Liberator aircraft then moved in and sank five U-boats, severely damaging another five. The total U-boat losses for May came to 41 and U-boats were temporarily withdrawn from the Atlantic. The U-boat threat was never entirely eliminated, German submarine production held up well and technological innovation always threatened to swing the advantage back to the predator, but the figures for tonnage lost to U-boats speak for themselves: 1942: 6,266,215; 1943: 804,277; 1944: 358,609; January–May 1945: 270,277.[11] The naval war in the Atlantic, lasting the entire duration of the Second World War, lacks the spectacular horror of the great land battles on the Eastern Front, though its horrors, dispersed across miles of ocean, were ghastly. Without allied victory in the Atlantic, however, Britain might have been defeated and D-day impossible.

The Eastern Front

Many have seen the German surrender at Stalingrad as marking the end of German hopes of victory in eastern Europe, but it did not spell the certainty of Soviet victory. The German army remained formidable. It was the great tank battle of Kursk that finally ended German hopes of stabilising the front and holding on to the bulk of their conquests in Russia.

During the winter of 1942–3, the Germans were pushed back along the entire front from the Baltic to the Black Sea, with the *Wehrmacht* being driven out of most of the Caucasus, while Leningrad was relieved, and a push from Moscow forced the invaders back west of the Don with the loss of the city of Kharkov. Stalin appears to have taken the rein of command from Zhukov and, intent on a vigorous pursuit which would allow no time for the enemy to regroup, overstretched the Soviet advance, permitting a powerful German counter-attack. Under the command of von Manstein, the Germans, although outnumbered by about seven to one, had not only halted the Russian advance, but thrown back the enemy on the southern part of the Eastern Front. Kharkov was retaken and a new line was established along the Donetz river. The *Wehrmacht* had made a remarkable recovery, but its losses had been considerable.

Any objective analysis suggests that Germany could no longer look forward to the defeat and conquest of the Soviet Union. The great gamble had failed. What was the alternative? The generals appear to have concurred that a largely defensive war was now the only option, though an overall defensive strategy did not rule out, and even demanded, limited offensives to strengthen the line. But what was Hitler's view? Historians are, as usual, divided over Hitler's hopes and plans. For R. A. C. Parker: 'Germany was on the strategic defensive, and from now on Hitler's hope was to separate the allies.'[12] Alan Bullock disagrees, arguing that 'The one thing Hitler would not look at was a political solution in any form. Among proposals he turned down [was] Ribbentrop's for putting out peace feelers towards Moscow'.[13] Gerhard L. Weinberg contends that though the German generals hoped at this time for little more than a stalemate: '... the *Führer* still thought of great victories ahead'.[14] Richard Overy suggests that Hitler was now prepared to accept advice and that: 'After Stalingrad his interest in the Eastern Front perceptibly declined.'[15] Alan Clark has commented:

> For the first time in twenty years Hitler was silent. He had no ideas. Looking back on Hitler's conduct in this period, we can see 1943 as a plateau of reason and orthodoxy standing between the extravagant ambitions of the post-Munich period and the nihilist defensive with which the war ended.[16]

It seems clear that, as the Germans had exhibited their ability to recover from their disarray after Stalingrad, the Russians were interested in a negotiated peace. This would have involved Germany evacuating all the territory it had conquered beyond the 1941 borders, but although both von Ribbentrop and Goebbels were prepared to consider this, Hitler still had confidence that he could hold on to his conquests. The campaign planned by the Germans for the summer of 1943 was a limited offensive. The Soviet advances had created a vast bulge or salient around the town of Kursk, at once a spearhead for the Soviet army and a trap should a German pincer movement cut it off. Although Hitler accepted von Manstein's plan for pinching out the bulge around Kursk, his insistence on delay destroyed its chances of success. The military mind when planning an offensive must necessarily weigh such contradictory factors as the advantages of surprise and the benefits of preparation, which may, however, also give the enemy time to prepare his defences. Hitler had, until 1943, consistently backed surprise over preparation; his new-found caution was disastrous.

Von Manstein proposed to attack in April or May, but Hitler forced a postponement until mid-June, and then again put it off until July.

This resulted in more German tanks being available, but gave the Russians time to work out, on the basis of British intelligence reports and their own, where the attack would come. Delay meant that the *Wehrmacht* had available Panther and Tiger tanks and the Ferdinand self-propelled gun, but the Germans roared in on 5 July to what was virtually a killing ground of carefully prepared defensive positions. During the next week the German armies struggled forward, and on 12 July, the Russians launched a counter-attack with two armies of tanks. There followed a great tank battle with some 1300 tanks on each side and German and Russian tanks advancing from opposite sides of a plain. Tanks can be seen as the horses of twentieth-century cavalry or as analogous to the chargers of mediaeval knights, and no battle does more to justify these comparisons than Prokhorovka, a small town which gave its name to the battle, where the opposing sides charged each other and order, command and planning gave way to a wild and bloody *mêlée*. Yet, the battle exposed the limitations of the tank and a major reason for the Soviet victory was that the Russians had been, because of the delay in the German attack and good intelligence, able to prepare minefields, dug-in infantry positions and anti-tank guns. The following day, Hitler called off the offensive, overruling von Manstein who pleaded for the remaining tanks in the reserve to be thrown into battle. The Soviets now launched offensives to the north and south of Kursk which the Germans were unable to block. Disregarding Hitler's orders to hold on to Kharkov at any cost, von Manstein conducted a skilful retreat back to the line of the River Dnieper.

From now on Germany would be permanently involved in defence on the Eastern Front. The Russians had always had superiority in numbers, but now they were superior in tanks and in the air, while US trucks gave their troops speed and flexibility. Russian numerical superiority was increased where it mattered because large German forces were maintained on the sidelines to the north and in the Crimea in order to keep allies, the Finns and the Romanians, in the war; such forces could have been far more effectively used in the central part of the front.

By September a general Russian offensive along all fronts west and south of Moscow was under way, and by mid-summer, Soviet forces had advanced an average of 50 miles along it. Hitler's strategy was now the construction of an East Wall to match the West Wall along the Rhine; it was supposed to run from the Sea of Azov to the Baltic and there was, he ordered, to be no retreat from it. By 30 September, however, the Red Army had five bridgeheads over the Dnieper. The long drawn-out battle for the River Dnieper continued through October to December. On 6 November Kiev was taken, and by the end of December, advancing Russian forces had cut off the German Army in the Crimea, which had been forbidden by Hitler to evacuate from its increasingly untenable position. While the desperate fighting for the Dnieper was taking place, divisions were actually being withdrawn by Hitler from Russia to send to Italy. Two days before the great tank battle at Prokhorovka, British and American forces had landed in Sicily. Stalin may not have got the second front he wanted, but the invasion of first Sicily and then the Italian mainland provided a new and pressing problem for Hitler. Allied operations in the Mediterranean had, indeed, resulted in weakened German strength for the eastern campaign for some time. Having failed to give Rommel sufficient support when it might have been effective, the Germans had in November 1942 committed some 150,000 troops to Tunisia and moved squadrons of bombers from the Eastern Front. As Weinberg argues: 'The diversion of effort [made it] impossible for the Germans to send a substantial army to the relief of Stalingrad.' Allied landings on the home territory of her Axis partner gave German problems a whole new dimension. Not only Italy but the Balkans were threatened with allied invasion.

Strategic Bombing

The Casablanca conference also witnessed a reaffirmation of allied commitment to its other offensive against the Axis – strategic bombing – and on 21 January, a directive was issued governing the operation of the allied bomber commands in Britain. Like its commitment to action in the Mediterranean, Britain's enthusiasm for strategic bombing went back to the time she had faced the Axis alone in 1940 and 1941. Churchill had, from before the war, been a believer in the effectiveness of bombing, and the policy of strategic bombing elicited an enthusiastic response both from Roosevelt and from a USAF anxious to establish itself as an independent service.

No aspect of allied policy has proved so controversial as the bombing of enemy cities, whether with the 'conventional' bombs that were able to inflict vast destruction on Hamburg, Dresden and Tokyo or the nuclear bombs which destroyed Hiroshima and Nagasaki. 'Strategic' is an innocuous enough word in comparison to 'terror' or 'indiscriminate'. However, the decision to use bombers not just in the tactical support of troops or ships, but to destroy or limit an enemy's capability to wage war – by attacking factories, communication systems and cities – was an escalation of the traditional means of warfare, a further move to 'total' war, a war against civilians. The distinction between strategic bombing, designed to destroy factories and railways, and terror bombing, which aimed to destroy civilian morale, was never watertight in theory, while in practice, because of the proximity of factories and homes and the lack of precision by bombers, there could be little difference.

Arguments about strategic bombing boil down to two: was it morally justified and did it work, though, if the answer to the second is yes, the two can be combined in the further question, was it morally justified because it worked and thus shortened the war? A subsidiary question is, who started it? Germany bombed Rotterdam in May 1940, though this could just about be held to be within the Geneva Convention as the raid was designed to break Dutch military resistance. The British had bombed Berlin prior to Hitler's order to the *Luftwaffe* to bomb British cities, an action which immediately justified any bombing of Germany in the minds of the British public. An escalating tit-for-tat had made the bombing of cities seem acceptable to both Britain and Germany.

In fact, the strategic bombing of Germany started on 15 May 1940, when RAF Bomber Command was authorised to attack strategic targets east of the Rhine. A major reason for its adoption was that it was one of the few offensive actions Britain could take. After July 1941 it was also a way of demonstrating to the Russians that Britain was doing something to help them. It soon became clear that there could be no real distinction between industrial and other civilian targets, such as housing, since the bombing raids were conducted at night (daylight bombing was soon all but abandoned by the British) and were only accurate enough to hit the broad targets of cities. By 1942 strategic bombing had achieved very little at a high cost of aircraft and lives, but the bombing programme was invigorated by the appointment early in the year of Air Chief Marshal Sir Arthur Harris to head Bomber Command and by the production of heavier bombers, most notably the Lancaster. The incendiary bomb raids on Lübeck and Rostock in March and April were followed by raids of over 1000 bombers on Cologne, Essen and Bremen; all were given great publicity and inflicted considerable damage, even if the amount of this was exaggerated.

Already, in 1942, the USAF had undertaken raids on France, Belgium and Holland by bombers based in Britain. The USAF differed from the RAF in believing that heavily armed bombers could defend themselves adequately in daylight raids and that such raids could achieve precision bombing on carefully selected targets.

After Casablanca the two allied airforces essentially pursued their favoured and complementary strategies, the Americans bombing by day and the British by night. The RAF developed the practice of hitting particular targets time and again, and these successive raids became known as 'battles': the Battle of the Ruhr (March–July 1943); the Battle of Hamburg (July–August 1943); and the Battle of Berlin (August 1943–March 1944). Meanwhile the USAF, from June 1943, began to attack industrial targets: the Focke-Wulf aircraft plant, the Messerschmitt works and the ball-bearing factories at Schweinfurt. The results were mixed: the firestorm started by the British raid on Hamburg on the night of 24 July undoubtedly shocked and demoralised the city's population; but the raids on Berlin resulted in heavy losses of bombers with little damage to the targets; while American losses were extremely heavy with two thirds of the force that attacked Schweinfurt on 14 October being destroyed or damaged.

By the end of 1943, the losses of the allied airforces were becoming unsustainable and German production was continuing to expand. It was only from March 1944 that, with escorts of P-51 Mustang fighters, the USAF's daylight bombing of Germany became effective. Mustangs, Thunderbolts and Lightnings fitted with long-range fuel tanks began to clear the air of German fighters, and in the last year of the war, precision bombing began to weaken, but did not destroy Germany's capacity to continue the war.

Much of the debate over strategic bombing has concentrated on whether it was effective in destroying either the enemies' morale or their productive capacity. David French has summed up the case against it: 'The strategic bombing offensive cost the lives of 100,000 British, Commonwealth and American aircrew and perhaps between three-quarters of a million and one million Germans. It was a major misapplication of resources.'[17] There can be little doubt that, especially in 1942 and 1943, the effects of bombing on Germany were exaggerated by allied commanders, but it does appear that the impact of the bombing of Italy played a considerable role in Mussolini's overthrow and the Italian surrender. A further dimension, however, is the effect of strategic bombing on German air-power. As Richard Overy has argued: 'From the middle of 1943 the defeat of the German airforce became a central objective.'[18]

Germany could and did defend its airspace, but the results of the decision to commit resources to this end were the withdrawal of fighters from the Russian front, and a relative decline in the production of the bombers needed to assist the *Wehrmacht*. Already in 1943 strategic bombing was having an effect on German air power and its ability to support German armies, while from March 1944 allied long-range fighters would win a decisive victory over the defending German fighters and Germany could no longer aspire to command of the air. The defeat of German air-power was to lead to a grave weakening of German strength on the Eastern Front and of the ability to resist an allied invasion of France, while, once the air over Germany was cleared of defending fighters, the USAF strategy of daylight bombing of specific industrial targets could at last become effective. We may conclude, perhaps, that strategic bombing failed to do what its architects claimed it could do, that is win the war by destroying Germany's ability to fight, but that, as much by its ancillary effects as by the destruction it wrought on towns, communications and factories, it made a significant contribution to allied victory.

Second Fronts

To the Russians, to most American military opinion, to a segment of contemporary British opinion, and to the majority of historians after the war, neither Operation Torch nor strategic bombing were substitutes for a *real* second front, which could only mean an invasion of France. The advantages of such an invasion were obvious: once a powerful allied force was landed in northern France and was in control of major ports, there was the opportunity for a direct attack on Germany, an attack which could be continually and relatively easily reinforced. The disadvantages were just as obvious for the Germans had been preparing to resist such an invasion of northern France, meaning the enterprise would be hazardous and, even if successful, costly in lives. The Dieppe Raid of 19 August 1942, from which more than two thirds of the 5000 troops who landed failed to return, had demonstrated just how costly a full-scale invasion might be.

Anglo-American differences ran deep. Britain was cautious, anxious to husband its strength, and was concerned not just with winning the war, but with its interests in a post-war world. Britain had, prior to the twentieth century, fought European wars from the periphery, attacking Napoleon via the Spanish Peninsular, rather than by invasion. The Mediterranean and the Middle East were seen as crucial British spheres of interest, which a Mediterranean strategy could safeguard, with Greece and Turkey being seen as particularly important to this end, while the possibilities of pushing on from Italy into the Balkans were a constant temptation to Churchill. Once in command, he had learned slowly with the assistance of General Brooke, what

Chamberlain always knew, the limits of British power; he was little inclined to risk his armies in what could be a costly failure and was concerned to safeguard Britain's strategic interests. The United States had not suffered the losses and humiliations that had been the British experiences from 1939 to 1941, had far greater resources to commit to the war, and was intent only on rapid victory rather than worried about her position after victory over Germany. To most of the American command, an invasion of France seemed more an opportunity than a risk, while other initiatives in the European theatre seemed a sideshow. For the moment, however, the difficulty of an invasion of France and the opportunities presented in Italy allowed British preferences to prevail.

The rapid fall of Sicily to the Anglo-American forces in Sicily in July 1943 precipitated the overthrow of Mussolini. The Italians, having suffered military defeats, been expelled from their empire and experienced heavy allied bombing raids, had lost faith in the *Duce*, who was dismissed from office by the Fascist Grand Council with the support of the king and the army. There was no immediate Italian surrender and the new government under Marshal Badoglio promised the Germans that it would continue the war, while secretly conducting negotiations with the allies. The Germans did not believe Badoglio and rushed all available troops to Italy. In early September, Anglo-American forces landed on the southern Italian mainland at almost the same time as the Italians surrendered, but met stiff German opposition.

Was a great opportunity missed? Was it the necessity for unconditional surrender or simply fear of their erstwhile German allies that caused Italian procrastination? A swift surrender after Mussolini's overthrow combined with allied landings in northern Italy, before the Germans had time to reinforce, might have avoided the long slog by Anglo-American forces up the peninsular. Allied plans, however, seem to have provided only for an occupation of southern Italy. If the 'soft underbelly of the Axis' existed at all, it was vulnerable in September 1943.

Historians have not, on the whole, been kind to British plans for offensives in the Adriatic and Aegean. There is an element of hindsight in this. Initiatives which fail are usually deemed to have been flawed from their conception. The attempt to take Italian-garrisoned islands in the Aegean in October and the landings at Anzio were failures, but the Americans refused assistance in the former and the fault of the Anzio landings lay in the failure of the US commander, General Mark Clark, to follow up the allies' early success. General

Alexander's later plan for the seizure of Trieste and an advance through the Ljubljana Gap towards Vienna may or may not have been fanciful. It was never tried. The failure of the Anzio landing, on 22 January 1944, to do more than establish a pocket south of Rome meant that the allied armies in Italy faced more than a year of fierce fighting against well-prepared positions in a terrain which favoured defence; the Germans were able to withdraw from one well-prepared and fortified line (the Bernhard, the Gustave and the Gothic Lines) to another.

If the lack of enthusiasm of the British for an invasion of France was responsible for its successive postponements, then this was fortunate. The chances of such a formidable undertaking succeeding were not good until successes against the U-boats enabled greater numbers of US troops and enormous amounts of equipment to reach Britain and until the *Luftwaffe* was greatly weakened. It was also essential that the number of German divisions in France should not be built up and the pressures of the Italian campaign contributed towards this, while the success of the Soviet armies ensured that large numbers of German tanks and men could not be switched from the Eastern Front. It was not until the early summer of 1944 that these prerequisites for success had been achieved and not until then that the necessary number of landing craft was available.

Such a massive undertaking did, however, have to be carefully planned and prepared for and, even after the Western allies had formally agreed in Washington in May 1943 to plan for an invasion a year later, Anglo-American differences arose as to its operation, while the British continued to regard the project as provisional. By August, when a strategic conference was held at Quebec, the planning staff under the British General, Frederick Wilson, had agreed on landing three divisions on the Normandy coast, between Cherbourg and the mouth of the Seine, and the British delegates, albeit with reservations, accepted this plan for 'Overlord'. The unanimity of Stalin and Roosevelt at the Tehran Conference of December 1943 on the need for Overlord to go ahead finally ensured Churchill's reluctant co-operation; he had to agree or be dangerously isolated. General Eisenhower was now appointed supreme commander, with Air Marshal Tedder as his deputy and three other Britons, General Montgomery, Admiral Ramsay and Air Marshal Leigh-Mallory, in command of the land, sea and air dimensions of the invasion.

Because the D-day landings succeeded, there seems a certain inevitability about their success, but a disaster was always a possibility. The English Channel was a formidable obstacle; the landings in Italy, where the Germans were less well prepared, had come close to failure; the weather was an important and uncertain factor; while much depended upon the speed and effectiveness of the German reaction. The Germans were well aware that an invasion was coming, but did not know where to expect it, while the allies spread misinformation and drew up an elaborate deception plan.

Early in 1944 Eisenhower and Montgomery altered the original plan to provide for the landing of five divisions on a wider stretch of the Normandy coastline. This inevitably added to the problems of logistics in view of the requirement for the almost simultaneous landing of so many tanks and men. The problem was not just the initial landings, but effective reinforcement once beachheads were established. Although it was hoped that Cherbourg would be swiftly taken, there could be no guarantee that the harbour would be useable, and ambitious and ingenious plans for floating harbours (mulberry harbours) were laid. A shortage of landing craft meant a brief delay while some which had been used at Anzio were brought to Britain and the date for D-day was extended to 5 June.

From the German point of view, the problem was how to dispose their forces so as to most effectively throw back landings when they did not know where those landings would take place. An invading force was going to be at its most vulnerable when it was on the beaches and before it had time to be reinforced and supplied. Rommel, appointed commander of the defence forces of northern France, set about strengthening the Atlantic wall of coastal defences and favoured keeping his Panzer divisions close to the coast. Von Rundstedt, Commander-in-Chief West and the tank commander, von Schweppenburg, disagreed and wished to concentrate the Panzer divisions inland, ready to strike with concentration in any direction. Given an equality in air cover, von Rundstedt's plan was probably better, but the allied superiority in the air was likely to destroy the mobility on which it depended. Hitler intervened and the result was a compromise which divided the Panzer divisions three ways: a reserve force was held well back from the coast; a third was placed at intervals along the coast; and a further four divisions were stationed in southern France. These dispositions represented a dangerous dilution of strength. Only one division was close to the Normandy coast since there was a general consensus that the main attack would come in north-eastern France in the Pas de Calais area.

Delayed by bad weather, the allied landings in the Bay of the Seine between Caen and Cherbourg took place on 6 June and were preceded by the dropping of paratroops near the two flanks. If the weather had threatened the enterprise, it also helped make the invasion unexpected and the vast Armada had almost completed its crossing before it was detected. Heavy bombers, naval guns and then medium bombers bombarded the defensive fortifications before the troops and tanks were landed. American forces landed on two beaches (code-named Omaha and Utah) on the western flank, while one Canadian and two British divisions landed further east on three beaches (Gold, Juno and Sword). Although the US force at Omaha encountered stiff resistance, all landings were successful, and by 11 June, 326,000 allied soldiers were on French soil.

Caen had been meant to be taken by the British on D-day itself, but was bravely defended for six weeks. Only after the RAF had dropped 2500 tons of bombs on the city, was it eventually taken. The bombing of the bridges over the Seine realised Rommel's fears that the German Panzers would not be able to fight a mobile war, and the main German forces to the east of the river had to make a difficult detour to engage the allied invaders. When reinforcements reached the area, they concentrated around Caen, perceiving that it barred the way to the Seine and Paris. Eisenhower was to complain at Montgomery's slow progress, but, in fact, the British were facing the bulk of the German forces and providing a shield for the Americans to the west. This was to enable General Bradley to take Cherbourg, punch his way into the town of Avranches, and clear the way for General Patton's Third Army to lead the Americans out into Brittany and then eastwards toward Le Mans and Chartres. A German counter-attack failed to cut the Avranches bottleneck, through which supplies were sent to Patton, and was almost caught in an allied pincer move-ment around Falaise, where some 10,000 Germans were killed and 50,000 taken prisoner. Falaise was a gigantic tank battle in which ten German Panzer divisions fought a fast-moving battle of manoeuvre against ten Allied armoured divisions. Even more than Kursk, where mine fields and anti-tank guns had played a great part in the German defeat, Falaise was a classic battle of tank against tank which lasted two weeks and ended with the US Third Army breaking through. By mid-August the battle not just for Normandy but for France had been decided and German forces were withdrawing eastwards before a rapid allied advance. American troops landed in the south of France on 15 August, Paris was taken on 25 August, Lyons on 3 September, and British troops entered Brussels and the Belgian port of Antwerp on 3 and 4 September.

The allied victories in France meant the fall of the Vichy govern-ment, opportunities for revenge and hopes for power or influence amongst the swelling Resistance, and a further period of hardship for the majority of the French population. There is little reason to believe that the Normandy landings were welcomed by this majority. The liberation of Paris was left to General Leclerc's Free French division, but the German commander had already decided to put up only a nominal defence and to disobey orders to destroy the city. The rapid surrender of Paris both saved the city and strengthened the Free French by cutting short a communist-inspired rising aimed at setting up a 'People's government'. De Gaulle arrived and, attending mass at Notre Dame, was greeted by cheering crowds; few cared to remember that Pétain had similarly gone to mass at Notre Dame some months earlier and that the cheering crowds had been larger. Although the defeat of the Germans in France was largely the work of American, British and Canadian troops, it immediately raised the question of a French government. De Gaulle's position was strengthened by his reception in Paris. He acted swiftly to gain control of the tattered, but intact machinery of the French state, at one and the same time both lauded and disarmed the Resistance, and gained the support of many of those who had supported Vichy and now saw in him a font of authority and order. He still, however, needed the recognition of the allies.

There had been no French government in exile in London, for the Free French under de Gaulle were recognised by the allies only as a Committee of National Liberation. To a large extent this was because the allies had realised that de Gaulle's claims to be the accepted leader of the majority of Frenchmen were dubious, that Pétain's authority was accepted by most of France, and that it might be necessary to negotiate with the Vichy government. Churchill was more enthusiastic for the recognition of de Gaulle and the Free French than was Roosevelt, partly because, in spite of an uneasy relationship with the general, he had some admiration for him, and partly because he was concerned that France should be reinstated as a great power, as rapidly as possible, to provide some counterweight to the USA and the Soviet Union. Immediately after the D-day landings, he urged that de Gaulle's administration should be recognised as the provisional government of France, but it was not until October that such recognition was accorded, a delay which was greatly resented by de Gaulle and which increased his dislike of the 'Anglo-Saxon' powers. Nevertheless the new French government was soon acting as a great power and full ally, providing divisions for the assault on Germany and even for the war with Japan, while it was to achieve parity of status as an occupying power in Germany at the end of the war in Europe.

Prelude to Defeat

Germany now had to fight a war on three fronts and was losing it. If the terrain of northern Italy was such as to enable the Germans to fight a tenacious defensive war, the allied Italian campaign tied up several German divisions. After Kursk, the Germans had been on the defensive in the east, and by the end of 1943, had been forced to give ground in the Ukraine to the south of their line and been pushed back towards the old Polish frontier in the centre. In January 1944 the Russians launched an offensive on the north end of the German line and raised the siege of Leningrad, a siege that had lasted 900 days.

At the beginning of 1944 the Germans were facing 5,000,000 Soviet troops. This was an army with weaponry that was no longer inferior, but which was often superior in quality and always superior in quantity. The Germans had lost control of the air and if their tanks and mechanised infantry were still a match for their enemy, their army as a whole was horse drawn and slow moving, as opposed to Soviet forces with their plenitude of US trucks. Now it was the German turn to face a new type of *blitzkreig*, by which instead of tanks spearheading the attack, artillery and infantry prepared the way for tanks. Germany's only advantage was the quality of its soldiers, especially its junior officers.

The Eastern Front was to a great extent a personal duel, fought with the weapon of millions of lives, between two warlords. Never, since Napoleon, had political and military leadership been so conflated, for both Hitler and Stalin were active supreme commanders, controlling, overruling and dismissing (in the Soviet case, if they were lucky) their generals. Hitler had exercised a certain military genius when it came to attack – surprise and a ruthless kill. As a commander in a defensive war, he was a disaster, unable to distinguish between military necessity and political *amour propre*; his commitment to static defence, exemplified by the creation of fortresses, which could not be surrendered, gave the initiative to the Russians. Stalin always expected too much, demanding advances on all fronts, more extensive than could be properly supplied, but by 1944, the Red Army was capable of meeting his demands for a continuous momentum.

At Tehran, Stalin had promised a new offensive to coincide with the landings in France. The June assault (Operation 'Bagration') against the centre of the German line, not as the German High Command had expected against their southern flank, involved 1, 500,000 men and 4000 tanks against which the German Army Group Centre could only oppose 500,000 men and around 600 tanks. Bagration, by which the Red Army destroyed Army Group Centre has been described as, 'the only operation in the preceding three years of combat which replicated in its form and effects the spectacular German triumphs of *Sichelschnitt* and Barbarossa'.[19] During the next months, the Russians made enormous advances. They smashed through the German centre and were outside Warsaw by the end of July. There they stopped.

A further offensive took place in the south and saw the invasion of Romania, which was followed by a coup on 3 August in which the young King Michael overthrew the pro-German Marshal Antonescu and then surrendered to the Russians. Soon Romania had declared war on Germany and, hoping to regain Transylvania, upon Hungary. This was the beginning of a general rush by Germany's allies to attempt to come to terms with the advancing Soviet forces. Bulgaria had never been formally at war with the Soviet Union but, on 5 September, Stalin declared war and power in Sofia was seized by a Communist-dominated coalition; on the same day Bulgaria declared war on Germany. German forces now began to withdraw from Greece and the Balkans as a whole. To the north, Russian armies overran the Baltic states and were driving German forces out of Finland. The Finnish President, General Mannerheim, broke off relations with Germany on 2 September, and on 19 September signed a peace treaty with the Soviet Union.

Aware that the Regent of Hungary, Admiral Horthy, was attempting to negotiate an armistice with Moscow and hoped to pull out of the German alliance on 15 October, the Germans acted as swiftly and efficiently as they had in Italy, kidnapping Horthy, taking over the country and instituting a new regime under the pro-Nazi, Ferenc Szalasi. As an attempted revolt in Slovakia was also successfully put down, the Germans were able to improvise a new front protecting central Europe, running through central Hungary, the eastern borders of Slovakia and central Poland. Along this line, the German defence stabilised, while the Soviet armies regrouped for the final push into central Europe and into Germany itself.

Germany had lost the war, but it would not end for another eight months. Could it have finished in 1944? There were two possibilities that could have led to a conclusion to the war in 1944: a coup by elements within the German armed forces, resulting in the overthrow of the Nazi regime and a German surrender; and a continuation of the rapid advance of the Western allies through France and the Low Countries into Germany.

The only important opposition to the Nazi regime within Germany was the secret opposition of sections of the officer corps of the *Wehrmacht*. Hitler's relationship with the army command had always been equivocal, and neither he nor the Nazi Party had ever achieved the complete subordination of the armed forces to leader and party that Stalin and the Soviet Communist Party maintained. For senior officers to contemplate the assassination of Hitler was not only dangerous, but it also went against the tradition of an officer corps which prided itself on loyalty. Hitler was the supreme commander to whom oaths of loyalty had been made and there was no king or kaiser in a cupboard who could, as in Italy or Romania, be brought out as the final focus of loyalty. Since 1942, however, there had been a group, largely composed of officers from aristocratic backgrounds, prepared to launch a coup, the first and essential step in which was the assassination of the *Führer*. Their motives were honourable but mixed: a higher duty to Christian morality and to the interests of the Fatherland. A series of assassination attempts failed or had to be aborted but on 20 July, a staff officer, Claus von Stauffenberg, placed a briefcase carrying a bomb under the table at which Hitler was sitting. Von Stauffenberg made an excuse and left, heard the bomb go off, saw bodies hurled in the air, and made for Berlin where Reserve Army Headquarters announced Hitler's death, while in Paris the army arrested SS and Gestapo officers. Hitler had, however, survived. His authority and charisma retained their force and he exacted a terrible revenge upon the plotters.

Whether the coup would have succeeded, even if Hitler had been killed, is uncertain, but its failure ensured that Germany would fight to the bitter end. The German people did not need Goebbels's expert propaganda to tell them that an occupation by Soviet forces would be a terrible experience, though he graphically articulated and fanned fear. Success for von Stauffenberg and his fellow plotters would have posed difficult problems for the Western allies. It would have produced the sort of situation sought by Britain and France in 1939: a defeated Germany under a moderate government, requesting negotiations which would take Germany back to her pre-war, pre-March 1939, or even pre-Munich frontiers. But things had moved on since then. All the Allies had signed up to unconditional surrender and implicit in any scenario involving a post-Hitler and essentially military German government was the desire to keep Germany intact, plus a marked preference for surrender to, or occupation by, the Western allies as opposed to the Soviet Union.

There was no possibility of Stalin temporising with such a German government now that Germany's defeat was in sight, although he had himself approved tentative communications with Hitler in 1943. Precisely because he had been prepared to consider a separate peace himself and because, at a time when Soviet relations with the Western allies were deteriorating, he could see the strategic advantages for them in an accommodation with Germany, Stalin was very suspicious. Public opinion in the Western democracies was not, however, in a mood to distinguish between Nazis and German generals or, indeed, Germans in general, even if Western leaders had sought to do so. Not just Hitler, but Germany had to be defeated before a new, if cold, war would persuade both the Western partners and the USSR to seek strength and support from the wreckage of a broken and divided nation. The best a post-Hitler government could have hoped for would have been a surrender, so arranged and timed as to facilitate the maximum amount of German territory being occupied by the troops of the Western allies. For the moment there was no alternative for most Germans but to fight desperately in a war that was lost, while the Nazi Party tightened its grip upon German society.

Hopes for a military victory in 1944 rested with the allied armies in France and the Low Countries. The German front in the east was temporarily consolidated, Soviet forces still paused before Warsaw, and the Soviet Army in the southern segment of the front needed time to resupply before its next push. It seemed, however, after the Western allies' rapid advance in August and September and the huge losses suffered by the German forces in the west, more than half a million of whom had been captured, that the Germans had little hope of defending their 600-mile frontier from Switzerland to the North Sea. Under the command of General Model, the German army achieved the seemingly impossible. The German defence was helped considerably by the allies' supply difficulties. The Germans had left garrisons in the Channel ports with orders to hold out and although Antwerp was taken, the Scheldt estuary was not and the port could not be used. The British and American armies were therefore still largely reliant upon Cherbourg for supplies and the further they advanced, the slower they could be refuelled and replenished.

In the face of stiffening German resistance, a bold plan of Montgomery's was adopted, the dropping of three airborne divisions behind the enemy lines in Holland to clear the way for the British 2nd Army to cross the Rhine. It was imperative, for the success of the plan, that a series of river and canal bridges were seized quickly, to allow the 2nd Army to thrust forward. Two American parachute divisions were dropped at Eindhoven and Grave, and the British First Airborne Division, later reinforced by the Polish Parachute Brigade, landed further north at Arnhem to capture the bridge there. British forces advancing behind them linked up with the American divisions, but their advance was then slowed by German harassment, while at Arnhem the British and Polish paratroopers became involved in a hopeless, but gallant battle with two SS Panzer divisions, which lasted for ten days before the survivors surrendered or escaped across the river. The failure at Arnhem put an end to the prospect of a swift victory. A push towards Aachen was repeatedly checked and the progress of the Western armies along the whole front was slow throughout September and October. Although the mouth of the Scheldt was cleared of German forces, thus enabling allied ships to unload at Antwerp, a general offensive in mid-November made disappointing progress at a heavy cost. What the allies were not expecting was the German counter-offensive that was mounted in December.

The Germans had managed to conduct their defence without engaging their mobile reserves, had been able to form new units, and had re-equipped Panzer divisions with fresh tanks. Hitler had, in short, enough for one last attempt, not just to drive back the Western allies but, in fevered fantasy, to drive them off the continent. Germany was back to the lines of early 1940, defending the fatherland from behind the Westwall. Could a brilliant offensive repeat, against all odds, the success of 1940? That an offensive could do much more than improve the German defensive position and postpone complete defeat was always wishful thinking, little shared by the generals, not least because of allied control of the air. But that a major offensive was possible at all testifies to the remarkable ability of the *Wehrmacht* to reorganise and maintain cohesion and fighting spirit after severe defeats.

As in 1940 the plan was to push through the wooded and hilly terrain of the Ardennes, towards and over the River Meuse, but this time, to make for Antwerp. Led by V and VI Panzer Armies, the attack, involving 200,000 troops, began on 16 December. The build up of forces had not been discovered and the surprise of the attack was aided by fog. The initial breakthroughs were successful, but the Germans could not maintain the impetus, while the Allies reacted and reinforced speedily. The offensive petered out short of the Meuse, the furthest distance advanced being some 60 miles. Although the German armies withdrew with skill once it was clear the attack had faltered and the allied forces were about to cut them off, Hitler's last throw had failed. In tactical terms, the 'Battle of the Bulge' was a draw, but in terms of strategy and its effect upon morale, it marked the end of Germany's coherent resistance: the *Luftwaffe* had put its last resources into a vain effort to counter allied air supremacy; the inferior mobility of the German army, with its horse-drawn body behind a motorised head, had been demonstrated; and if the offensive had disrupted allied plans for the invasion of Germany, its failure demonstrated to German soldiers that the future held nothing but hardship and ultimate defeat.

The Pacific War

Though the Battle of Midway is usually seen as the turning point in the Pacific War, the moment when the seemingly irresistible advance of the Japanese Empire was halted, there is, as we have seen, a case for seeing the battle for Guadalcanal as equally important, the moment when it became clear that the advance could be reversed. Midway blunted the Japanese advance in the central Pacific, but in the south Pacific, the Imperial Army still persevered with its attempt to take Port Moresby. With relatively slender forces, General MacArthur, Commander South-West Pacific, directed landings at Guadalcanal on 7 August 1942, the first objective in a plan for the recapture of the Solomon Islands. The Japanese decision to reinforce their small garrison – once the American landings had begun – drew them into a costly battle of attrition, which lasted some six months, weakened their air and naval capacity, and diverted their forces from more strategically important offensives.[20]

The ferocity of the Japanese resistance demonstrated how difficult the allies would find the task of breaking through the Japanese defensive perimeter and pushing the enemy back towards the home islands. In the naval engagements and the fighting on land the Japanese more than matched the Americans until, in December, three US Army divisions were landed on the island to reinforce the marines who had made the initial landings. The fighting on Guadalcanal did, however, distract the Japanese from the critically important objective of Port Moresby. It also prevented any serious attempt at co-ordinating their strategy with that of the Germans in the Indian Ocean. German victories in North Africa in June opened up the only real opportunity, if a Japanese attack on Russia was ruled out, for Axis collaboration. An increase in their naval strength in the Pacific Ocean might enable the Japanese to cut British supply lines to Egypt and India, and the supply line to the Soviet Union across Persia. Accordingly, Japan directed a number of submarines to the Indian Ocean and promised further forces would be sent in the autumn, but the need to defend and reinforce Guadalcanal meant that even the submarines in the Indian Ocean had to be recalled. Gerhard L. Weinberg has commented that 'the opportunity to meet her [Japan's] European allies by an advance into the Indian Ocean slipped by unutilised; it was an opportunity that both Tokyo and Berlin saw at the time and which never came again'.[21] By the end of 1943, Japanese forces in the Solomons were encircled by Admiral William F. Halsey's actions at New Georgia and Bougainville, as well as at Guadalcanal, and were isolated at Rabaul by MacArthur's campaign in New Guinea, New Britain and the Admiralty Islands.

The pace of the war against Japan was to a considerable extent dictated by the 'Europe First' strategy to which Britain and the USA were committed and which limited offensive operations. One interpretation of 'Europe First' would have been to stay on the defensive altogether, but in practice, the war in Europe and the war in the Far East were fought simultaneously, though the European theatre was accorded priority. British efforts focused upon the defence of India and the recapture of Burma; the American Navy, commanded in the central Pacific by Admiral Chester Nimitz, pursued a policy of amphibious attacks against Pacific islands; while MacArthur, with American and Australian forces, concentrated on expelling the Japanese from New Guinea, preparatory to taking the Philippines.

As in Europe, there were strategic differences between the British and the American governments, and between British and American military commanders. In the Pacific and China there was also considerable tension between US commanders, caused partly by disagreements over strategy and partly by personal ambitions and mutual dislikes: in addition to the army-navy rivalry of MacArthur and Nimitz, there was the mutual contempt between General Joseph Stilwell, the US commander in the China-Burma theatre, and General Claire Chennault, head of the US air force in China.

Apart from the perennial American dislike of the British Empire, which led Roosevelt to press for Indian independence, there was the high regard the Americans had for Chiang Kai Chek and his Nationalist government, a regard that was not shared by the British. The American view was that China was capable of playing a major role in the war against Japan and that it was essential to send as much equipment as possible to Chiang Kai Chek's forces. This could best be achieved by close co-operation between the British and Chinese in recapturing Burma, thus enabling supplies to be sent to China via the 'Burma Road'.

If the British and Americans had differing views and priorities, so did the Imperial Japanese Navy and the Imperial Japanese Army and such differences constituted a perennial weakness in Japan's strategy. Unwilling to commit forces to the navy's plans in the Indian Ocean, the army placed great importance on the invasion of Burma. Not only would control of Burma cut the supply route between Rangoon and Kunming for Chiang Kai Chek's government and thus assist the army's war in China, but it would also assist moves to destroy British control of India. The army also saw a considerable opportunity in taking advantage of what it saw as anti-British and nationalist opinion via the idea of a Co-Prosperity sphere, a regional organisation for the co-operative development peoples of East Asia. The initial plan was to simply take control of air bases in the south of Burma but this soon changed to a policy of occupying the whole country, which was done after the capture of Rangoon on 8 March, 1942. Both the Anglo-American differences and those between the two branches of Japan's armed forces came to a head over attitudes to China.

During 1943, it became increasingly clear that the Chinese nationalists had little appetite for offensives against the Japanese and were more concerned with consolidating their position against the Chinese communists, in preparation for the time when Japan had been defeated by the Western allies. Roosevelt's initial confidence in Chiang Kai Chek was already badly dented by the time a Japanese offensive in China in the spring of 1944 wiped out whole Chinese armies and captured many US airbases. In any case it was obvious that, after the failure of the first British attempt at a counter-offensive against the Japanese in Burma in late 1942, that the country's reconquest would be difficult.

British policy during 1943 was to defend India, but a reconquest of Burma was not high on the agenda. General Orde Wingate's small force of around 3000 men penetrated deep into Burma in the spring of 1943, cutting lines of communication and harassing Japanese outposts. This did something to boost the morale of British forces which were demoralised after the humiliation of the Singapore surrender, the initial ejection from Burma and the failure of the first counteroffensive, but achieved no tangible military results. In October 1943 Admiral Lord Louis Mountbatten was appointed to command the newly formed South East Asia Command.[22] There were few more glamorous wartime commanders than the dashing naval officer with royal connections, but the reconquest of Burma was to owe more to General Bill Slim, who was put in command of the new Fourteenth Army. Slim, who had experienced two retreats from Burma, appreciated the tactical and logistical weaknesses that had led to defeat and set about organising and training his forces for jungle warfare.

The Japanese controlled the main transport routes in Burma and were in a strong defensive position and it was an ill-judged Japanese offensive towards the Burma-Indian border by the Japanese Fifteenth Army, commanded by General Reya Mutaguchi, that played into British hands.

It is a tribute to Slim, to the powers of recovery of the British Army, and to the loyalty of the Indian Army to the Empire, that when the Japanese launched this invasion of India in early 1944, the British defence was tenacious and, relying on air supplies, units held out even when in danger of being cut off. The battles for the important bases of Kohima and Imphal raged from March to June, and after both had been relieved, the British Fourteenth Army then inflicted the most crushing defeat the Japanese had experienced on land, with only a handful of their 150 000 troops limping back to Burma. Chinese forces under Stilwell's command, together with a small but effective detachment of US troops, had meanwhile made progress with an attack into Burma from the north, while Chindits were operating behind the Japanese lines. At the same time as Mutaguchi was retreating, however, the Japanese offensive in southern China was proving so successful that the Americans feared Chiang Kai Chek's government might collapse. Nevertheless, by the end of 1944 as Slim's army crossed into Burma, the Japanese, who had earlier in the year had hopes of the conquest of India, were steeling themselves for a desperate defence of the shrinking perimeter of their conquests. The battles for Burma were among the greatest military defeats Japan suffered at the hands of the Western allies and were for Britain a revenge for the Malayan campaign and the fall of Singapore, though they pale in comparison to the last great battle of the war, when the Red Army annihilated the Kwantung Army in August 1945. They did not determine Japan's eventual defeat, however, for events elsewhere made it clear that that Japan would not long survive the imminent defeat of her Axis partner, Germany.

General MacArthur and Admiral Nimitz followed separate roads to Tokyo, coming together in the Philippines in October 1944 and then separating again, but both roads were long and hard. There was a pattern to the US advances across the Pacific, in which sea battles decided the long-term outcome by preventing the Japanese supplying and reinforcing their island garrisons, but did not prevent a bloody short term, in which such garrisons put up brave and desperate, if hopeless, resistances. Thus the Battle of the Bering Sea in March 1943 decided the fate of the Aleutian Islands and the Battle of the Bismarck Sea in the same month, together with further naval engagements in August and November, facilitated US landings and denied supplies to Japanese defenders in New Guinea and the Solomons, but were preludes to fierce land-fighting. In the central Pacific, Nimitz orchestrated attacks, combining ships, carrier-borne aircraft, landing craft, marines and the army, on successive chains of islands – the Gilbert Islands, the Marshall Islands and then the Marianas. US Marines landed on the Island of Saipan in the Marianas on 15 June 1944, but the success of the campaign was secured by the major naval and air battle of the Philippine Sea, which broke Japanese naval air power. Naval victories made US invasions irresistible but did not break the Japanese will to resist. A total of 26,000 Japanese died in the defence of Saipan, and the last defender of Guam was to emerge from his jungle hideout to give himself up in 1972.

US Navy Commander Admiral King, with Admiral Nimitz, had wanted to bypass the Philippines and make for Formosa, but MacArthur, for military and personal reasons, insisted that the islands he had been ejected from in 1942 be taken and his assault was supported by Nimitz's forces. Landings began on 20 October at Leyte Gulf, but once again land fighting was to be accompanied by a naval engagement. The Battle of Leyte Gulf was, in terms of ships engaged, the largest naval battle ever fought. At the end of it the Japanese, who had thrown everything including suicide, *Kamikaze* or 'Divine Wind', aircraft into the fray, had lost their last four aircraft carriers, as well as three battleships and six cruisers. As ever, the near certainty of defeat did not weaken Japanese resistance and it was not until March 1945 that Manila, the Philippines' capital, fell to the US forces.

A characteristic of the Pacific War after 1942 was the technological superiority of the US war machine. This resulted in an enormous number of Japanese deaths, while Allied losses were far less than in the war in Europe.[23] In the European War, the *Wehrmacht*, whether it was advancing or retreating, consistently killed more of its opponents than the number of men it lost itself. The Japanese, in contrast, suffered far higher casualties than their Western opponents. Nevertheless the determination of Japanese defenders ensured that American casualties were not getting any lighter as the Japanese home islands were approached. If there was no longer any question that Japan would be defeated, the question as to how many Allied lives would need to be sacrificed to achieve that defeat was increasingly pertinent.

Chapter 6:   Unconditional Surrender

Fractures in the Alliance

Hitler and the Nazi leadership continued to hope that total defeat could be avoided despite the desperate military position. These hopes were based on a correct perception that the alliance against Germany was increasingly under strain. What they failed to grasp was that they had become so hated and unacceptable that even an incompatible alliance would remain intact until after the destruction of German power. As Norman Davies has written: 'Though the anti-Nazi alliance was to be wrapped in the verbiage of freedom, democracy, and justice, the Big Three were bound together by cynical convenience.'[1] The closer the Allies came to victory, the more differences as to the geopolitical shape of post-war Europe overshadowed the straightforward goal of victory. Nothing did more to expose the fundamental differences between the allies than the question of Poland, the very state for which Britain had, ostensibly, gone to war.

On 1 August 1944, with the Red Army on the verge of Warsaw, the Polish Home Army rose against the German occupiers. This was no loose grouping of partisans, but a well-organised secret army of more than 400,000 men directly responsible to the Commander-in-Chief of the Polish forces in London. On 29 July Moscow Radio broadcast a message from Molotov, calling on the inhabitants of Warsaw to rise against the Germans. It was a trap. Once the rising was under way, its leaders were denounced by the same Moscow Radio as a gang of criminals. The Soviet forces sat back and waited, while German reinforcements were summoned to smash the rising and brutally kill insurgents and ordinary citizens alike. The rising lasted for 94 days, 250,000 Poles were killed, and after the surrender, Hitler ordered the demolition of the city. It was not until the following January that Soviet forces entered Warsaw's ruins.

Nothing better illustrates the blinkers of war, the censorship and self-censorship of press and politicians in Britain and the USA, and the myopia or selective vision of generations of historians, than the reaction to, or lack of reaction to, this ghastly episode.[2] Stalin, well aware that no Polish government with any basis of popular support would be pro-Soviet, allowed the Germans to do his work for him, the destruction of the bravest and most patriotic elements in Polish society.

Poland, a member of the original alliance of 1939, had always been the most likely issue over which the allies would fall out. In 1941 and 1942 the Russians had pressed for an acceptance by the west that the eastern Polish frontiers would have to be withdrawn in the USSR's favour. Britain had gone to war in 1939 because of her guarantee to Poland, but had never guaranteed Poland's exact frontiers, and as the war continued, Churchill and Eden began to put pressure on the Polish government to accept the loss of land to the east and be recompensed to the west. They believed that such a readjustment of territory was inevitable and hoped that if the Poles accepted it, Stalin might be prepared to allow a post-war Poland a degree of independence. Certainly, if the Poles had been persuaded in 1941 that they would have to give up the eastern territories, gained by the Treaty of Riga in 1921, relations with the Russians would have been easier, but the rearrangement of frontiers was the least of the USSR's demands for it sought nothing less than the complete subordination of Poland.

In truth, Poland became an embarrassment to both Britain and the United States. It was best not mentioned that the Soviet Union, along with Hitler, had carved up Poland in 1939. It was most unfortunate that Stalin had ordered the massacre of Polish officers in March 1940; even more unfortunate that the Nazi authorities in Poland had revealed the discovery of a mass grave containing the bodies of some 4500 Polish officers murdered by the Soviets in Katyn forest; and more unfortunate still that the Polish government in London wouldn't keep quiet about it. In April 1943 the Soviet Union had withdrawn recognition from the Polish government, and increasingly favoured its own tame group of Poles, the Union of Polish Patriots, who were prepared both to accept Poland's eastern frontier as the line drawn by Ribbentrop and Stalin, – more or less corresponding to the line drawn by Lord Curzon in 1918 – and whatever form of 'liberated' Poland Stalin cared to devise. At Tehran Churchill had accepted the Curzon line as the probable eastern frontier of a post-war Poland. The Poles, it has been said, were 'the nation who really lost the Second World War'.[3] Neither the Western leaders nor their public were prepared to make a stand for the interests of the inconvenient Poles. Britain, because of expediency and because it could do little to prevent Stalin's determination to impose a compliant regime on Poland, was to move, nudged on by the USA, towards what can only be regarded as a betrayal – both of Britain's ostensible reason for going to war and of the Polish forces fighting with Britain. Roosevelt, his eyes fixed upon a wide-ranging post-war settlement involving a United Nations, a US economic hegemony and a US-Soviet political hegemony, was also prepared to brush aside Polish concerns, especially when the 1944 presidential election was over and he no longer had to worry about several million Polish-American voters. Poland was the most conspicuous and most emotive rock on which the alliance was to founder, for as Soviet forces advanced, it became clear that territory conquered by the Red Army was to be shaped into frontiers and political regimes to the taste of the USSR. Stalin could, of course, respond that the Western allies were not consulting him as to the political shape of the territories they conquered or liberated.

As Roosevelt rejected Churchill's urgings that there should be Anglo-American negotiations with Stalin to set limits to Russian control of eastern Europe – negotiations which would stand a better chance of success while the Soviet Union still needed Western assistance – Churchill attempted to play a lone hand. He and Eden flew to Moscow on 9 October 1944. The so-called Percentage Agreement, worked out on half a sheet of paper between Churchill and Stalin in Moscow in October 1944, gave the Soviet Union effective control over Romania and Bulgaria, the two powers a supposed equality of influence in Hungary and Yugoslavia, and Britain the decisive say in Greece.

The 'Percentage Agreement' should be seen in the light of British interests and ambitions in the eastern Mediterranean. Churchill was seeking to conserve British power and preserve some independence for Britain and her empire. Since 1940 the Mediterranean had been the area where Britain had invested her maximum effort,[4] and late in 1944, he, General Alexander and Harold Macmillan, Alexander's political adviser, were still pressing for an Adriatic offensive. He was concerned to preserve a British sphere of influence, including Italy, Greece, and if possible, Yugoslavia and Hungary. To this end, he was prepared to put pressure on the London Polish government to give in to Russian demands and to write off any hopes of regaining influence in Romania. The disposition of British forces at the end of the war ensured that the only country on the half sheet of paper where Britain enjoyed post-war influence was Greece, but here Stalin kept his word, withdrawing support from the Greek Communists. Roosevelt continued to resist the idea of spheres of influence and to refuse to consider making military decisions in the interests of political influence. His ambitions were focused upon a new world order based on the United Nations. As the Soviet forces advanced ever further westwards, the difficulty of persuading the USSR to co-operate with that world order became increasingly apparent.

When the leaders of the three principal allied powers met at Yalta in the Crimea in February 1945, the war in Europe was as good as won. Britain, the Soviet Union and the United States had embarked on war with Germany at different times and under very different circumstances. The pretence was that they were all fighting for the same reasons, but their views on a post-war settlement and on the structure of the post-war world were by no means harmonious. However, Yalta maintained a facade of harmony, largely because it combined real concessions by Britain and the USA *on behalf of* Poland (and an agreement on Germany which provided for four allied zones of occupation, but little else) with more lofty innovations and sentiments: the inauguration of the United Nations, foreshadowed at the 1944 Dumbarton Oaks conference; and the Declaration on Liberated Europe which bore witness to a verbal adherence to democracy and self-determination. The high-flown sentiments of the declaration obscured, while they contradicted, the 'realism' of the provisions for Poland.

At Yalta the two Western powers not only agreed to changes in Poland's frontiers that ran counter to the Atlantic Charter, but by accepting Stalin's proposal that the communist controlled Lublin Committee should become the basis of Poland's future government, they also repudiated the government in exile for which Britain had gone to war. Yalta was indeed Churchill's Munich. Yet the choice was stark for, as Norman Davies has written, 'At Yalta ... there was no way that Churchill and Roosevelt, *by diplomatic means*, could have deflected Stalin from his chosen solution.'[5] As the American, General Ed. Hull later put it, 'All that Yalta did was recognise the facts of life as they existed'.[6] British and American public opinion, nurtured on a wartime propaganda diet of amity with the Soviet Union, would have taken much persuading that any other than 'diplomatic' means should have been employed. But that same public opinion would have winced at a frank admission that Stalin could do what he liked with the Poles and eastern central Europe as a whole. Stalin's promise of free elections in Poland after the war, which was scarcely credible, was accordingly accepted.

Stalin's achievement at Yalta was considerable. As Michael Dockrill has written:

> [H]e believed that the West had accepted Soviet control over Poland and eastern Europe, although he realised this would have to be achieved behind a facade of self-determination. Roosevelt had said nothing at Yalta which disabused the Soviet leader of this impression. Stalin was willing to pay lip-service to western principles by encouraging the formation of so-called 'people's' democracies in eastern Europe whereby communists formed coalition governments with anti-Nazi left and centrist parties. In countries under Red Army control real power of course rested with the Communists.[7]

The political boundaries of post-war Europe were to be decided, not by statesmen, but by the extent of the Red Army's advance at the end of hostilities. By the spring of 1945, Russian troops were in control of all of Poland, the Baltic States, East Prussia, the Karelian peninsular (previously Finnish territory), eastern Germany, northern and eastern Austria (including Vienna), Hungary, Romania and Bulgaria, and the Soviet Union was a dominant influence, via indigenous communist forces, in Yugoslavia and Albania. Having gone to war to prevent an alarming expansion of German power, Britain and, indeed, western Europe, now found that Russian power had penetrated into the centre of Europe and the countervailing power of Germany had disappeared.

What could the Western allies have done during 1942–5 to curtail a developing Soviet hegemony over eastern and central Europe? The options, at least in theory, were: to use their position as the suppliers of aid and war materials to the Soviet Union to extract firm commitments from Stalin on the shape and character of post-war Europe; to come to a realistic understanding with Stalin on a *quid pro quo* basis as to spheres of influence; to align their military strategy so as to pre-empt Soviet control in as much of eastern and central Europe as possible; or to encourage forces within Germany, especially within the *Wehrmacht*, to overthrow the Nazi regime and thus facilitate an armistice, separately from the Soviet Union if need be, with a new German government. As we have seen, none of these options was seriously pursued, largely because the United States under Roosevelt was not prepared to recognise that there was a problem. Determined to avoid the fate of Woodrow Wilson, Roosevelt felt that American public opinion would not wear agreements, secret or otherwise, over post-war territorial arrangements or spheres of influence. He also distrusted the British, disliked the British Empire, was preoccupied with the war in the Pacific, and trusted that the post-war international organisation (the outline of the United Nations Organisation had already been agreed at Dumbaton Oaks in 1944) would be able to curtail Soviet actions.

Relations between Britain and the USA, the latter increasingly the senior partner in the alliance, bore some similarity to those between the US and its allies in the First World War. In 1941 Roosevelt had put forward a loose concept of a post-war world based on the rights of all peoples to self-determination and had secured Russian and British association with it. Such a concept recalls the views of Woodrow Wilson, but Roosevelt was conscious that Wilson's policies had been repudiated by Congress's rejection of the Treaty of Versailles, caused in part by the gap between Wilsonian idealism and the self-interested aims of the European powers. Roosevelt pursued both a lofty idealism and American self-interest, which he tended to see as synonymous, and was determined to avoid Wilson's fate by dissociating himself and America from any carving up of Europe into spheres of interest.

Roosevelt was both opposed to the British Empire and suspicious of Britain as a practitioner of a worldly approach towards international relations involving the pursuit of self-interest modified only by the need for a balance of power. He had, at the same time, no illusions that the Soviet Union's preoccupations with its security and world communism would make it a satisfactory partner in implementing a world order based on self-determination. He, however, placed high hopes on the establishment of a close personal relationship with Stalin, and was convinced that America's economic power and ability to grant economic aid would prove persuasive. His own policy, so far as Europe was concerned, was to content himself with a lofty moral conception of the future, to concentrate on winning the war against Germany, and largely to ignore the question of the future territorial and political arrangements for eastern and central Europe, even as that question became steadily more pressing. He hoped that the Soviet Union would be contained by a combination of moral pressure and economic need.

The most well established reading of US policy is, as above, one which emphasises its missionary and moral zeal, but suggests that it was unrealistic. An alternative Machiavellian reading is to see the refusal to consider war as, in Clausewitz's dictum, the continuance of diplomacy by other means, as due to the USA's ambitions being so far-reaching that they made the territorial boundaries and the political characters of European states seem unimportant. The charge is that the US was seeking to use its military and economic might to impose a *pax Americana* upon the world. Conscious of its immense economic power, but aware that the end of the war could bring a crisis of over production if it could not reach markets throughout the world, American sought a global free market that it could effortlessly dominate. The world economic system proposed by the USA at the Bretton Woods conference in July 1944, which involved the establishment of the International Monetary Fund and the World Bank, was to be a force for economic stability in the post-war world, but the view of it as an attempt to impose a dollar global hegemony is understandable.

Even had the United States lacked either a missionary or a Machiavellian plan for shaping the post-war world, it is improbable that it would have been able to withdraw into isolation. Its economic strength and strategic position would have ineluctably led to its becoming the dominant world power. At the time of Yalta, however, Roosevelt did not foresee the degree to which the attempt to implement his vaguely formulated plans for a new economic and political order would involve a continuous and active, political and military involvement overseas. In pursuit of great goals, the USA felt it could remain aloof from the undignified jostling for position that marked Soviet and British policy. Where armies met, questions of frontiers, and of the political complexion of regimes, in eastern central Europe were of minor importance because the post-war world would exist within an international, democratic and liberal political-economic structure. A fundamental misreading of the nature of Stalin and the Soviet Union led Roosevelt to believe that the USSR would not stand clear of an essentially liberal-capitalist post-war system.

Views of Stalin's aims and policies tend to divide on whether he was motivated by Marxist ideology or acted, much as Tsars before him, within the traditional perception of Russia's national interests, and on the question of whether he aimed for a political-geographic settlement, which would safeguard the Soviet Union's security, or was determined on a Soviet dominated communist Europe. Such questions go to the heart of the causes of the division of Europe and of the Cold War, which alternatively have been seen as lying primarily and inescapably in ideology, in the clash between liberal capitalism and Marxist socialism, or in the conflict of great powers with opposed geopolitical ambitions, who also happened to have conflicting political ideologies. The problem is that it is often difficult to see whether ideology was the servant or the master of the policies of states. This is particularly so in respect of the Soviet Union. The case for continuity with Tsarist policy is a strong one: the desire to regain territory lost at the end of the First World War; the drive for hegemony in eastern central Europe; the push into Manchuria in 1945, recalling the eastward expansion of the Russian Empire; the attempt to detach the province of Azarbaijan from Persia (Iran), which can be seen as a continuation of the long Russian advance down the shores of the Caspian Sea in the eighteenth and nineteenth centuries; and Stalin's demand at Potsdam for a base on the Dardanelles for control of the Black Sea Straits had been a consistent aim of nineteenth-century Russian foreign policy. A Red Tsar seemed to want much the same things as his White predecessors. Yet, if Soviet policy makers were convinced that a future world communism depended on the Soviet Union and that the revolutionary struggle for socialism was synonymous with the advance of soviet power, ideology and the traditional great power aims of Russia could go hand in hand.

While it would be ridiculous to argue that the U-turns of Soviet policy and rhetoric between 1939 and 1948 were dictated by Marxist ideology, it would be wrong to dismiss the Marxist arguments that justified them as so much window dressing. Ideology may not have been the motivation for actions, but it is significant that ideological justifications had to be found for them. The Second World War was described by Stalin at different times as: 'a struggle of predatory imperialist nations over the control of world markets'; 'a great patriotic war of freedom-loving nations against fascism'; and 'an inevitable result of the development of world economic and political forces on the basis of modern monopoly capitalism'. The difference between these descriptions, or rather between the second and the other two, can largely be explained by their dates: 20 June 1940, 3 July 1941 and 9 February 1946. Once victory over Germany was assured, the control of the Party over the state, of socialism over the nation, and of the Marxist-determinist historical scenario over neo-Tsarism was reasserted. Yet whether ideology dictated, justified or merely cloaked policies is still debateable, as is whether Stalin became more bellicose and Marxist in opposition to Western reactions to what he considered was the USSR's modest exploitation of a hard-won victory, or whether he simply reverted to his true colours.

Whatever the answers to these questions, the US view that the USSR would not stand apart from a free-market world economy and a liberal supra-national world order was illusory. Almost immediately after the Yalta Conference, it became clear that Roosevelt's hopes were ill-founded. Free elections in Poland were not forthcoming and the leaders of the Polish underground were arrested, while in Romania a communist coup was organised by the Soviet Army.

The End of the War in Europe

The last months of the Third Reich retain a dramatic if horrifying fascination. Hitler seldom emerged from his command post, a bunker under the Chancellery in Berlin. He seems to have lost all sense of reality and to have alternated between grim despair and hopes that some miracle could still save him and his regime. A Germany he had come to despise – because it had failed him – still obeyed him. This was, in part, because he was still trusted, even loved, by a substantial section of the population; in part because the Nazi Party was more powerful and more ruthless than it had ever been; and because, although nearly everyone knew defeat was inevitable, its reality was greatly feared.

The Soviet advance did, indeed, bring terrors and not only to Germans, but also to the other peoples of central Europe, for freedom from Nazi domination brought a new and remorseless tyranny. If the first terrors were those of rape and pillage – it has been estimated that some two million German women were raped by Soviet troops – the second wave, brought by the NKVD in the wake of the advancing army, were those of political control and the elimination of dissent and these were to last for generations.

Even on the brink of defeat, the Reich could hurt its enemies as civilians in Britain and in allied-occupied Europe found when first the V-1 flying bombs, and then V-2 rockets, rained on them. The real damage, however, was being inflicted upon Germany as British and American bombers turned cities and towns into rubble. Hitler and the more fanatical Nazis seem to have taken a certain satisfaction in this devastation, for if *they* were doomed, it seemed fitting that, rather than survive them, the German people should perish with them. Of all the interpretations of Hitler, that which portrays him as a black romantic and perverted artist-turned-politician best suits him in the last months of the Reich; the man who had spent so much time pouring over plans for the great buildings and cities of the Reich of the future took a grim satisfaction in the destruction of the existing Germany.[8] The invasions of Germany by the Western allies and the Soviet Union were not co-ordinated. Marshal Zhukov's offensive was launched in January, and by the end of February, nearly all of Poland and much of Hungary had been overrun. In the south the Germans were forced back to Austria. Vienna fell on 11 April and the Soviet forces moved on to Prague. Two Soviet armies under the commands of Marshals Koniev and Zhukov made for Berlin.

The Anglo-American offensive was marked by disagreements between Montgomery and Eisenhower. The former wished to be given command of the bulk of the allied forces for a thrust across the Rhine north of the Ruhr; his plan was to cut the Ruhr off from the rest of Germany and then to drive on to Berlin. Eisenhower, refusing to allow political considerations to influence him, adopted a much more cautious plan involving two lines of attack across the Rhine and a more flexible approach aimed at the destruction, entrapment and surrender of German forces rather than the occupation of the maximum of territory. The Rhine still represented a formidable obstacle to the Anglo-American forces and the Rhineland campaign lasted from 8 February to late March. The American's were fortunate in finding a bridge at Remagen, near Bonn, that the Germans had not destroyed and crossed it on 7 March; to the south of Remagen, General Patton's army secured crossings on the 22 March; and Montgomery with his British and Canadian forces, the main force in the offensive, crossed on the 22 and 23 March. By early April the Americans had surrounded the Ruhr, trapping over 300 000 German troops; British tanks had broken through the German lines and Montgomery was making for the northern cities of Bremen and Hamburg; while US armies advanced east and south. On 23 April Patten's forces and Soviet forces met in Saxony. By 25 April the Allied advance was deep into Germany and had reached the Elbe in the north, the Mulde in the centre and the Danube in the south. Meanwhile on the Italian front, an offensive had opened on 9 April and by late April the allies were close to Venice and Milan.

The end of the war in Europe was now very close, but neither the President of the United States nor the two Axis leaders were to witness its final days. On 12 April Roosevelt, whose health had been deteriorating for some time, died while resting at a health resort and was succeeded by his Vice-President, Harry S. Truman. On 28 April Mussolini and his mistress, Claretta Petacci, were shot by partisans and their bodies strung up in a Milan square.[9] Two days later, having on 29 April married his mistress, Eva Braun, Hitler committed suicide along with her. Soviet troops were only 200 yards away. Germany's unconditional surrender followed on 9 May when – with due regard to the pride of the individual allied powers – three separate ceremonies took place as German delegations surrendered to Montgomery on Luneberg Heath, to Eisenhower near Reims and to Zhukov in Karlshorst. The German people paid a high price for their support for Hitler. The Reich had planned for the resettlement of others as part of its search for living space in the East, but in 1944 and 1945 columns of German refugees limped after the retreating German army while others desperately sought passage down the Baltic on overcrowded ships. As Eastern Europe moved west, Germans were expelled from their farms and homes in East Prussia, Poland and Czechoslovakia. They returned, if they were lucky enough to get there, to a Germany being systematically looted and, metaphorically as well as literally, raped by Soviet forces. Within what became occupied Germany there was a further rush westward as families sought the less harsh rule of the Western allies.

Only recently have historians described in full the horrors of the last months of the war, the attrition of the last battles on the road to Berlin, and the excesses of the Red Army.[10] Few in the victorious nations had in 1945 any sympathy with the suffering of the Germans who were seen as reaping the consequences of their own expansionism and brutality.

Victory Over Japan

Early in 1945 the Western allies had estimated that the war against Japan would last for another year and a half. This prospect, combined with the success of the Japanese against Chiang Kai Chek's forces in 1944, seemed to make Soviet entry into the war highly desirable and may well explain the degree to which Roosevelt was accommodating to Stalin at Yalta. Stalin had promised that the USSR would declare war against Japan as soon as Germany surrendered. Roosevelt was determined he should keep his promise because Soviet armies might be needed to defeat the large Japanese forces in Manchuria and China. The British, too, were keen on the Soviet Union joining in because they planned a campaign to reconquer Malaya, and Soviet intervention might divert Japanese troops from there to Manchuria. Stalin also promised to give support to Chiang Kai Chek's government. His price for intervention was the restoration of Russia's losses after the Russo-Japanese War in 1904–5, a recognition that Mongolia was to be a Russian satellite, and the Soviet Union's acquisition of the Kurile Islands from northern Japan.

Victory in the Far East was, however, to be much quicker than expected and by August 1945, when the Soviet Union did declare war – two days after the atomic bomb had been dropped on Hiroshima on 6 August – Soviet entry into the war no longer looked necessary or even desirable to the Western allies. By March 1945 most of the Philippines, including Manila, where the combined effect of house-to-house fighting and massacres by the Japanese had resulted in the deaths of 100,000 Filipino civilians, were in American hands, although Japanese forces continued to hold out in several parts of the islands. Nimitz's forces had also continued their progress towards Japan by taking the atoll, Iwo Jima, in what was, relative to the numbers involved, the most costly battle of the war for America with 2500 killed or wounded.

The taking of Iwo Jima further facilitated what had begun in the autumn of 1944 after the taking of the Marianas Islands, the bombing of mainland Japan from island bases. The 'Doolittle' raid of 1942, when land-based planes took off from carriers and landed in China, had been significant largely in demonstrating to the Japanese that the home islands could be attacked, while later bombing raids from bases in China had not inflicted a great deal of damage. From the Marianas the new heavy bombers, the B-29 Super Fortresses, were able, against inadequate air defences, to inflict terrible destruction on Japan's cities. From October 1944 onwards, Tokyo and other cities were regularly bombed; on 9–10 March the first incendiary attack on Tokyo took place and started a firestorm amongst the vulnerable, flimsy housing; and from April to the end of the war, an intensification of the bombing devastated Japan's cities. The Japanese population was already suffering dreadfully, and many came close to starvation as the allied blockade grew ever more effective and internal communications were disrupted by air-raids. Yet they endured and the war was not to be brought to an end by internal unrest.

In Burma the Fourteenth Army, made up of British and Indian Army divisions, drove southwards and crossed the Irrawaddy river in perhaps the most brilliant assault crossing of the war, while other British forces seized the port of Akyab. Racing on in anticipation of the imminent monsoon rains, the Fourteenth Army took Mandalay on 20 March and Rangoon fell on 3 May. The humiliations visited upon the British forces in Malaya and Singapore in 1942 are often highlighted; not so often remarked upon is the effectiveness of the defence of India and the success of the Burma campaign. Historians, aware of the post-war demise of the empire, have too often underestimated its cohesion and resilience during the war. The British Empire could, and did, strike back.

National and personal considerations played a part in the plans for Japan's defeat. The retaking of the Philippines was important to the Americans and especially to General MacArthur for symbolic rather than strategic reasons, while the British were for similar reasons set on an invasion of Malaya and a triumphant entry into Singapore. The Americans had little time for the planned Operation 'Zipper' an amphibious landing by British and Indian forces on the Malayan coast. Despite the opposition of the Anglophobe Admiral King, the British insisted that their Pacific Fleet was deployed at Okinawa.

On 1 April the Americans landed on Okinawa, which has been referred to as: 'the last stepping stone on what had been the long road to mainland Japan'.[11] The battle for Okinawa demonstrated that if Japanese resistance was now desperate, it was still formidable. There was no longer enough of an Imperial Navy to oppose the landing, but General Ushijima Mitsuru had over 100 000 men with which to defend the island, and a simple but sound strategy. He would not attempt to meet the invaders on the beaches, but would establish strong defensive positions inland, where naval guns would not assist the attackers; the Americans would be held in front of these positions and would be dependent on supplies from sea. As there were few naval forces to attack their supply ships and attendant warships, aircraft, especially *kamikaze* suicide bombers, flown from Kyushu would do the job of destroying the American ships and once the US troops were running short of supplies, the Japanese would counter-attack. The struggle for Okinawa, basically, consisted of three battles: a debilitating, slow and bloody advance by the American troops, in which every yard of land was defended to the death; the attacks by aircraft and *kamikaze* on the allied ships, in which the thicker decks of the Royal Navy aircraft carriers, which had come to reinforce the American fleet, proved more resilient than those of the US Navy carriers; and the final throw of the brave and professional Imperial Japanese Navy, which sent out to its doom the giant battleship, *Yamato*, supported only by a light cruiser and destroyers, and without air cover.

Okinawa is not a large island, yet fighting lasted nearly three months until late June. Japanese casualties were enormous (estimates vary between 50,000 and 100,000) and in addition to soldiers, tens of thousands of civilians died. Some 7000 Americans were killed, 32,000 wounded and there were a further 26,000 'non-battle' casualties, largely consisting of troops suffering from mental breakdown under the stress of battle.[12] This was seen as not a good precedent for an invasion of Japan itself for the home islands would be even more tenaciously defended, but the Okinawa casualty figures do underline the fact that the Japanese were reduced to throwing flesh against an enemy with an immense superiority in weaponry.

The Americans and British were planning three massive invasions, operations 'Olympic', 'Coronet' and 'Zipper'. Olympic, originally planned for September 1945, was the code for landings on the southern island of Kyushu, to be made by US troops, supported by British and American naval forces and bombers. Coronet, the invasion of the main island of Honshu, required a massive force of 25 divisions to be composed of US armies in the Pacific, US forces moved from Europe, and British and Commonwealth divisions. Zipper, intended for December 1945, was designed to take Singapore and to take place at the same time as Coronet. As the battle for Okinawa drew to an end, the dates for these invasions had already been put forward in the light of Japan's continued capacity for fierce resistance, and it was increasingly clear that all three were likely to result in huge allied casualties.

It was in these circumstances that the decision to use the new weapon that British and American scientists had been developing was taken. The atomic bomb promised to be a weapon many times more powerful than any existing munition. Since 1942 the Anglo-American team of scientists had been working together on the Manhatten Project, but it was not until July 1945 that a successful test was carried out in a New Mexico desert. The secrecy surrounding the development of the bomb is demonstrated by the fact that Vice-President Truman of the USA, knew nothing about it until his sudden elevation to the Presidency on Roosevelt's death in April 1945. It fell to Truman, however, to make the decision to use it against Japan.

Truman's decision to use the new weapon came after the Potsdam Declaration of 26 July, in which the American, British and Soviet leaders, meeting at the Potsdam Conference, called upon the Japanese to surrender. When the Declaration was dismissed by the Japanese, atomic bombs were dropped on Hiroshima and Nagasaki on 6 August and 9 August respectively. Whether the atomic bombs alone were decisive in forcing the Japanese surrender of 15 August is debateable, for the Soviet Union had declared war on 8 August and, on the same day as the bomb was dropped on Nagasaki, had launched a massive invasion of Manchuria which inflicted major defeats on the Japanese Army there.

Why were the bombs dropped? The answer of the American and British governments of the time, that they were dropped to end the war without an invasion of the home islands, which would have resulted in enormous American and British casualties, is still largely accepted by historians. There are, however, dissenting voices, who point to other means of ending the war – and reasons other than the avoidance of heavy casualties in an invasion of Japan for dropping the bombs.[13]

One argument is that a Japanese surrender could have been achieved without either an invasion or the use of the atomic bomb. A combination of the blockade of Japan and the continuation of 'conventional' bombing raids would have wrung a surrender from a Japanese cabinet that was already convinced that there was little alternative to surrender. Japan was largely cut off from necessary food supplies and raw materials by the destruction of her merchant marine and navy and the allies' control of the seas. The bombing raids, which had intensified since April, were already destroying Japanese cities and killing Japanese at an alarming rate. The Americans who had, in Europe, argued for the accurate bombing of economically important targets had, without much discussion, gone over to the blanket bombing of Japanese cities, and had been very efficient. One authority has reckoned that

> [T]he B-29s destroyed 40 per cent of Osaka and Nagoya; 50 per cent of Tokyo, Kobe and Yokohama; and 90 per cent of Aomori. At least 241 000 persons died, and 313 000 were injured in the raids against the homeland. Conventional bombing killed almost as many people as did the two atomic bombs in August.[14]

It can therefore be argued that a Japanese surrender would have come without the use of atomic bombs. The Japanese culture of collective decision making and the almost priestly position of the emperor made such a momentous decision as surrender difficult, but it would have come. If the Potsdam Declaration had modified unconditional surrender to provide for an explicit continuation of the emperor system it might have proved acceptable. As it was, even after Hiroshima and Nagasaki, unconditional surrender had to be fudged, when the allied response to the Japanese surrender offer of 10 August implicitly accepted the emperor's authority.

Other reasons for the dropping of the atomic bombs that have been suggested include: the influence of General Leslie R. Groves, director of the Manhatten Project, who wished the bombs to be dropped to justify the expense and prove the importance of the project; the aim of bringing the war to a speedy end in order to forestall Russian advances deep into China; and the desire, in the incipient Cold War that was developing, to impress upon the USSR the military strength of the USA. It had been a major mistake of the Western Allies to persuade the USSR to declare war on Japan, not that with tempting prizes available Stalin took much encouraging.

Many discussions, of what has seemed, in hindsight, a momentous decision, fail to take account of contemporary circumstances: neither Truman nor many of his military advisers thought of the bomb as anything but a very big bomb, rather than as a weapon with horrifying implications for the health of generations to come; nor do they take account of a public opinion in the USA and Britain, which thought that nothing was too bad to be visited upon the Japanese, especially as the horrifying evidence of the treatment by the Japanese of POWs and captured civilians was coming to light. Nevertheless, if it seems unlikely that the bombs were dropped primarily to impress Stalin and to avoid Soviet forces penetrating deep into China, there is strong evidence that these were at least ancillary motives. The oddity is that such motives should seem particularly extraordinary or suspect, either to those who attribute them or reject them. What is certain is that the nuclear bombing of Hiroshima and Nagasaki hastened the end of the war against Japan and that the speedy end of that war strengthened the US position in the Far East.

The British had for some time favoured the preservation of the Japanese emperor system, and by August 1945, the American government had reluctantly agreed that this was necessary. When the emperor's voice, only half-intelligible to most of his listeners because of his quaint, court-manner of speech, announced the need to surrender, it marked a temporary assumption of executive power by a semi-divine authority. The emperor's role also ensured that the surrender was legitimate and had to be accepted by all the Japanese people. If the surrender ceremony on the deck of the US battleship, *Missouri*, on 2 September made clear the defeat of Japanese militarism, the continued rule of the emperor enabled Japan to accept militarism as an aberration from, rather than the essence of, Japan's character. The Americans would occupy Japan and MacArthur be a Shogun for half a decade, setting Japan on the path to further westernisation, but there was to be a symbolic continuity with Japan's past.

Peace

Victory over Japan was a relief rather than a cause for great celebration. It marked the end of Japan's attempt to dominate the Far East and, for Britain and America, it brought peace after, respectively, six and three and a half years of war. Japan's defeat had, however, been long discounted and the burgeoning Cold War in Europe had already suggested that the Second World War had been no 'war to end war'. In the Far East there was unsettled business: the conflict between Kuomintang and communist parties in China; Soviet influence in North Korea; and whether the colonial powers would regain their Asian possessions.

Nevertheless, if war was not over, the World War was. The developing Cold War might threaten an even more dreadful global conflict, but in Europe there was peace, even if it was an uneasy peace and accompanied by hardship and austerity in the west, and a grim and gloomy authoritarian Communism to the east. It was an odd peace in that there were no great peace treaties. This was in part because the unconditional surrender of the Axis powers had left no authorities to sign a peace with, and in part because of the disintegration of the alliance of the victorious powers at the moment of victory. Peace treaties were signed between some of the belligerents within a few years, but there was never a proper settlement with Germany and the Japanese Peace Treaty of 1951 was not signed by the Soviet Union or China.

A feature of the post-1945 settlement, if settlement is not an inapposite term, was the brutal displacement of populations. Whereas in 1919 the attempt had been made to make frontiers coincide with ethnic or national divisions, the less civilised world of 1945 made peoples fit frontiers. In particular, millions of Germans were expelled from East Prussia, from the German territory ceded to Poland and from the Sudetenland, while there were parallel movements of Poles from the territory ceded to Russia into that gained from Germany. Eastern Europe moved west. The main decisions were made by the conference at Potsdam, 17 July to 2 August 1945. There the allied leaders decided that there should be an Inter-allied Council to co-ordinate the four occupied zones of Germany; Austria should be independent; France should be given Alsace-Lorraine, and Czechoslovakia the Sudetenland; and Poland's western frontier should be the Oder-Neisse line.

A novel feature in terms of ending a war was the decision by the victorious to make the defeated stand trial. The Nuremberg Trials revealed the full horror of the Nazi regime, its conduct of the war and its genocidal treatment of the Jews. It can be argued that they were a necessary means of bringing home to the German population the nature of the state they had fought for, and there was widespread support for the trials in Britain and America. However, Nuremberg administered what was, in the final analysis, a selective victor's justice. Its legal basis and its conduct look more suspect with the passage of time. The full panoply of justice, the exemplary procedure, the judges and the defence lawyers, even the fact that some defendants were found not guilty, did not disguise the fact that the victors provided the judges, prosecutors and hangmen. That the Soviet Union provided judges added a special irony. Andrei Vyshinsky, Stalin's chief prosecutor in the show trials of the thirties, exemplified the Soviet attitude with his toast, 'Death to the Defendants'.[15] Churchill's view that the leading Nazis should simply have been shot when captured was more honest than the elaborate trials and subsequent executions. It was not that most of those condemned at Nuremberg did not richly deserve their sentences, but rather that the selectivity of a trial that only considered war crimes by the defeated and ruled evidence as to allied conduct out of order, made Nuremberg more an arm of Allied policy than a court of international justice.

The cleanliness of the hands of even the Western allies was sullied by the forcible repatriation to the Soviet Union and Yugoslavia of soldiers, anti-communist partisans, and often their families, who had fought on the German side. The British in northern Italy and southern Austria were particularly zealous in thus sending to their deaths White Russians, Cossacks and Croatians. This was done as the result of agreements with the Soviet government, and of local arrangements between British and communist Yugoslavian commanders, by which each country was to get back its own nationals. The forcible repatriations by the British were comprehensible, if unforgivable, in the circumstances of the day: in May 1945 Stalin was a popular figure in Britain; there were several thousand British prisoners of war who were in Russian hands, having been liberated by the Soviet army; and the Western allies were concerned to keep on reasonable terms with Stalin, who could restrain or encourage attempted coups by communist resistance movements.

Horrible as these enforced repatriations were, they were just one of the many horrors of the last months of the war and of the immediate aftermath of peace. The Soviet Army exacted a terrible revenge on the civilian populations of enemy nations. Resistance movements vied with each other for power and position, and exacted their revenge on collaborators. In Yugoslavia Tito's communist partisans, who had received assistance from the British, were in an unassailable position and mopped up royalist partisans, while Greece erupted into full-scale civil war with the British supporting the royalists against the communists. In those countries 'liberated' by the Soviet Army, the process of destroying opponents of client regimes was under way. In Poland and the Baltic states anti-communist resistance would continue till the end of the decade. Populations had been on the move in much of Europe since 1939. The Nazi 'New Order' had seen an ambitious and ruthless attempt to change the ethnic map of Europe with the expulsion of Czechs, Poles and Slovenes from lands incorporated into Germany. Great movements of population within the Soviet Union had also been taking place, as the populations of the Baltic states were removed by successive waves of deportations that would continue after the war, and Volga Germans, Circassians, Chechens and many other peoples were uprooted from their homelands. Soviet victories reversed the movements instituted by the Nazis, and in late 1945, much of western Europe swarmed with refugees pushed eastwards by the Soviet advance, expelled with the revision of frontiers, marooned after being used as forced labour by the Germans, or just washed up by the tide of war. It has been estimated that the war resulted in the movement of some 25 million people in Europe; not even good guesstimates are available for the great population movements in the Far East.

An estimate for deaths due to the war is that the global figure probably reached 60 million, with civilian far exceeding military casualties.[16] The combined figure for civilians and military killed in the Soviet Union was almost certainly around 25 million, but many millions more were killed during deportations, by executions at the hands of the Soviet authorities, during imprisonment in the Gulag,[17] and while repatriates and inhabitants of territory that had been occupied by the Germans were undergoing post-war screening.[18] China may have lost 15 million. The death toll of the Axis powers was: 2 million Japanese, 4 million Germans and 400,000 Italians. The USA lost 300,000 military personnel, while Britain suffered about 250,000 military and 150,000 civilian deaths. The ferocity of the war in Yugoslavia is testified to by the death toll of 1.5 million. The number of Jews killed in the Holocaust is variously estimated as being between 4 and 6 million.

Everywhere that fighting had raged and bombs had been dropped exhibited holes in the physical fabric. Whole cities seemed to have been destroyed. If atomic bombs had done this most completely at Hiroshima and Nagasaki, incendiaries and high explosives had done a thorough job at Dresden, Hamburg and Tokyo, while towns which were fought over, like Stalingrad, Manila, Warsaw and Berlin, had also been almost completely destroyed. Central Europe was particularly affected for there the Germans had battled for every mile, but every part of Europe where there had been fighting exhibited its wounds: Poland and Russia, Yugoslavia, and Greece, Italy and northern France, Belgium, Holland, Germany, Austria, Hungary and Czechoslovakia. Britain might have seen no land battles, but air-raids had done damage enough. That many in Europe wondered whether reconstruction in some areas was possible is illustrated by the case of Berlin:

> Ninety-five per cent of its urban area lay in ruins. There were 3000 broken water mains ... 149 of the city's schools had been demolished, and not one of its 187 Evangelical Churches was untouched. In the streets were over 400 million cubic metres of rubble; one estimate reckoned that if 10 trains a day with 50 wagons each were used to remove it, the process would take 16 years.[19]

The physical and economic recovery of Europe was to be quicker than most expected and that of western Europe was to be spectacular, but the immediate post-war years were to be austere and the outlook bleak. As the Grand Alliance against Germany dissolved, two new mutually hostile alliance systems emerged as the lines where the Soviet Army and the Western armies met became the demarcation lines of the Cold War.

As part of his last desperate campaign to persuade the Germans to keep fighting, Goebbels had warned in March 1945 that the Soviets would occupy the whole of eastern and South-eastern Europe, plus the largest part of the Reich, and that in front of these territories, 'an iron curtain would come down'.[20] Churchill too would use this analogy, most notably in his speech at Fulton, Missouri, in 1946 when he talked of the iron curtain that had descended across the continent 'from Stettin in the Baltic, to Trieste in the Adriatic'. As Chamberlain had feared, war would overturn the old order. Perhaps, however, ice is a better analogy than iron. If Hitler had indeed been Stalin's 'icebreaker', the ice had refrozen with Soviet power deep in central Europe and western Europe's security was dependent upon the USA. The Cold War also petrified interpretations of the Second World War, leaving a frozen perspective of 'winners' history which saw the origins of the war and its early stages forgotten for several decades.

Conclusion

The Cold War provided a structure, lasting for nearly half a century, within which major developments, the end of colonialism, the creation of the European Union, and even the emergence of the Pacific economies, were opposed or supported, accommodated, articulated and interpreted. To a considerable degree it also imposed a perspective upon the great conflict which preceded it. Most obviously, because it seemed to make ideology the key to the present, the Cold War perspective emphasised the ideological dimension of the Second World War, conceiving of it as a clash of ideologies. Thus the concept of a war against fascism, rather than of a war between states wedded to different ideologies and systems, was influential. The fact that none of the allies had, in fact, gone to war to crusade against fascism was not allowed to interfere with what was, essentially, a convenient fiction.

The effect of the fiction was to gloss over the real reasons why the allies had found themselves engaged in a common struggle and to limit analysis of the early years of the war. There was room for debate as to where the responsibility for allowing Nazi Germany to embark on its campaign for world domination lay, who had been most consistent in opposition to Germany, and who had been most culpable in the search for advantage, which had resulted in the break up of the alliance and the beginning of the Cold War, but little recognition of the fluidity of the positions adopted by the powers before and during the early years of the war. Appeasement of Germany by France and Britain was seen as, at worst, a failure of nerve or a culpable misreading of Hitler's intentions and, at best, as a means of buying time for rearmament. Stalin's agreement with Hitler in 1939 was viewed with some indulgence as an understandable expedient, with much of the blame for the Nazi-Soviet Pact being placed on Britain's and France's reluctance to embrace an alliance with the Soviet Union. Even the ideological dimension was skewed by the need to justify the post-June 1941 line up, so that the triangular nature of the conflicting ambitions of the democracies, the Soviet Union and the Third Reich, which had been the salient characteristic of power relations before *Barbarossa*, was modified to emphasise the common interests of two sides of the triangle, the democracies and the Soviet Union. The eventual pattern of a grand alliance against Hitler was seen as merely awaiting birth.

Paradoxically, the effect of the Cold War, which polarised interpretations of the post-war world, was to perpetuate a largely consensual 'allied' interpretation of the Second World War. Even at the height of the Cold War, the memory of the alliance against Hitler continued to inform historical accounts by most Western historians. What the alliance had been against rather than what it had been for set the agenda, while the corollary was that the pattern of post-1941 was accepted as inevitable rather than a continuation of the changing and fluid power relations that had marked the early years of the war. If the coming of the Cold War and the future enmity of the partners in the great alliance lay as a contrapuntal theme across accounts of the final years of the war and the eventual victory of the allies, yet still the very facts of the alliance and its victory tended to privilege the Soviet Union. The Soviet Union had not only been essential to allied victory, but it had been adulated as a gallant ally and, therefore, it could never be equated with Nazi Germany. Its sins and ambitions were glossed over, and not only by communists and fellow travellers. Even works which demonstrated the true nature of the Soviet regime – and the great number of its own citizens who perished under it – were rarely integrated into accounts of the war.

The memory of the alliance correspondingly diminished and devalued not only those peoples and states who had fought on Germany's side for their own specific reasons (Ukrainians, Cossacks and Estonians; Romanians, Hungarians and Finns), but also those who had fought on the allied side yet been as anti-Soviet as they were anti-Nazi, such as royalist Yugoslavs and patriotic Poles. The peoples of eastern central Europe had not so much been fighting for either 'side' as pursuing their own ambitions. The defeat of Russia and then of Germany in 1918 had given them an opportunity to free themselves from empires, establish states, further their national ambitions and trample on the national ambitions of their neighbours. From 1921 to 1938 an uneasy and uncertain order had pertained. The *Anschluss* inaugurated a period in which, alongside the rivalries of great powers and under their feet, the competing nationalisms of eastern central Europe had to support, or be destroyed by, Germany and at the same time attempt to pursue their own interests. The leader of the Yugoslavian royalists, General Milhailovic, spoke for many when, at his farce of a trial, he said he had been caught up in the 'gale of the world'. The ideological perspective imposed by the Cold War tended to downgrade the importance of nationalism, arguably a more potent and more resilient focus of loyalty than socialism, liberalism or any other 'ism' of the modern world. Now, when the map of eastern Europe after the implosion of the Soviet Union more resembles that of the wake of Brest-Litovsk than that of 1989, when General Vlasov, who fought with Hitler, is regarded as a hero in his native Ukraine, and when old sores and ambitions have torn apart the former Yugoslavia, the role of nationalism in the Second World War can be better appreciated.

The European perspective on the war was much influenced by the way in which the context of Cold War Europe seemed immutable. The geopolitical divide between East and West remained, set largely by where the allied armies had met in 1945; the opposing hegemonies of two super-powers armed with nuclear weapons seemed to make changes to that map impossible; while few, not even many Germans, conceived that a reunited Germany was a possibility. If it seems astonishing now to remember that, just over 30 years ago, the end of the Second World War in Europe and the Cold War which succeeded it were jointly incarnate in a divided Berlin garrisoned by troops of the victorious powers, it was difficult then to imagine the dissolution of a structure which had lasted for over 40 years.

Among the effects of this perspective were: a tendency for historical enquiry to centre almost obsessively on the nature of Hitler's ambitions and of the Nazi state; a corresponding tendency to underplay the ambitions and interests of the other great powers; a distaste for interpretations of the war which emphasised the long-term historical context and geography, or conceived of the powers as acting within the tradition of their national ambitions; a general underestimation of nationalism rather than ideology as a motive force; and a dismissal of the importance of the roles of the peoples and states of east and central Europe. The divide between eastern and western Europe, with central Europe disappearing as a cultural and political concept, subconsciously destroyed major dimensions of the war as memory, while the growth of the European Union, necessarily a purely western European development, was accompanied by selective amnesia as to the history of Hitler's Europe.

If, in eastern Europe, there was essentially only one structure of power, since Soviet power was dominant economically, politically and militarily, in western Europe there were two. Firstly, the NATO Alliance defended the West – keeping the USA physically present and providing Britain with the major secondary role, with France as semi-detached – resembling the western half of the alliance at the end of the war. Secondly, the EEC, soon to become the European Union, provided a parallel power system dominated by the German Federal Republic and France, with Britain loosely and reluctantly attached. Protected militarily by the Anglo-Saxon powers and locked in a strong French embrace within the EEC, one half of the state which had been defeated in 1945 had become the most powerful economic entity in Europe. In its combination of first-class status as an economic power and its negligible military strength, West Germany resembled its old ally, Japan. The events of 1989 and 1990, which resulted in German unification, caused consternation in both London and Paris, raising once more the problem which had troubled Europe since 1871, the predominant power of Germany.

The perspective from the Far East was less ossified for, if the Cold War provided an ideological and geopolitical framework for developments in south and east Asia, there were major developments and new wars. The Second World War had to be looked at retrospectively, from beyond the victory of Communism in China, the Korean War, post-colonial nationalisms, the Vietnam War and the remarkable emergence of Japan as a first-class economic power. The Second World War could be integrated into the longer history of the region and could lose its unique and privileged position.

Europe, or at least western Europe, had achieved a certain comfort in the limitations of its present and the accompanying limitations on considerations of its past consequent upon the Cold War. Few, perhaps least of all Western experts on eastern Europe, had realised the weakness of the Soviet empire behind the facade and had foreseen its dissolution. The myth of two super-powers, where one could provide a modern economy with a high standard of living for its citizens *and* military might, and the other was, essentially, a third-world economy and society with military might, was exposed with brutal suddenness, leaving Europeans flabbergasted rather than euphoric. Rather than the end of history, problems and ambitions quiescent for nearly half a century came flooding back.

It is not just the post-Cold War perspective that, despite the tens of thousands of books on aspects of the subject, makes the interpretation of the Second World War more pertinent and relevant than ever. Old men talk rather than forget, Western archive material survives time-limited embargoes, and new regimes in the East release long-concealed papers. Skeletons tumble out of cupboards: Soviet skeletons giving greater details of the Molotov-Ribbentrop Pact or of peace overtures between the Soviet Union and Germany after 1941; French skeletons confirming the popularity of Vichy, French complicity in the export of Jews to their death, and the degree of continuity between Vichy and post-war France; Britain's dark secret, the repatriation of the Cossacks; and even the dealings of the banks of neutral Switzerland with the Nazi regime. In 2010 Russia released the collective death warrant for the Polish officers who perished at Katyn, complete with Stalin's signature.

It is, however, the end of the Cold War perspective which, above all, enables us to reconsider the Second World War and see it – for all its horrors and monsters, and without denying the effects of great or malign individuals – in a more long-term context: that of the persistent rivalries of peoples and states, of balances of power, the rise and fall of great powers, the opportunism of minor powers, and the static structure of geography. We no longer live in a post-war world and yet the comforting certainties that, in the 1990s, seemed to have succeeded it have proved illusory. Churchill's glorious account of the Second World War is defunct, and so is the immediate post-Cold War perspective that saw a world eventually made safe for liberal democracy and the free market under the beneficent hegemony of the United States, a deferred fulfilment of the Woodrow Wilson-Roosevelt scenario. If it is unlikely that that there will be successor theses, so tidy and compelling, the importance of the war, both in history and as formative of the contemporary world, will ensure new, if less elevated, competing narratives.

Notes

Introduction

1. Norman Davies, *Europe At War* (2006), p. 2.
2. Cato, *Guilty Men* (1940), a polemical attack on Chamberlain and Baldwin by three journalists, Michael Foot, Frank Owen and Peter Howard, writing anonymously as Cato.

Chapter 1: The Origins of the Second World War

1. David Reynolds, *In Command of History: Churchill Fighting and Writing the Second World War* (2004).
2. See F. Fischer, *Germany's Aims in the First World War* (1967), p. 7.
3. Analogous to the war of 1618–48.
4. See P. M. H. Bell, *The Origins of the Second World War in Europe* (1967); and Michael Howard, 'A Thirty Years War? The Two World Wars in Historical Perspective', *Transactions of the Royal Historical Society*, 6th ser. (1991).
5. A. Lentin, *Lloyd George, Woodrow Wilson and the Guilt of Germany* (1986), p. 132.
6. Adam Tooze, *The Wages of Destruction: The Making & Breaking of the Nazi Economy* (2006), p. 660.
7. See V. Suvorov, *The Icebreaker* (1972).
8. Norman Stone, *Europe Transformed 1878–1919* (1983).
9. Bell, op. cit., p. 66.
10. F. Fischer, *From Kaiserreich to Third Reich* (1986), p. 84.
11. E. Eyck, *A History of the Weimar Republic*, vol. 2 (1967), p. 25.
12. See, for instance, K. Hildebrand, *The Foreign Policy of the Third Reich* (1973).
13. Adam Tooze, *The Wages of Destruction: The Making and Breaking of the Nazi Economy* (2006).
14. M. Brozart, *The Hitler State: The Foundation and Development of the Internal Structure of the Third Reich* (1981); and H. Mommsen, 'National Socialism: Continuity and Change' in *Fascism* (ed.) W. Laqueur (1976).

15. See T. Mason, 'Labour in the Third Reich 1933–39', *Past and Present*, Vol. 33 (1966).
16. B. H. Klein, *Germany's Economic Preparations for War* (1959).
17. This view has been argued persuasively by R. J. Overy in 'Hitler's War and the German Economy: A Reinterpretation', *Economic History*, 2nd ser., vol. 35 (1982) and in his *The Road to War* (1989).
18. Two divergent views of Chamberlain's policies are provided by John Charmley, *Chamberlain and the Lost Peace* (1984) and, who sees his policies as rational and realistic, R. A. C. Parker, *Chamberlain and Appeasement* (1993), who considers they stifled serious chances of preventing the Second World War.
19. See Richard Overy, *1939: Countdown to War* (2009).

Chapter 2: A European War

1. Lord Alanbrooke, *War Diaries 1939–45*, eds. A. Danchev and D. Todman (1992), pp. 10–11.
2. H. R. Kedward, *Occupied France, Collaboration and Resistance 1940–1944* (1985), p. 18.
3. John Charmley's *Churchill: The End of Glory* (1993) is the best-known example of this.
4. Ibid., pp. 401–6 and 423–4.
5. Colin Smith, *England's Last War Against France: Fighting Vichy 1940–1942* (2009).
6. Some 42,000 civilians were killed and 50,000 seriously wounded by German bombing in the course of the war. See R. A. C. Parker, *Struggle for Survival* (1989), p. 52.
7. Tom Harrison, *Living Through the Blitz* (1976), p. 15.
8. Peter Myers and Malcolm Smith, *Cinema, Literature and Society* (1987), p. 234.
9. See Keith Jefferies, *The History of the Secret Intelligence Service 1909–1949* (2010).
10. See Andrew Roberts, *Masters and Commanders* (2008), p. 273.
11. Gerhard L. Weinberg, *A World at Arms* (1994), p. 158.
12. See, for instance, H. W. Koch, 'Hitler's "Programme" and the Genesis of Operation *Barbarossa*', in *Aspects of the Third Reich* ed. H. W. Koch (1985).
13. Quoted in H.W. Koch in 'Hitler's "Programme"'.
14. See Wolfgang Michalka, 'From the Anti-Comintern Pact to the Euro-Asiatic Bloc: Ribbentrop's Alternative Concept of Hitler's Foreign Policy Programme' in *Aspects of the Third Reich*, op. cit.
15. Quoted in Alan Bullock, *Hitler and Stalin: Parallel Lives* (1991) p. 767.
16. Koch, 'Hitler's "Programme"', p. 321.
17. See Adam Tooze, *The Wages of Destruction* (2006)

18. Tooze, Ibid.
19. Ian Kershaw, *Hitler 1936–45: Nemesis* (2000), p. 388.
20. Sheila Lawlor, *Churchill and the Politics of War 1940–41* (1994), p. 256.
21. Viktor Suvarov, *Icebreaker: Who started the Second World War?* (1990). See also, Edward Razinski, *Stalin* (1996).
22. H. W. Kovh has summarized Suvorov's evidence in 'Operation *Barbarossa* – the current state of the debate', *The Historical Journal*, vol. 3, no. 2 (1988).
23. Two defences of the established view are Gabriel Gorodetsky, *The Grand Delusion* (1999) and David Glantz, *Stumbling Colossus* (1998).
24. Quoted in Bullock, p. 786.
25. Tooze, *The Wages of Destruction*, pp. 454–5.
26. Radzinski, p. 454.
27. Norman Stone, *Hitler* (1980), p. 112.
28. Adam Tooze, *The Wages of Destruction*, p. 488.

Chapter 3:   A World War?

1. See Saki Dockrill, 'Introduction: ' One step Forward – A Reappraisal of the Pacific War' in *From Pearl Harbor to Hiroshima: The Second World War in the Pacific, 1941–45*, ed., Saki Dockrill (1994).
2. See Evan Mawdsley, *World War II: A New History* (2009).
3. Norman Davies, *Europe At War 1939–1945*, op. cit. p. 16.
4. For opposing views on Hirohito's role see Herbert P. Bix, *Hirohito and the Making of Modern Japan* (2000), which argues for the Emperor's culpability, and Stephen Large, *Emperor Hirohito and Showa Japan* (2005), which sees the Emperor as distant from decision making.
5. See W. G. Beasley, *The Rise of Modern Japan. Political and Economic Change Since 1850* (1990), Ch. 2.
6. The modern method expressing Chinese names in English makes the name Jiang Jieshi but it is as Chiang Kai Chek that he remains best known in the English-speaking world.
7. Ian Nish, 'Anglo-Japanese Alienation Revisited', in *From Pearl Harbor to Hiroshima*, op. cit., pp. 11–23.
8. Kosmas Tsokhas, 'Dedominionisation: The Anglo-Australian experience, 1939–1945', *The Historical Journal*, vol. 37, no. 4 (1994).
9. See John Chapman, 'The Imperial Japanese Navy and the North-South Dilemma', in *Barbarossa*, ed. John Erikson and David Dilkes (1994).
10. Quoted in Gerhard L. Weinberg, *A World at Arms* (1994), p. 260.
11. See Robert B. Stennett, *Day of Deceit* (1999).
12. Ikuhito Hata, 'Admiral Yamamoto and the Japanese Navy', in *From Pearl Harbor to Hiroshima*, p. 65.
13. Churchill, *The Second World War*, vol. iv, p. 344.

Chapter 4: Behind the Lines

1. R. A. C, Parker, *Struggle for Survival* (1989), p. 86.
2. Richard Overy, *Why the Allies Won* (1995).
3. Paul Kennedy, *The Rise and Fall of Great Powers* (1986), pp. 353–4. Brackets signify production figures for countries not yet in the war.
4. Overy, *Why the Allies Won*, pp. 193–7.
5. Kennedy, p. 355.
6. Norman Davies, *Europe At War, 1939–1945*, p. 216.
7. J. M. Roberts, *Europe 1880–1945* (1974), p. 527.
8. Correlli Barnet, *The Audit of War; The Illusions and Reality of Britain as a Great Nation* (1986).
9. Figures taken from Kennedy, pp. 357–8.
10. Richard Overy, 'Great Britain: Cyclops' in *Allies at War*, eds D. Reynolds, W. F. Kimball and A. O. Chubarian (1994), p. 134.
11. Overy, 'Cyclops', p. 198.
12. William Carr, *A History of Germany 1815–1945* (1969), p. 388.
13. Toby Abse, 'Italy', *The Civilians in War*, ed. Jeremy Noakes (1992), p. 107.
14. Max Hastings, *Nemesis*, p. 37.
15. Kennedy, p. 352.
16. Overy, 'Cyclops', p. 201.
17. John W. M. Chapman, 'From Allies to Antagonists' in *The History of Anglo-Japanese Relations 1600–2000*, vol. III, *The Military Dimension*, eds, Ian Gow and Yoichi Hirama (2003), pp. 160–1. See also Eiji Seki, *Mrs Gerguson's Tea-Set, Japan and the Second World War* (2007).
18. Draft memorandum by von Renthe-Fink of the German Foreign Ministry, 1939. Quoted in John Laughland, *The Tainted Source: The Undemocratic Origins of the European Idea* (1997), p. 35.
19. Norman Stone, *Hitler* (1980), p. 124.
20. Norman Davies, *Europe. A History* (1996), p. 1015.
21. John Keegan, *The Battle for History: Refighting World War II* (1995), p. 108.
22. See E. Nolte, 'Between Myth and Revisionism', in *Aspects of the Third Reich*, ed. H.W, Koch, p. 405.
23. M. Broszat, 'Hitler and the genesis of the Final Solution', in *Aspects*, Ibid., p. 405.
24. Adam Tooze, *The Wages of Destruction: The Making and the Breaking of the Nazi Economy* (2006).
25. Davies, *Europe At War*, p. 166.
26. David Irving, *Hitler's War* (1977).
27. See D. J. Goldhagen, *Hitler's Willing Executioners: Ordinary Germans and the Holocaust* (1996).
28. S. Friedlander, *Nazi Germany and the Jews: The Years of Persecution 1933–39* (1997).

29. Crimes perpetrated by Asians on Westerners are, however, in a different category and in post-war Britain the revolting treatment of British POWs by the Japanese was felt more keenly than the fate of the Jews in Europe.
30. Arthur Marwick, *War and Social Change in the Twentieth Century* (1974) and *Total War and Social Change* (1988).
31. Harold Perkins, *The Origins of Modern English Society* (1972).
32. For the role of monarchies in the war, see A. W. Purdue, *Long to Reign? The Survival of Monarchies in the Modern World* (2005), Chapter 9.
33. Joan Bright Astley, *The Inner Circle: A View of War at the Top* (1971), p. 28.
34. See Paul Addison, *The Road to 1945* (1975).
35. Cato, *The Guilty Men* (1940).
36. See for instance, Angus Calder, *The People's War: Britain 1945–1946* (1971).
37. Andrew Thorpe, 'Britain' in *The Civilian in War* (1992), ed. Jeremy Noakes, p. 32.
38. By the end of the war there were estimated to be about 7 million foreign workers: 5 million civilians, and 2 million prisoners of war.
39. The question of the employment of women in Germany has been the subject of much debate. See Mark Roseman, 'World War II and social change in Germany', in *Total War and Social Change*, ed. Arthur Marwick (1988) for the view that the Nazis were reluctant to employ women in war work; and Richard Overy, 'Hitler's War and the German economy. A reinterpretation', *Economic History Review*, 2nd series, vol. 35, no. 2, for a contradiction of this.
40. Mark Harrison, 'The Soviet Union', in *The Civilian at War*, p. 69.

Chapter 5: Roads to Victory 1943–4

1. Norman Stone, *Hitler* (1980), p. 153.
2. Robert Spector, 'American seizure of Japan's Strategic Points' in *From Pearl Harbor to Hiroshima*, p. 79. See also Richard B. Frank, *Guadalcanal* (1990).
3. Weinberg, p. 347.
4. Max Hastings, *Nemesis. The Battle for Japan, 1944–45* (2007), p. 5.
5. Norman Davies, *Europe at War*, pp. 20–1.
6. See Andrew Roberts, *Masters and Commanders* (2008).
7. The British seem to have been more purist than the Americans about not talking to the Germans, even to dissident factions. Churchill banned all embassies in neutral countries from contact with the enemy, but the German diplomat Rheinhard Spitzy talked to the American representative, Allen Dulles, at Berne in the Spring of 1944. See Rheinhard Spitzy, *How We Squandered the Reich* (1997).
8. See Weinberg op. cit., p. 610.
9. Richard Overy, *Why the Allies Won*, p. 32.

10. Ibid., p. 46.
11. J. Costello and T. Hughes, *Battle of the Atlantic* (1977), p. 304.
12. R. A. C. Parker, *Struggle for Survival* (1989), p. 112.
13. Alan Bullock, *Hitler and Stalin* (1993), p. 60.
14. Weinberg, p. 457.
15. Overy, p. 87.
16. Alan Clark, *Barbarossa: The Russian-German Conflict* (1965), p. 312.
17. David French, 'Warfare and National Defence' in *A Companion to Modern European History 1871–1945* (1997), p. 69.
18. Overy, p. 129.
19. John Keegan, *The Second World War* ((1989), p. 407.
20. See Richard B. Frank, *Guadalcanal* (1990) for an account of the battle and an assessment of its significance.
21. Weinberg, p. 345.
22. Mountbatten remains a highly controversial figure. See Philip Ziegler (1985) and Andrew Roberts, 'Lord Mountbatten and the Perils of Adrenalin' in *Eminent Churchillians* (1994).
23. Max Hastings, *Nemesis* (2007) estimates American losses in the Pacific War at about 103,000 killed, while about 30,000 British servicemen perished. The US army alone suffered some 143,000 deaths in Europe and North Africa while 235,000 British servicemen died fighting the Germans.

Chapter 6:   Unconditional Surrender

1. Norman Davies, *Europe: A History*, p. 1028.
2. The Western leaders failed to put any pressure on Stalin on behalf of their Polish ally. Churchill did suggest to Roosevelt that if Stalin did not allow the Poles to be supplied via Soviet air-bases they should threaten 'drastic action' but the American President did not want to upset Stalin. Norman Davies is a notable exception to the tendency of historians to play down the iniquity of the Soviet role.
3. Adam Zamoyski, *The Polish Way* (1987), p. 371.
4. See Sheila Lawlor, *Churchill and the Politics of War, 1940–41* (1994) for an account of how British policy first became preoccupied with retaining influence in Greece.
5. Norman Davies, *God's Playground. A History of Poland* (1981), p. 15.
6. Quoted in Andrew Roberts, *Masters and Commanders* (2008), p. 556.
7. Michael Dockrill, *The Cold War 1945–1963* 1988), p. 22.
8. See J.P. Stern, *Hitler. The Fuhrer and the People* (1975).
9. Mussolini's death was convenient for the Italians, who feared that a trial by the Western Allies would be as much a divisive investigation into Italy's recent past as a trial of the *Duce*. It has also been suggested that it was convenient for Britain in view of an alleged correspondence between Churchill and Mussolini.

10. Anthony Beevor, *Berlin: The Downfall 1945* (2002) is an outstanding account of the last days of the Third Reich.
11. Charles Messenger, *The Century of Warfare; Worldwide Conflict from 1900 to the Present Day* (1995), p. 256.
12. R. A. C. Parker, *Struggle for Survival* (1989), p. 232. Such figures do seem to be subject to quite large disagreements. Mark A. Sloler gives a figure of 12,500 US deaths on Okinawa in, 'The United States: the Global Strategy' in *Allies At War*, ed., D. Reynolds, W. F. Kimball and A. O. Chubarian (1994).
13. See G. Alperovitz, *The Decision to use the Atomic Bomb* (1995); and R.J. Lifton and G. Mitchell, *Hiroshima in America: 50 Years of Denial* (1995).
14. A. Coox, *Cambridge History of Japan*, vol. vi, The Twentieth Century, ed. P. Duus, p. 369.
15. Norman Davies, *Europe*, p. 1055.
16. Weinberg, p. 894.
17. Anne Applebaum, *Gulag: A History of the Soviet Camps* (2003) exposes the nature of the Soviet concentration camps and their affinities with their Nazi counterparts.
18. Davies, *Europe*, p. 1529.
19. R. Mayne, *The Recovery of Europe: From Devastation to Unity* (1970), p. 30.
20. Goebbels in an article in *Das Reich*, quoted in *H. Thomas, Armed Truce: The Beginnings of the Cold War 1945–6* (1986), p. 699.

Annotated Bibliography

The literature on the Second World War is vast and ranges from the broadest outlines of events to the most detailed analyses of particular battles. What follows is a guide to further reading in published secondary sources in English rather than an attempt at a comprehensive bibliography. Readers concerned to pursue in depth specific aspects or features of the war, its causes, campaigns, the war aims and internal politics of the combatants, or the many biographies of leaders and generals, will find that the books listed here have their own bibliographies and that these will lead them to further books and articles, to sources in languages other than English and indeed to archival primary material.

History of the war

Gerhard L. Weinberg, *A World at Arms* (Cambridge 1994) is probably the best one-volume history of the war. In more than a thousand pages, it combines a global perspective with detailed accounts of each theatre of the war. R. A. C. Parker, *Struggle for Survival. The History of the Second World* War (Oxford 1989) is more compact, but still comprehensive as are Evan Mawdsley, *World War II* (2009) and Spencer C. Tucker, *The Second World War* (2004).

Martin Gilbert, *Second World War* (London 1989) also provides a full and authoritative, if conservative, account of the war. An accessible military history of the whole war is provided by John Keegan, *The Second World War* (London 1989). Paul Kennedy, *The Rise and Fall of the Great Powers* (London 1988) puts the war in the long-term context of great power ambitions and fears. Norman Davies, *Europe A History* (New York 1996) is recommended to those who wish to consider the war in the light of Europe's conflicts over the centuries and his *Europe At War 1939–1945* (2007) is a stimulating critique of traditional interpretations of the war in Europe.

War atlases and Dictionaries

The Times Atlas of the Second World War (London 1989) is an invaluable guide to the course of the war in all theatres: while David Smurthwaite, *The Pacific War Atlas 1941–1945* (London 1945) and John Man, *The Penguin Atlas of D-Day and the Normandy Campaign* (London 1994) illuminate these crucial campaigns. Stephen Pope and Elizabeth-Anne Wheal, *Dictionary of the Second World War* (1997) is a useful and reliable reference work.

Origins of the war

For the origins of the war, Sir Winston Churchill's *The Second World War, vol. 1, The Gathering Storm* (London 1948) remains an essential starting point. Like the other volumes in the series it should be read in conjunction with David Reynolds, *In Command of History: Churchill Fighting and Writing The Second World War* (2005). A. J. P. Taylor's *The Origins of the Second World War* (London 1961) has been massively influential though it remains controversial. For the Versailles Settlement, A. Lentin, *Lloyd George, Woodrow Wilson and the Guilt of Germany* (1986) and Alan Sharp, *The Versailles Settlement. Peacemaking in Paris 1919* (2008) are incisive studies. Two books which provide both detailed analyses of the war's origins and influential interpretations are: P. M. H. Bell, *The Origins of the Second World War* (London 1986); and Richard Overy with Andrew Wheatcroft, *The Road to War* (London 1989). There are many good brief guides, but R. J. Overy, *The Origins of the Second World War* (London 1987) is one of the best.

Hitler and the Third Reich

The aims and ambitions of Adolf Hitler, and the nature of the Third Reich and National Socialism, remain central to the question of responsibility for the war and for its development. Few subjects have attracted so many historians and the historiography is best initially approached via 'seminars in' or 'introductions to' studies which summarise the historiography and debates. John Laver, *Hitler. Germany's Fate or Germany's Misfortune* (London 1995); and D. G. Williamson, *The Third Reich* (New York 1995) are both useful. Two books by K. Hildebrand, *The Foreign Policy of the Third Reich* (London 1973), and *The Third Reich* (London 1984) provide valuable interpretations of the aims and ambitions of Nazi Germany from an 'instrumentalist' viewpoint; while Martin Brozart, *The Hitler State. The Foundation and Development of the Internal Structure of the Third Reich* (London 1981) takes the 'structuralist' view. I. Kershaw, *The Nazi Dictatorship* (London 1985) provides a balanced analysis of the nature of Nazi Germany. The revisionist essays in H. W. Koch (ed.), *Aspects of the Third Reich* (London 1985) set out to 'de-demonise' Hitler. Ian Kershaw's *Hitler 1889–1936: Hubris* (1998) and *Hitler 1936–1945: Nemesis* (2000) constitute the best biography of Hitler. Adam Tooze, *The Wages of Destruction: The Making and Breaking of Nazi Germany* (2006), challenges many traditional views with the argument that Germany's economy was fatally weak.

British foreign policy

On British foreign policy: Martin Gilbert, *Roots of Appeasement* (London 1966) sets out the classic Churchillian case against British 'Appeasement'; which Maurice Cowling, *The Impact of Hitler* (Cambridge 1975) does much to modify; while John Charmley, *Chamberlain and the Lost Peace* (London 1989) rehabilitates Chamberlain and his policies. R. A. C. Parker, *Chamberlain and Appeasement. British Policy and the Coming of the Second World War* (London 1993) provides a sophisticated defence of the anti-Appeasement case.

French and Italian foreign policy

For France: A. P. Adamthwaite, *France and the Coming of the Second World War* (London 1977); and R. J. Young, *In Command of France: French Foreign Policy and Military Planning 1933–40* (Cambridge, MA 1978) are recommended. D. Mack Smith, *Mussolini's Roman Empire* (London 1979); MacGregor Knox, *Mussolini Unleashed 1939–41* (Cambridge 1962); Richard Lamb, *Mussolini and the British* (London 1997); and Jasper Ridley, *Mussolini* (London 1997) all give contrasting accounts of Mussolini and Italian foreign policy.

Poland

On Poland: R. Leslie, *The History of Poland since 1863* (Cambridge 1980); and the relevant chapters in Norman Davies, *God's Playground. A History of Poland*, vol. 2, 1795 to the present (Oxford 1981) provide sympathetic studies of Poland's political and strategic dilemmas.

German-Soviet relations

An informative, if personalised, view of German-Soviet relations is given in Alan Bullock's *Hitler and Stalin* (London 1993); while essays in *Aspects of the Third Reich*, ed. H. W. Koch, op. cit. discuss German policy towards the USSR and the origins *of Barbarossa*. Alan Clarke's *Barbarossa: The Russian-German Conflict* (London 1965) is accessible and is written with panache; while J. Erikson's two books, *The Road to Stalingrad: Stalin's War with Germany* (London 1975), and *The Road to Berlin: Stalin's War with Germany* (London 1987) are well-established accounts but Anthony Beevor, *Stalingrad* (London 1998) and *Berlin: the Downfall* (London 2002) are less deferential to standard

Soviet interpretations. Viktor Suvorov, *Icebreaker. Who Started the Second World War?* (1990) has challenged orthodoxy with his claim that the USSR was about to attack Germany when Hitler launched *Barbarossa.*

The Pacific or Far Eastern War

Dick Wilson, *When Tigers Fight: The Story of the Sino-Japanese War 1937–1945* (New York 1983) provides an accessible account of the long war between China and Japan and Ronald H. Spector, *Eagle Against the Sun. The American War with Japan* (New York 1985) is a good one-volume study of America's war with Japan. E. P. Hoyt, *Japan's War: The Great Pacific Conflict* (London 1986) is a good general history of the war in the Far East. For Britain's part in the Pacific War there is Christopher Bailey and Tim Harper, *Forgotten Armies. Britain's Asian Empire and the War with Japan* (London 2004) and two books by Louis Allen, *Singapore 1941–42* (London 1977) and *Burma: The Longest War, 1941–1945* (London 1986). Max Hastings, Nemesis (London 2007) is a study of the last year of the war against Japan.

US foreign policy

A. A. Offner, *The Origins of the Second World War: American Foreign Policy and World Politics 1917–1941* (New York 1975) provides a broad view of US foreign policy; while R. Dallek, *Franklin D. Roosevelt and American Foreign Policy 1932–45* (New York 1979); and P. Hearden, *Roosevelt Confronts Hitler* (Dekalb, Illinois, 1987) concentrate more specifically on Roosevelt. J. G. Utley, *Going to War with Japan* (Knoxville, Tennessee, 1985) deals with American policy in the Far East and Pacific up to Pearl Harbour. Akira Iriye, *The Origins of the Second World War in Asia and the Pacific* (London 1987) considers Japanese and Chinese as well as American perspectives.

Japan

R. Storey, *A History of Modern Japan* (London 1960) and W. Beasley *The Rise of Modern Japan* (London 1990) are excellent accounts of Japan's modern development, while Ian Nish, *Japanese Foreign Policy 1869–1942*, holds the field as an analysis of Japan's path to war.

Socio-economics

Alan Milward, *War Economy and Society* (London 1977) is the standard work on wartime economies; while Richard Overy, *Why the Allies Won* (London

1995) brings strategy, economics and weaponry together in an analysis of the reasons for allied victory. On home fronts, Jeremy Noakes (ed.), *The Civilian in War: The Home Front in Europe, Japan and the USA in World War II* (Exeter 1992) is useful and wide-ranging. A. Marwick, *Total War and Social Change* (London 1988) is a broad treatment of the question of the impact of war upon society; while H. L. Smith (ed.), *War and Social Change: British Society in the Second World War* (Manchester 1986) provides a selection of views on the war's effects on Britain.

Leadership and the Grand Alliance

Contrasting views of Churchill's wartime leadership, and of the grand alliance, can be found in Martin Gilbert, *Winston S. Churchill. Vol. IV: Their Finest Hour 1939–41* (London 1983), and *Vol. V The Road to Victory 1941–45* (London 1988); and in John Charmley, *Churchill's Grand Alliance: The Anglo-American Special Relationship 1940–57* (London 1995). J. M. Burns, *Roosevelt the Soldier of Freedom 1940–45* (New York 1970) remains a sound study of Roosevelt's strategies and leadership; while A. B. Ulam, *Stalin the Man and his Era* (London 1989) provides useful chapters on the wartime alliance with Britain and the US. Andrew Roberts, *Masters and Commanders* (London 2008), is a study of the relationships between Churchill Roosevelt, Alanbrooke and Marshall.

Military history

While I make no attempt to provide a detailed guide to the military history of the war, books which are accessible introductions to dimensions of warfare are: Max Hastings, *Bomber Command* (London 1987), and *Overlord* (London 1984); J. Rohwer, *The Critical Convoy Battles of March 1943* (London 1987); P. Padfield's biography of Admiral Donitz, *Donitz, The Last Führer* (London 1984); and R. Lewin, *Ultra Goes to War* (New York 1978). H. Feis, *Japan Subdued. The Atomic Bomb and the End of the War in the Pacific* (Princeton 1961) should be compared with G. Alperovitz, *The Decision to use the Atomic Bomb* (New York 1985).

Vichy France

For Vichy France: H. R. Kedward's Historical Association study, *Occupied France. Collaboration and Resistance 1940–44* (Oxford 1985) can be contrasted with Ian Ousby, *Occupation: The Ordeal of France 1940–44* (London 1987) and Robert O Paxton, *Vichy France: Old Guard and New Order 1940–44* (New York 2001); while, for the Resistance in occupied Europe as a whole, H. Michaels, *The Shadow War* (London 1972) is a good general survey.

The Holocaust

There is a vast literature on the Holocaust, but G. Fleming, *Hitler and the Final Solution* (London 1985) is a useful starting point; while D. J. Goldhagen, *Hitler's Willing Executioners. Ordinary Germans and the Holocaust* (London 1996) should also be consulted.

The Cold War

The fractures in the grand alliance which ultimately led to the Cold War are well covered by M. L. Dockrill and M. F. Hopkins *The Cold War* (London 2005); and H. Thomas *Armed Truce: The Beginnings of the Cold War 1945–46* (London 1986).

Index